UNIVERSITY OF NOTRE DAME

PUBLICATIONS IN MEDIAEVAL STUDIES

VOLUME XVII

THE LINEAGE OF LADY MEED

THE DEVELOPMENT

OF MEDIAEVAL VENALITY-SATIRE

PUBLICATIONS IN MEDIAEVAL STUDIES
THE UNIVERSITY OF NOTRE DAME
EDITOR: PHILIP S. MOORE, C.S.C.
ASSOCIATE EDITOR: JOSEPH N. GARVIN, C.S.C.

——————————————XVII——————————————

The Lineage of
LADY MEED

THE DEVELOPMENT
OF MEDIAEVAL
VENALITY SATIRE

BY JOHN A. YUNCK

MICHIGAN STATE UNIVERSITY

UNIVERSITY OF NOTRE DAME PRESS 1963

PUBLICATIONS IN MEDIAEVAL STUDIES

I. The Works of Peter of Poitiers. *By Philip S. Moore.*

II. Commentarius Cantabrigiensis in Epistolas Pauli e schola Petri Abaelardi. *By Arthur Landgraf.*

   1. In Epistolam ad Romanos.

   2. In Epistolas ad Corinthios 1^{am} et 2^{am}, ad Galatos, et ad Ephesios.

   3. In Epistolas ad Philippenses, ad Colossenses, 1^{am} et 2^{am} ad Thessalonicenses, 1^{am} et 2^{am} ad Timotheum, ad Titum, et ad Philemonem.

   4. In Epistolam ad Hebraeos.

III. Petri Pictaviensis Allegoriae Super Tabernaculum Moysi. *By Philip S. Moore and James A. Corbett.*

IV. Johannis Dominici Lucula Noctis. *By Edmund Hunt.*

V. Sachsenspiegel and Bible. *By Guido Kisch.*

VI. Saint Bernward of Hildesheim. 1. His Life and Times. *By Francis J. Tschan.*

VII. Sententiae Petri Pictaviensis I. *By Philip S. Moore and Marthe Dulong.*

VIII. The 'Summulae logicales' of Peter of Spain. *By Joseph Patrick Mullally.*

IX. The Cyprus Passion Cycle. *By August C. Mahr.*

X. Pseudo–Philo's Liber Antiquitatum biblicarum. *By Guido Kisch.*

XI. Sententiae Petri Pictaviensis II. *By Philip S. Moore, Joseph N. Garvin, and Marthe Dulong.*

XII. Saint Bernward of Hildesheim. 2. His Works of Art. *By Francis J. Tschan.*

XIII. Saint Bernward of Hildesheim. 3. Album of All Extant Works. *By Francis J. Tschan.*

XIV. Student Life in Ave Maria College, Mediaeval Paris: History and Chartulary of the College. *By A. L. Gabriel.*

XV. Summa Contra Haereticos. *By Joseph N. Garvin and James A. Corbett.*

XVI. Navigatio sancti Brendani Abbatis. *By Carl Selmer.*

XVII. The Lineage of Lady Meed. The Development of Mediaeval Venality Satire. *By John A. Yunck.*

In Preparation

Sententiae Petri Pictaviensis. III–V. *By P. S. Moore, J. N. Garvin, and M. Dulong.*

Stephani de Longuotona Cantuariensis archiepiscopi Quaestiones. *By J. N. Garvin.*

Aurora, Petri Rigae Canonis Rhemensis Biblia versificata. *By P. E. Beichner.*

Udonis Summa super Sententias Petri Lombardi. *By J. N. Garvin.*

The Summa "Breves dies hominis." *By J. N. Garvin.*

PREFACE

The type of thematic study which follows has seemed to me the most fruitful and practicable way of dealing with a centuries-long literary tradition whose individual contributors only rarely achieved distinction. Many of the most characteristic examples of medieval venality-satire are difficult to date and written by authors unknown, whose very nationalities cannot always be guessed. They probably reached the eyes of most medieval readers thus anonymously, divested of the historical contexts which produced their protests, simply as faceless representatives of a familiar and gratifying moral-satirical tradition and diverting expressions of an ancient theme.

The Middle Ages were enormously rich in venality-satire. Fortunately much of it has gradually found its way into print, especially during the past century. I have quoted from this material with great freedom: though I have worked almost wholly from printed sources, these are so scattered and often so inaccessible that I have tried thus to provide the reader with a small anthology of venality-satire. For many this may be the most useful part of the study. The texts themselves best suggest the true flavor and mood of the satire, as well as its conventionality and sense of tradition. Usually I have cited the most easily available editions of texts, even when these are not the best. Textual variations rarely affect the broad sense or even the detailed imagery of this satire, and in the growth of a literary tradition the corrupt texts which circulated are quite as significant as the author's own. I have translated all prose quotations, but have preferred to leave verse passages from the Latin and medieval French in the original. Too much disappears in translation.

My debts are many. Professor Margaret Schlauch, now of the University of Warsaw, a dozen years ago suggested the subject of this study and pointed out its significance. Professor John H. Fisher directed my doctoral dissertation on the subject at New York University in 1951-52. His firm, friendly guidance and careful criticism helped me reduce my sprawling investigations to some degree of order, and taught me much about the techniques of scholarship. In the past several years my research has been aided by a grant from the American Philosophical Society and grants from the All-University Research Fund of Michigan State University. I wish to thank also the editors of *Modern Language Quarterly*, *The American Bar Association Journal*, and *Mediaeval Studies* for permission to use material which first appeared in those journals, and Mrs. Barbara Goretzka, who generously undertook the demanding and unpleasant task of indexing the volume.

The present synthesis leans heavily on the work of scholars too numerous to list: literary historians like Manitius and Raby, editors of texts like Hilka and Strecker, students of attribution like Hauréau and Wilmart, the indefatigable antiquaries and editors of an earlier century like Wattenbach and Thomas Wright. I wish to mention specifically my indebtedness to Professor Paul Lehmann, whose distinguished studies in medieval parody have been a constant guide. Professor G.R. Owst's studies of the medieval sermon have been almost as valuable.

I am further indebted to my colleagues at Michigan State University: Professor Arnold Williams, whose wisdom and scholarly judgment have repeatedly come to my assistance, and Professors Robert J. Geist and Herbert Weisinger, who have read the manuscript and made valuable suggestions. The learned and generous advice of the Reverend Joseph N. Garvin, C.S.C., of the University of Notre Dame has saved me from a number of serious errors. I owe a special debt of gratitude to the Reverend Philip S. Moore,

C.S.C., the editor of PUBLICATIONS IN MEDIAEVAL STUDIES, for his willingness to include this study in the series, for his kindness and patience during the process of publication and for his several suggestions for the improvement of the first draft of my study.

Finally, I wish to express my deepest gratitude to Mrs. Ursula Karsten Franklin of the *Centennial Review*, Michigan State University, for kindness and encouragement more valuable than I can express. Without her constant and gracious aid this study would not have been completed.

East Lansing, Michigan
1 May 1962

CONTENTS

IV

Nummus Vincit, Nummus Regnat: The Flowering of the Venality-Theme in Latin Satire

V

L'Amour de Dan Denier: The Venality-Theme in the Vernacular

VI

Who is a Maister Now But Meede: The Venality-Theme in English and Other Vernaculars

VII

The Lineage of Lady Meed: the Culmination and Significance of the Theme

I

RADIX OMNIUM MALORUM: THE NATURE AND

BACKGROUND OF THE THEME

ONE

The Nature of Venality-Satire

Most of the common literary types of the Middle Ages have
attracted thorough scholarly and critical attention during the
past fifty years. Fable and *exemplum,* liturgical and guild drama,
heroic poetry and saga, romance and Breton lay, fabliau and
conte, ballad and song, have been fully canvassed, sometimes
beyond their ability to support the learned superstructure. Medieval satire ·alone has been relatively neglected, or has received
merely incidental consideration. Yet the period was one of the
great ages of satire, however rarely the type reached literary
distinction. The satirical spirit swept aside differences in form and
insinuated itself into all literary types. It was the essence of most
fabliaux, the heart of many sermons, the cause of those parodies
of sacred subjects which were so popular in the Middle Ages.
It walked hand in hand with edification in collections like the
Gesta Romanorum. It usurped allegory and dream vision, provoked
digressions in erotic romances and asides in serious chroniclers,
rose to greatness in the tradition of Reynard the Fox, in Chaucer,
and parts of the *Romance of the Rose,* the *Divine Comedy,* and *Piers
Plowman.* Eighty years ago Lenient commented on its impor-

tance in medieval France: "Jamais peut-être, dans aucun temps ni dans aucun pays, la satire n'a été plus universelle et plus variée. Elle revêt toutes les formes, parle tous les langages: vielle, plume, pinceau, ciseau, sont autant d'instruments à son usage. Elle lance sur la place publique, par la bouche des ménestrels, les premières hardiesses de la liberté moderne; elle s'accroche grimaçante et capricieuse au portail des cathédrales et jusque sur la pierre des tombeaux; elle ramène au sein de l'Église les restes de la saturnale antique, dresse ses tréteaux profanes en face des mystères sacrés, et inaugure ce terrible pouvoir de l'esprit qui a tué tant de choses en France, et qui leur a survécu."[1]   Lenient's comments apply equally well to all the medieval literature of Western Europe.

Fortunately it is no longer necessary to apologize for a discussion of satire in an age of faith, to explain it away as exceptional, as idiosyncrasy or errant genius, to identify it as Protestantism before the fact or exorcise it as a vagrant "precursor of the Renaissance." We have learned that faith and the critical spirit are not mutually exclusive, and that the Middle Ages were richly endowed with that spirit of caustic surveillance which flowers in satire. Yet the history of medieval satire remains to be written. Much, indeed, has been said on the satire of Chaucer, Dante, and a few other major figures, but we have only begun to see their work as part of the main body and to discover their common bonds with the unknown, workaday satirists who produced, for example, the huge volume of barbed medieval Latin verse, good and poor. Some attention has been given, too, to certain of the most popular medieval satirical themes and devices. We appreciate, for example, Francis Lee Utley's penetrating analysis of the antifeminist theme, and Paul Lehmann's distinguished studies in parody.[2]

---

[1] C. Lenient, *La satire en France au moyen âge* (Paris, 1883), p. 6.
[2] F. L. Utley, *The Crooked Rib* (Columbus, Ohio, 1944), pp. 3–90. P. Lehmann,

Though the satirical literature is rich, it will require much discussion in detail before we can arrive at a full synthesis of the subject. I believe that for the present the most fruitful approach to medieval satire is through the analysis of its individual themes, by tracing their development and evaluating their significance as *specula temporum*, by savoring their literary and doctrinal flavor. In this volume I propose to contribute to that approach by examining one of the most important of these themes, that of human venality and the power of money.

> My theme is alwey oon, and evere was—
> Radix malorum est Cupiditas.

Thus Chaucer's Pardoner—one of literature's most vivid portraits of the venal soul—introduces himself. His favorite text, metrically misquoted from St. Paul, will serve well enough to introduce this book. I am not concerned with the cardinal sin of avarice in all its manifestations, but with that aspect of it which issues in human venality, in graft, simony and barratry, in the extortions connected with these vices, and in the timeless phenomenon of the Almighty Dollar.

The theme is obviously not peculiar to the Middle Ages. Satirical assaults on greed and venality had formed a venerable tradition long before Paul uttered his strictures, and warnings against these vices are scattered throughout the Old Testament. The earliest Greek poets had pointed the paradox that the Golden Age was an age without gold. Then the haunting figure of Judas placed the spectacle of venality forever in the Christian account of the

---

Die Parodie im Mittelalter (Munich, 1922). A. R. Heiserman's important *Skelton and Satire* (Chicago, 1961), which arrived too late for use in this study, should also be mentioned. The author provides valuable surveys of all the medieval satirical themes used by Skelton, generally confining himself to material of English provenance.

very redemption of mankind. The cash-centered soul, the fiscal villain, innocence and decency crushed by the might of money, are common data of human experience. Hence the theme survived the Middle Ages. The Renaissance especially, along with its Machiavels and its power politicians, had its literary Economic Men: Shylock and Marlowe's Barabas, for example, Milton's Mammon, even personifications like Spenser's Lady Munera and Barnfield's Lady Pecunia. "Our *summum bonum*," wrote Burton in the seventeenth century, "is commodity, and the goddess we adore *Dea Moneta*, Queen Money, to whom we daily offer sacrifice, which steers our hearts, hands, affections, all, that most powerful goddess, by whom we are reared, depressed, elevated, esteemed the sole commandress of our actions, for which we pray, run, ride, go, come, labor, and contend as fishes do for a crumb that falleth into the water."[3] Burton's money-goddess was probably inspired by the Roman poets, but she might equally well have descended from similar personifications which proliferated in medieval satire, for the passage in which she appears is thoroughly medieval in tone. Whatever her lineage, she has since reappeared in numberless characters of later literature.

Though the theme is universal, it nevertheless achieved a peculiar preeminence in the Middle Ages, exercised more fascination over writers and caused more anger than it has done in other periods. It provided a major attack on the intrusion of the City of Mammon into the City of God, the temptations of the World for the Christian. It seems to have reflected, too, the inability of conservative thinkers, oriented to feudal and Christian ideals, to understand the very nature or power of money, and to have voiced their contempt for a policy which would use barren coin as an instrument of secular or religious rule. Complex, then, in its

---

[3] *The Anatomy of Melancholy* (London, 1891), pp. 33–34.

causes, medieval venality-satire achieved a typical unity and a distinctive flavor, the result of a long tradition which reached its English culmination in the striking episode of Lady Meed in Langland's *Piers Plowman*. In the following pages I will examine the development of this tradition, considering the literary aspects of the theme and certain social, economic and political conditions which helped produce it. I will concern myself with the common literary sources, classical and scriptural, which it absorbed; with the religious and moral principles behind the theme; with the special groups against whom the satire was directed; and with examples of the satire both in Latin and the vernacular tongues, especially those directly associated with the English literary tradition.

Satire is notoriously difficult to define, but a rigid definition is hardly necessary for the purpose of this study. The distinction between satire and sermon, between mockery and moralizing, has always been blurred, and it was especially so during the Middle Ages, when even the most irresponsible railers were disposed to assume the mask of the preacher. I have not found Peter's recent distinction between satire and literature of protest, nor his tendency to disqualify the Christian moralist for satire, especially fruitful.[4] Much of the material examined on the following pages may be best described cautiously as moral-satirical. It is virtually never mere personal diatribe; the satirists who compose the tradition insist on the immense social and spiritual significance of the fiscal vices which they attack.

I have mentioned the importance of *Piers Plowman's* Lady Meed as a medieval image of human venality. Meed, the familiar of courts and popes, clerks, justices, false friars, mayors and merchants,

---

[4] J. D. Peter, *Complaint and Satire in Early English Literature* (Oxford, 1956), pp. 1–39.

assizers, summoners and others of all estates, dominates three *passus* of the poem, playing a major role in the *Visio* section, which deals with the world of affairs.[5] Her episode is a vivid allegorical dramatization of the power of money, of the secret and insidious effects of "graft" and venality in blunting justice, oppressing the poor, the weak, and the peaceful, undermining piety, concealing and supporting commercial fraud and all the sins of the senses, gaining high position for the unworthy in the State and especially in the Church. Human venality is a basic problem of *Piers Plowman*; the satirist sees it as a major obstruction on the road to Eternal Life. Before probing the origins and development of the theme, we can best characterize it by a brief summary of the Meed episode.

At the beginning of *Passus* II, Holy Church shows the dreamer a woman gorgeously dressed, whom she identifies as "Mede the mayde," daughter of False,[6] about to be married, through the efforts of Favel and Liar, to False Fickle-tongue. Rich retinues assemble for Meed's bridal: knights, clerks, beadles and bailiffs, tradesmen, summoners, sheriffs and their clerks, advocates:

> Ac Symonye and Cyuile   and sisoures of courtes
> Were moste pryue with Mede   of any men, me thou3te.
> Ac Fauel was the first   that fette hire out of boure,
> And as a brokour brou3te hir   to be with Fals enioigned.

---

[5] William Langland, *The Vision of William Concerning Piers the Plowman*, ed. W.W. Skeat (2 vols., Oxford, 1886). In the B Text the episode covers *Passus* II–IV. All citations, unless otherwise noted, are from the B Text.

[6] In the A Text the daughter of Wrong, in the C Text the daughter of Favel. Either of these is more appropriate, since Meed is represented as betrothed to "Fals Fickel–tongue." On the scriptural backgrounds of Meed cf. D.W. Robertson and B. Huppé, *Piers Plowman and Scriptural Tradition* (Princeton, 1951), pp. 49–56.

Whan Symonye and Cyuile   seiȝ here beire wille,
Thei assented for siluer   to sei as bothe wolde.

(II, 63-67)

In a mock charter witnessed by Wrong, Piers the Pardoner, Bette the Bedel and other traditionally disreputable characters, Guile grants the betrothed couple lordship over the realms of sin. But Theology is outraged by the approaching wedding and asserts that Meed should follow truth and justice, not falsehood: though Meed's father is False, on her mother's side she is noble, "of Amendes engendred" (II, 118). Theology demands that the case be brought to court, and all agree amid a scene of promiscuous bribery:

Thanne fette Fauel forth   floreynes ynowe,
And bad Gyle to gyue   golde al aboute,
And namelich to the notaries   that hem none ne faille,
And feffe False-witnes   with floreines ynowe;
'For hc may Mede amaistrye   and maken at my wille.'

(II, 143-147)

Lady Meed then leads a grotesque procession to London, all mounted on appropriate steeds: Meed herself on a sheriff "shodde all newe," False on an assizer, Favel on a flatterer. Summoners, deans and archdeacons also serve as mounts:

Lat sadel hem with siluer   owre synne to suffre,
As auoutrie and deuorses   and derne vsurye,
To bere bischopes aboute   abrode in visytynge.

(II, 174-176)

But Soothness and Conscience warn the king, who issues orders that Meed be taken and brought before him. The party breaks up in panic. False flees to the friars, Guile to the merchants, Liar to the pardoners. The whole entourage disappears, and Meed is seized, alone and trembling.

Meed is courteously received by the king. Awaiting her hearing, she becomes the center of attention at court, especially among lawyers and justices, and showers her rewards where they will help her most (III, 1-24). The clerks too are attentive to Meed, and a friar offers her painless shrift, no matter how terrible her sins. Meed confesses to him,

> Tolde hym a tale   and toke hym a noble,
> Forto ben hire bedeman   and hire brokour als.

(III, 45-46)

She agrees to help with the friars' expenses if they will look lightly on the frailties of the flesh.

The king calls Meed into his presence and reproves her for her misdeeds, but promises to forgive her if she will amend her ways and marry Conscience. Meed readily agrees; but Conscience indignantly rejects the offer, accusing Meed in a long, climactic speech which summarizes all the evils wrought by misused rewards in the world of *Piers Plowman*. Meed teaches women lechery, and damages Holy Church; she is the friend of assizers and summoners; she causes men to lose life and property, lets the guilty escape, condemns the innocent; she fears no excommunication, for she is the mainstay of the consistory courts, and is shriven as she pleases; she can accomplish more in a month than the king's seal in four; she and Sir Simony even seal the papal bulls. She appoints ignorant bishops and permits evil priests to live in adultery. If a king loves her, she ruins his kingdom. She corrupts judges and destroys the whole legal process. In fine, she brings all estates to sorrow and subdues learning to the service of avarice (III, 124-164).

Meed angrily denies the charges: indeed, when the king's father fought in France it was Conscience who ruined him rather than Meed. But for Conscience, the king might now be ruler of France. Further, Meed has a true place in court and country. Emperors, kings, popes, prelates all must use meed as an instrument of policy (III, 208-226).

Conscience counters by distinguishing between two types of meed: one, the heavenly reward granted through God's grace to those who have led good lives on earth; the other, sheer corruption (III, 240-249). The laborer's wage is not *meed* but *mercede;* and the shopkeeper's profits represent mere mutation of form, from goods into money.[7] After supporting himself by Scripture, Conscience concludes with the vision of a kingdom ruled by reason in which men, guided by charity and conscience, faithfully perform the duties of their own estates. Meed will no more be master, but rather love and humility and loyalty together (III, 288-290). Meed tries to answer Conscience by a similar appeal to Scripture, quoting passages out of context; but Conscience reveals her deceit.

Conscience refuses reconciliation with Meed without the advice of Reason, who is thus brought to court, not without an attempt by Waryn Wisdom and Witty to bribe him. But now the king's deliberations are interrupted by the appearance of Peace, who complains of the violence offered him by Wrong—the lawless violence of officialdom and high station. Peace—wronged, beaten, and helpless—is supported in his plea by Conscience. Wisdom and Witty advise Wrong to "make his pees with his pens." When the king forestalls the attempt to bribe the judges, Meed tempts the victim himself,

> And profred Pees a present   al of pure golde:
> 'Haue this, man, of me,' quod she   'to amende thi skathe,
> For I wil wage for Wronge   he wil do so namore,'
>   (IV, 95-97)

----

[7] The C Text (IV, 335-409) makes an elaborate distinction between *meed* (reward or bribe, not earned as recompense) and *mercede* (wages, or recompense for work done). This is developed by a characteristically medieval grammatical analogy.

Now Peace himself, bought by Meed's gold, begs for the release of Wrong; but the king will not permit the settlement. Corrupt courtiers, however, try to interpret the ruling for the king's private benefit, and Meed gets the support of the venal men of law (IV, 152-156). Nevertheless, the righteous majority agree with Reason and abandon Meed. With the king's decision to rule by the counsel of Reason and Conscience (IV, 171-179), Lady Meed disappears from the poem, her fate unannounced.

This, then, is Langland's fullest portrayal of the power of money in fourteenth-century England. Meed the Maid, with all the graces of a heroine of romance, is clearly an excellent embodiment, as Nevil Coghill has suggested, of "the notion, ancient and modern, that money is the root of all evil."[8] Her dealings offer a colorful and pungent vision of corrupt administration in Church and State in any age. Meed and her tame officials smirk and wink at one another, and laugh together as Peace, Truth, and Loyalty languish under their corruption. Yet despite the evil she produces, Lady Meed is an ambiguous figure, like the word which constitutes her name. Meed can be just: there is a place for just reward. And so Lady Meed is of an honorable mother, Amends, and can defend herself strongly against the attacks of Conscience, until Conscience makes the necessary distinctions.

This ambiguous nature of Meed reflects admirably the perplexity of Langland's whole era, from the eleventh century onward, about the morality of money and a money economy. The new economy was an inescapable fact, but it was confusing, often apparently immoral, and almost always terrifying. Sometimes Meed appears wholly evil; sometimes her dual nature forces itself on Langland's attention, and he attempts to clarify her ambiguity.[9]

<hr />

[8] N. Coghill, *Visions from Piers Plowman* (London, 1949), p. 132.
[9] The discerning comments of A. G. Mitchell, *Lady Meed and the Art of*

Langland considers meed as something beyond mere wages, over and above what the recipient can claim for services performed, whether it be magnanimous reward or shameful bribe. It was difficult during this period to distinguish extortion from tax, bribe from honorarium, graft from stipend. Much of the difficulty grew from the habit of feudally-minded thinkers of identifying office and person. To such men political obligations and responsibilities depended almost wholly on direct personal loyalties. Payments were made to the person, not to the office or function, and confusion was easy. Stated in modern accounting terms, personal monies and public monies were mingled freely, both in fact and in the feudal mind. But whatever the problems in distinction, it is clear from the length and management of Langland's Meed episode that venality and the power of wealth were a formidable—probably the fundamental—social problem to the poet. Lady Meed, the polar opposite of Holy Church, is in that sense a manifestation of Antichrist. She is the focus of Langland's whole indictment of the world of affairs.

The Meed episode is merely the heart of the venality-satire of *Piers Plowman*. Langland recurs to the problem throughout the work in scattered passages which must be discussed later. He directs his money-satire almost wholly against certain groups: the clergy, from the Court of Rome down to the least chantry priest; the officials concerned with the administration of the law, civil or ecclesiastical; and officials of the royal courts. Other groups were rarely in a position to incur the guilt of scandalous venality. Finally, Langland's satire issues in generalizations about the power of money or meed in his time.

'*Piers Plowman*' (Third Chambers Memorial Lecture, London, 1956), cast light on the art of the Meed episode and especially on the implications of its allegory.

The venality-satire of *Piers Plowman* was not an isolated phenomenon in Langland's century. The theme appeared in numerous contemporary sermons, pious treatises and literary works, the outgrowth
of three centuries of money-satire in poetry and prose, in Latin
and the vernacular tongues. Meed the Maid in one form or another had become, as Coulton has remarked, a medieval commonplace by the time *Piers Plowman* was written.[10] No doubt pious
men had distrusted money and hated venality from the beginnings
of Western Christendom. But social satire, if we associate the
term with some literary pretensions, with the ridicule of faults
or vices common to a group, and with a reasonably learned or
sophisticated audience, was hardly to be found in the Middle
Ages before the eleventh century. Satirical poetry, remarks de
Ghellinck, "suppose un niveau de culture qui lui assure, avec
la liberté des idées et du langage, des lecteurs assez instruits pour
comprendre ses productions souvent chargées d'allusions, et assez
cultivés pur les goûter. Ce stade de développement était atteint
au XIIe siècle, par-ci par-là déjà à la fin du XIe."[11] De Ghellinck
suggests that the sudden outburst of satire which marked the
twelfth century resulted from the influence of the cathedral schools,
where clerks studied and imitated Horace, Martial and Juvenal.
Raby agrees, noting that twelfth-century France had produced
the conditions necessary for satire: "a society which has reached a
high state of development, a civilization of towns, and considerable freedom of thought."[12]

[10] G.G. Coulton, *Five Centuries of Religion* (4 vols., Cambridge, 1923–49),
III, 519–520.

[11] J. de Ghellinck, *L'essor de la littérature latine au XIIᵉ siècle* (2d ed., Brussels,
1955), pp. 446–447.

[12] F.J.E. Raby, *A History of Secular Latin Poetry in the Middle Ages* (2d ed.,
2 vols., Oxford, 1957), II, 45.

Centuries before the medieval satirists began to write, the themes of bribery, venality, and the power of money had been fully and energetically developed. The satirically-minded cleric of the eleventh century could draw inspiration from two important traditions, both rich in materials on these subjects. The Latin classics, as de Ghellinck and Raby have mentioned, formed one. The other was Scripture, with its immense body of accumulated comment in sermons, exegetical works and other pious treatises. It will be useful to consider both these traditions.

TWO

THE ROMAN SATIRICAL TRADITION

We know the great popularity of the Roman poets—Virgil, Ovid, Horace, Juvenal, Persius, and Martial—as models for the eleventh and twelfth-century *litterati*, though it is difficult to determine how much of this medieval erudition was the reflected glow of the *florilegia*.[13] A discussion of the Roman influence on medieval venality-satire might well begin with the common classical concept of the Golden Age. The idea was congenial to the medieval writer (who liked gardens) because of its obvious parallel with Eden, as Dante's Matilda so charmingly indicated near the close

[13] On the Latin classics during the eleventh and twelfth centuries cf. C. H. Haskins, *The Renaissance of the Twelfth Century* (Cambridge, Mass., 1928), pp. 93–126; J. E. Sandys, *A History of Classical Scholarship* (3d ed., 3 vols., Cambridge, 1921), I, 517–559; M. Manitius, *Geschichte der lateinischen Literatur des Mittelalters* (3 vols., Munich, 1911–1931), III, 12–17; E. R. Curtius, *Europäische Literatur und lateinisches Mittelalter* (Bern, 1948), pp. 56–62; E. K. Rand, *Ovid and his Influence* (New York, 1928), pp. 108–149. On the role of the cathedral schools in spreading the Latin classics cf. Haskins, pp. 47–53, 368–383; Sandys, I, 517–523; Raby, *Secular Latin Poetry*, I, 307–355.

of •the *Purgatorio* (XXVIII, 139-148). There Virgil and Statius smile appreciatively at the identification of Eden and the Golden Age; and indeed the image of that unfallen age lies hauntingly just beneath the surface of many of Virgil's own lines. It is explicit in the Fourth Eclogue, so popular with medieval Christendom, and is mentioned in the *Aeneid* (e.g., VIII, 319-327). One of the glories of the Golden Age was its freedom from wealth and the struggle for wealth. Later ages brought war, civil commotion, and *amor habendi*, the love of possession (*Aeneid*, VII, 326-327). Virgil tended to identify the Golden Age with his agrarian ideal and his distrust of Roman luxury and commercialism. The farmers of the Golden Age knew neither gold nor trade; likewise Virgil's ideal philosophical farmer could create for himself a sort of golden age, peacefully plucking the fruit of his trees, far from the "mad market-place" (*Georgics*, II, 500-502). With this ideal the poet contrasts the Roman of his day, and his feverish race for wealth and power, in terms that suggest the baser activities of Langland's Field Full of Folk. "Some men," he says, "stir the blind seas with oars, or rush upon iron, or cross the thresholds and courts of kings";

> one seeks to destroy a city and bring its hearths to misery, so that he may drink from gems and sleep on Tyrian purple; another hides his wealth and guards his buried gold. . . . Sprinkled with the blood of their brothers they rejoice, and exchange their homes and sweet thresholds for exile, and seek out a land lying under an alien sun.   (*Georgics*, II, 503-512)

Virgil, too, sees avarice as the root of all evil. When Aeneas recounts the murder of the Trojan Polydorus for his wealth, the memory produces the poet's most famous words on the subject: "quid non mortalia pectora cogis,/auri sacra fames!—To what lengths do you not drive the hearts of men, accursed hunger for gold!" (*Aeneid*, III, 56-57). Readers of Dante will recall the curiously distorted echo which that cry produced in the *Purgatorio* (XXII, 40-41).

Medieval humanists found a more systematic account of the Four Ages in Ovid's *Metamorphoses* (I, 88-162). Avarice appeared in the Iron Age, basest of all times, an age of "treachery and deception, deceits and violence, and the wicked love of possession (*amor sceleratus habendi*)" (I, 131). Virgil's *amor habendi* had found its first echo as early as Ovid. The poet describes the Iron Age's frenzied search for wealth:

> nec tantum segetes alimentaque debita dives
> poscebatur humus, sed itum est in viscera terrae:
> quasque recondiderat Stygiisque admoverat umbris,
> effodiuntur opes, irritamenta malorum.
> iamque nocens ferrum ferroque nocentius aurum
> prodierat. . . .
>
> *(Metamorphoses*, I, 137-142)

The poet's "irritamenta malorum" is a strikingly close pagan parallel to the "radix malorum" of his near-contemporary, Saint Paul. Ovid's account of the decline of man from Golden Age to Iron Age was in great part an account of the progress of avarice and the power of gold.

The satirical poets of Rome were especially useful to the learned satirist of the twelfth century. They supplied him with a number of *sententiae*—memorable tags—and *exempla* on venality and the power of money which were popular enough to recur repeatedly in medieval literature, and which gave, as it were, a pagan benediction to the Christian moralizing. Horace was a favorite source of this wisdom, though when he wrote of money he was usually dealing with those stereotypes of Roman satire, the inheritance-hunter, the wealthy miser and the youthful spendthrift.[14] It is

---

[14] For the *captator* cf. *Sermones*, II, v; for the spendthrift and the miser, *Sermones*, II, iii. The types occur frequently in Horace.

hard to believe that many medieval clerks had the experience to understand these decadent types of the urbane early Empire, but some of the passages caught the eye of the imitator or collector of aphorisms, especially when the poet used heavy irony. One of these was Horace's personification of money, which appealed strongly to medieval taste:

> scilicet uxorem cum dote fidemque et amicos
> et genus et formam regina Pecunia donat,
> ac bene nummatum decorat Suadela Venusque.
>
> (*Epistulae*, I, vi, 36-38)

His mildly cynical observations on the ways of commercial ambition were likewise attractive:

> "o cives, cives, quaerenda pecunia primum est;
> virtus post nummos": haec Ianus summus ab imo
> prodocet, haec recinunt iuvenes dictata senesque,
> laevo suspensi loculos tabulamque lacerto.
>
> (*Epistulae*, I, i, 53-56)

In one of the two odes which Horace wrote on the evils of money and the vice of avarice (II, ii; III, xxix) an image comparing avarice to dropsy caught the fancy of the medieval venality-satirists:

> crescit indulgens sibi dirus hydrops,
> nec sitim pellit, nisi causa morbi
> fugerit venis et aquosus albo
>   corpore languor.
>
> (*Carmina*, II, ii, 13-16)

But though Horace produced other quotable tags (e.g., *Epistulae*, I, x, 47-48; I, xvi, 67-68) and an amusing attack on feminine venality in Tiresias' cynical explanation of Penelope's chastity (*Sermones*, II, v, 79-83), his attitude toward venality was generally too mild, and his temperament too genial, for the more severe views of his medieval successors.

The iron bitterness of Juvenal was more agreeable to the mood of the twelfth and thirteenth century satirists. His aphoristic brusqueness was more imitable than Horace's balanced urbanity. Juvenal provided much ammunition for assaults on the power of money. In his hands the *Regina Pecunia* of Horace becomes a very goddess; only her temples and altars remain to be built:[15]

> expectent ergo tribuni,
> vincant divitiae, sacro ne cedat honori
> nuper in hanc urbem pedibus qui venerat albis,
> quandoquidem inter nos sanctissima divitiarum
> maiestas, etsi funesta pecunia templo
> nondum habitat, nullas nummorum ereximus aras. . . .
>
> (*Saturae*, I, 109-114)

The savage first satire deals freely with the power of money in raising the slave-born, the criminal and the vile to rank and dignity. The power of wealth brings a scramble for money at any cost, since money once gotten can buy off the crime and infamy committed in obtaining it: "quid enim salvis infamia nummis?" (I, 48).

Much of Juvenal's attack on Roman life in the third satire is centered, too, on the power of money in Rome. In Rome a man without money is helpless; it is no place for the poor and honest. Everyone is judged by wealth alone:

> protinus ad censum, de moribus ultima fiet
> quaestio. "quot pascit servos? quot possidet agri

---

[15] Saint Augustine, twitting the pagan Romans about their multifarious minor gods, finds *Pecunia* among their *deos* "*minusculatios.*" Moreover he finds that Jupiter himself is occasionally called *Jupiter Pecunia.* "But do you hear," says Augustine, "their reason for this name? He is called Pecunia (say they), coin, because he can do all things. Oh, fine reason for the name of a god! Nay, he that does all things is basely injured that is called Pecunia, coin." From *The City of God*, tr. J. Healey and R. Tasker (London, Everyman's Library, 1945), VII, xi–xii.

iugera? quam multa magnaque paropside cenat?"
quantum quisque sua nummorum servat in arca,
tantum habet et fidei.

(Saturae, III, 140-144)

What poor man at Rome can improve his position by marriage
or inheritance or politics? In short, "omnia Romae cum pretio"
—everything at Rome has its price (III, 183-184).

These blasts at venal Rome were especially gratifying to the
medieval critics of the papal city, for it was Roman venality
which became the chief target of medieval satire on the power
of the purse. The cry of the poor clerk without preferment and
the accusations of ecclesiastical venality found their prototypes
in Juvenal. The tone, and indeed the very words, of the third
satire were repeatedly paralleled in the twelfth and later centuries.
By then the papal Curia had become the bottomless pit into which
supplicants poured their money.

Elsewhere Juvenal describes how a few hundred thousand
sesterces will transform a man's reputation. From a cipher he
becomes the friend of all and the recipient of the most slavish
services, the most absurd honors. The passage is capped by a
much-quoted apostrophe to money: "o nummi, vobis hunc praestat
honorem, /vos estis fratres.—O Money, he pays *you* this honor,
you are his brothers!" (V, 136-137).

The heart of the fourteenth satire is likewise devoted to an
attack on avarice, with a long description of the avaricious man,
containing lines much quoted in the Middle Ages:

interea pleno cum turget sacculus ore,
crescit amor nummi quantum ipsa pecunia crevit,
et minus hanc optat qui non habet.

(Saturae, XIV, 138-140)

Though this growing thirst leads men to the most unnatural
crimes, today's greedy father advises his son to go about quickly

making himself rich. If the son fears war let him become a common merchant, not worrying too much about the dignity of his trade; rotting hides and fine unguents smell equally sweet to those they enrich; only the lucre matters, not its source (XIV, 204-207). Such men undergo incredible exertion, discomfort and danger, by land and sea, in search of pelf (cf. Virgil, *Georgicon*, II, 503–512, and Horace, *Sermones*, I, i, 27-40). Yet the wealth gained by such pains must be preserved by still more. The only escape from this madness is to confine our wants to the demands of nature, with perhaps a bit more for pet luxuries (XIV, 256-331).

Persius, who also deals with the Roman love of gold (e.g., *Saturae*, II, 44-60), may have found imitators in some medieval satirists, though he was far less popular than Horace and Juvenal. His most memorable lines on venality are probably those of his fifth satire, where he personifies Avarice boldly, in the manner of the medieval moralities, as a slave-driver forcing his victim to rise early, work feverishly, undergo all sorts of hazard, and ignore the basic precepts of morality, all for wealth (*Saturaé*, V, 132-139).

But it was Ovid who became and remained—next to Virgil—the medieval favorite among the Roman poets. Traube has well described the twelfth and thirteenth centuries as the *aetas Ovidiana*,[16] when "Ovidius Ethicus" was regularly invoked by moralists and satirists. "Juvenal," remarks Rand, "seems an utter contrast to Ovid, but Ovid has the makings of a moralist, as the Middle Ages were aware. He does not cry sermons from the housetops, but his works are stored with acute observations on men and morals which, if the context be forgotten, might be fitted into a letter of St. Paul's or a satire of Juvenal's." [17] Certainly he became the

---

[16] Quoted in Rand, *Ovid and his Influence*, pp. 112–113.
[17] Rand, p. 111.

medieval satirists' ally and armorer, though he had frequently to be "moralized" for the occasion.

Because of Ovid's levity and his sometimes cruel epicureanism, medieval moralists detached his ethical aphorisms from their frequently questionable contexts; hence his work appears most often as *sententiae*. The *Metamorphoses* was useful to the moralist, however, not for its *sententiae* but for its *exempla*. Thus Midas (*Metam.*, XI, 100-149) became a type of unbridled avarice, and the episode of Polymestor, Polydorus, and Hecuba's revenge (XII, 545-564) an example of the destruction born of that vice. The tale of Jupiter and Danäe (IV, 611-616) became an example of father and maiden corrupted by love of gold; Ovid himself so interpreted it. The episode of Procris (VII, 720-750) suggested also the idea that no woman's virtue was proof against meed, and Hippomenes' conquest of Atalanta (X, 560-580) developed the same idea. The power of the golden bough in the underworld (XIV, 113-115; also Virgil, *Aeneid*, VI, 136-148) hinted that even the goddess of hell was amenable to gifts.

Other works of Ovid were rich in sardonic *sententiae* for the later satirists. In the *Fasti*, Janus, asked why he receives gifts of cash at his festival, laughs and answers in Ovid' strongest satirical tone: You are much misled if you think that honey-offerings are sweeter than hard cash. Even in the reign of Saturn lucre was sweet to everyone; but now much sweeter:

> tempore crevit amor, qui nunc est summus, habendi:
> vix ultra, quo iam progrediatur, habet.
>
> . . . .
>
> in pretio pretium nunc est: dat census honores,
> census amicitias: pauper ubique iacet.
> tu tamen auspicium si sit stipis utile, quaeris,
> curque iuvent vestras aera vetusta manus?
> aera dabant olim, melius nunc omen in auro est,
> victaque concessit prisca moneta novae.
>
> (*Fasti*, I, 195-196, 217-222)

Some of the money-passages most popular during the Middle Ages came from Ovid's amatory poems. In the *Ars amatoria*, the poet remarks that the wealthy need no instruction in love, and develops the theme in lines which the later period found attractive. The lover, he says, should not pain himself to write tender verses for the beloved: poetry may be praised, but great gifts—*munera magna*—are sought after. A barbarian, if only he is wealthy, will be pleasing enough:

> aurea sunt vere nunc saecula: plurimos auro
>   venit honos, auro conciliatur amor;
> ipse licet venias Musis comitatus, Homere,
>   si nihil attuleris, ibis, Homere, foras.
>
>   (*Ars amatoria*, II, 277-280)

The final line of this passage became a common vehicle for the cynical sentiments of numerous frustrate medieval clerks.

The *Amores*, too, contained lines conveniently detachable from their contexts for general use. The eighth elegy of the first book—the old hag's advice to a young beauty—abounds in them. The advice is centered on the ways of extracting the most possible wealth from a lover. Let the lover be judged by the value of the gifts he brings (I, viii, 38):

> qui dabit, ille tibi magno sit maior Homero:
>   crede mihi, res est ingeniosa dare.
>
>   (I, viii, 61-62)

Let your doors be deaf to those who merely beg, but open to the bearers of gifts (I, viii, 77). The same cynical doctrine appears in the eighth elegy of Book III, where the poet complains of being jilted for a *nouveau riche* knight. The liberal arts have succumbed to lucre; now the greatest barbarism is to have nothing (III, viii, 1-4). Better a crude soldier rich from the spoils of war than a good poet. Even Homer would have found more favor that way. Ovid then moralizes the tale of Danäe:

Iuppiter, admonitus nihil esse potentius auro,
   corruptae pretium virginis ipse fuit:
dum merces aberat, durus pater, ipsa severa,
   aerati postes, ferrea turris erat;
sed postquam sapiens in munera venit adulter,
   praebuit ipsa sinus et dare iussa dedit.

                      (III, viii, 29-34)

The poet contrasts the wealthless and agrarian Golden Age with
the corrupt Empire:

eruimus terra solidum pro frugibus aurum;
   possidet inventas sanguine miles opes;
curia pauperibus clausast; dat census honores:
   inde gravis iudex, inde severus eques.

                      (III, viii, 53-56)

Fragments of Ovid's verse are imbedded in the works of medieval venality-satirists more frequently than those of any other Roman poet. But commonly the tone of the medieval writers was closer to that of the philosophical-ethical prose works of Cicero and Seneca, who had some popularity among learned men in the twelfth century,[18] though it is difficult to assess their influence. Cicero in the *De officiis*, probably one of the most popular of his treatises in the twelfth century, laments the corruption of character in public administration and suggests that the chief problem of government is to avoid the least suspicion of venality in public officials (II, xii-xxii). Such remarks may well have helped form the unpleasant picture of the corrupt judge, the hired witness, and the venal lawyer which persisted throughout the Middle Ages.

[18] Haskins, *Renaissance*, pp. 111-114.

THREE

SCRIPTURAL SOURCES

The classical authors, then, frequently provided the medieval Christian satirist with literary seasoning. He might parade his learning by calling the ancients to his support, by making centos out of them, or stanzas *cum auctoritate*; but his true inspiration was likely to come from Holy Writ, and after it from the scriptural commentary of the Christian tradition. Scripture itself furnished sufficiently strong and specific condemnation of avarice, fiscal corruption, and the power of money in the world. The prophetic books abound in attacks on corrupt magistrates and lawgivers. Isaias, for example, in a passage later popular with medieval moralists, laments the corruption of Jewish civic life in his time:

> Thy princes are faithless, companions of thieves: they all love bribes, they run after rewards. They judge not for the fatherless; and the widow's cause cometh not in to them.[19]

He hurls his threat at corrupt judges: "Woe to you . . . . that justify the wicked for gifts, and take away the justice of the just from him" (V, 22-23).

Ezechiel, too, makes meed prominent in his summary of the crimes of Jerusalem: "They have taken gifts in thee to shed blood: thou hast taken usury and increase, and hast covetously oppressed thy neighbors . . . ." (Ezechiel, XXII, 12). The complaints of Amos are similar:

---

[19] Isaias, I, 23. All Biblical quotations are from the Douai–Rheims translation of the Vulgate.

> Thus saith the Lord: For three crimes of Israel, and for four I will not convert him: because he has sold the just man for silver, and the poor man for a pair of shoes.
>
> (Amos, II, 6)

> Because I know your manifold crimes, and your grievous sins: enemies of the just, taking bribes, and oppressing the poor in the gate.
>
> (V, 12)

Michaeas storms against the bribed magistrate, the venal priest, the hired prophet:

> Her princes have judged for bribes, and her priests have taught for hire, and her prophets divined for money: and they leaned upon the Lord, saying: Is not the Lord in the midst of us? no evil shall come upon us.
>
> (Michaeas, III, 11)

The didactic books are even richer in protests and warnings against venality. Eliphaz the Temanite in the Book of Job threatens the venal: ". . fire shall devour their tabernacles, who love to take bribes" (Job, XV, 34). The Psalms furnish one of the most influential warnings against the briber:

> Take not away my soul, O God with the wicked: nor my life with bloody men: In whose hands are iniquities: their right hand is filled with gifts.
>
> (Psalms, XXV, 9-11)

The use of the psalm in the *Lavabo* of the Mass made the verse dealing with meed—"dextera eorum repleta est muneribus"—especially popular with the satirists and exegetes.[20]

The Book of Proverbs warns repeatedly against relinquishing righteousness for riches (XVI, 8, 16, 19), and against the power of the venal corruptor of justice:

---

[20] Langland, e.g., uses it in the Meed episode, III, 245.

The wicked man taketh gifts out of the bosom, that he may pervert the paths of judgment.

(XVII, 23)

He that maketh presents shall purchase victory and honour: but he carrieth away the souls of the receivers.[21]

(XXII, 9)

Ecclesiastes likewise frequently condemns avarice and the vanity of wealth (esp. V-VII). One passage closes with a cynical phrase as popular with the medieval satirist as many *sententiae* from the Roman poets: "et pecuniae obediunt omnia—all things obey money" (X, 19). Ecclesiasticus, too, emphasizes that getting and spending are the source of much sin (XXVII, 1-3; X, 10), and that meed corrupts justice: "Presents and gifts blind the eyes of judges, and make them dumb in the mouth, so that they cannot correct" (XX, 31).

The venal judge corrupted by bribes is the most common target of the attacks on venality in the Old Testament. The idea appears in the Mosaic laws: "Neither shalt thou take bribes, which even blind the wise, and pervert the words of the just" (Exodus, XXIII, 8). It is repeated in the codifications of Deuteronomy (XVI, 19). It provides an *exemplum* of venality in the sons of Samuel, who forced the people of Israel to demand a king: "And his sons walked not in his ways: but they turned aside after lucre, and took bribes, and perverted judgment" (I Kings, VIII, 3).

But the Old Testament *exemplum* of venality most useful to medieval moralists was the story of Giezi. In the Fourth Book of Kings, Naaman, a captain of the Syrian armies, is stricken with leprosy. Eliseus by God's power cleanses him of the disease and refuses any reward for the miracle. But Giezi, one of Eliseus' servants, resolving to profit from the occasion, runs after Naaman

---

[21] Quoted in *Piers Plowman*, III, 333.

and by a subterfuge begs from the thankful officer two talents of silver and two changes of garments. Eliseus is aware of the deception, and the servant is himself afflicted with the leprosy of which Naaman was cured (IV Kings, V). For medieval commentators this passage came to typify the sale of the gifts of the Holy Spirit, and provided the Old Testament complement to the New Testament crime of Simon Magus which gave simony its name. Giezi tried to sell, Simon to buy, the gifts of the Holy Spirit.

New Testament passages also inspired venality-satire. The episode of Simon Magus (Acts, VII, 18-24) was obviously important to the commentators, but the central act of venality was that of Judas, which brought despair and suicide in its train (Matth., XXVI-XXVII). Since clerical venality was looked upon as the sale of the gifts of the Holy Spirit, or of God Himself, the names of Giezi, Simon and Judas loom large in medieval venality-satire. Though there were many other New Testament passages on the subject (e.g., Luke, XVI, 19-26; Matth., XX, 21-24; St. James Cath. Epist. V, 1-3), one of the most popular with the satirists was Saint Paul's identification of avarice with idolatry: "For know you that no. . . covetous person (which is a serving of idols) hath inheritance in the kingdom of Christ and of God" (Ephesians, V, 5; also Colossians, III, 5). The most popular of all New Testament *sententiae* on the subject was Paul's comment on the root of all evils, which helped provide Chaucer's venal Pardoner's income: "Radix enim omnium malorum est cupiditas" (I Timothy, VI, 10).

This brief survey of classical, Jewish and New Testament comment on venality and the power of money suggests how rich a tradition of moral and satirical commonplace was available to later satirists, and how fundamental, in any civilized society, is the ethical problem they describe. At the root of the problem lies the clash, potential and actual, between man's material necessities and his spiritual standards, between subsistence and integrity.

The psychic balance is precarious and the demands of the material can at any time break into a cancerous growth at the expense of the spiritual. Yet the problem is eternal, demanding to be solved for each generation—indeed, for each individual—since it originates in that most fundamental paradox of human existence, man's dual nature. Hence the money-satirist necessarily probes beyond the inconsequentialities of manners and customs to the essential paradoxes of human conduct. It is this aspect of venality-satire which gives it significance, no matter how repetitious, uninspired, or even frivolous its exponents.

To the medieval clerical satirist especially, the dangers of Meed were obvious and frightening. On the one hand was the spotted world of Meed and Mammon, on the other the ideal of Apostolic poverty and Christian renunciation. He knew that the latter was for few Christians—certainly not for most Christian laymen—but it appeared to him that coming to terms with Mammon meant becoming his slave. The danger seemed especially great to his fellow clerics, and their failure to heed it was a rich source of indignation to him. If *femina dulce malum* represented the temptations of the Flesh *par excellence*, certainly Lady Meed, *Regina Pecunia, Dea Moneta*, best represented the temptations of the World. History has seen the ideals of this utopian satirist go down to defeat. But the final full development and recognition of a money economy —capitalistic or socialistic—has not solved his problem. It has frequently seemed, indeed, more like surrender than solution.

FOUR

THE EXEGETICAL TRADITION

The early centuries of Christianity developed a fairly clear and conventional exegetical tradition around the scriptural texts

which dealt with the giving and receiving of "munera," a tradition which inevitably influenced the later satirists. Saint Jerome's
comment on Isaias, I, 23-25 (cf. p. 23 above) provides a good example
of the characteristic exegesis of these early years. He warns his
readers that "we should beware, lest by taking meed from worldly
men, who have gathered their wealth through oppression and
the tears of the unfortunate, we be called, not indeed thieves
ourselves, but the companions of thieves." Accepting gifts is not
wrong in itself, but the priesthood of the young Church must
keep its hands free from offerings of tainted money. Seeking
after gifts, Jerome notes, is reviled by Isaias; not the mere taking
of offerings, which is often necessary, but the attitude that our
only friends are those bearing gifts, and the belief that those only
are holy whose purses are at our disposal. He quotes Ecclesiastes
on the insatiability of avarice, and characterizes certain Christians
he has observed: "They pursue remuneration in such a manner
that they praise those from whom they have gotten anything,
or at least will give nothing to anyone except those from whom
they think they will get something back."[22] Already Jerome's
picture contains a hint of the *modus operandi* of Sir Hubert, Chaucer's
wheedling friar.[23]

Jerome's comment suggests that for the Church Fathers the
problem of "munera" went well beyond simple venality, the

[22] S. Eusebius Hieronymus, *Commentaria in Isaiam prophetam*, I, i, 23. In
J.-P. Migne, ed., *Patrologiae cursus completus, series latina* (PL), (Paris, v.d.),
XXIV, 39-40. Where textual considerations are not primary, works available
in PL will be cited from that source for convenience of reference.

[23] There was more of the satirist in Jerome than in many later medieval
satirists. Readers will recall the acid image of the sycophantic, meed-seeking
society-priests in the letter to Eustochium (PL, XXII, esp. 414-415), which
in turn recalls Juvenal's bitter portraits of sycophancy in the earlier Empire.
Jerome was a part of the satirical tradition as well as the exegetical.

obvious crimes of bribery and extortion. It involved the question of how fully the Christian, and especially the clergy, should accept the support of those not of the City of God. In general, moralists of Jerome's stamp agreed that offerings from the treasure of iniquity should be refused. The problem remained important for later moralists, casuists and canonists, and became more difficult as society grew more complex and the Church more important, more worldly, and more wealthy. It lay at the heart of many later attacks on simony, and indeed represented one of the most obvious aspects of the general problem of the relation between Church and Civil Power, the City of God and the City of Mammon, the secular realm and the spiritual realm. The problem, as we have said, is as paradoxical and as permanent as the dual nature of man, in which it has its roots. It provided medieval spiritual history with some of its most curious ironies. The rejection of all possessions by the mendicant ideal, for example, ultimately produced satires attacking the friars as venal—because they were mendicant.

St. Augustine's attitude is similar to Jerome's. He mocks the pagans' *Jupiter Pecunia* (cf. n. 15) in his *City of God*, and indignantly contrasts gold with true riches: "But avarice gave him [Jupiter] this name, that he that loved money might say his god was not any sort of god, but the king of all the rest." Why name a god after what no wise man desires? The best name for a chief god would be wisdom, which cures men of avarice.[24]

Augustine's comment on Psalm XXV, 9-11, is pertinent. He notes that "munera"—meed—is not merely money or material gifts; nor do those who accept such things necessarily accept "munera." St. Peter, and even Christ, accepted gifts. What then is it to accept *munera*?

[24] S. Aurelius Augustinus, *De civitate Dei*, VII, xii. In PL, XLI, 204.

For the sake of meed to praise or fawn on a man, to wheedle him with flattery; for the sake of meed to judge counter to the truth. What meed? Not only gold or silver or anything of that sort; but even he who judges badly for the sake of praise accepts meed, than which there is nothing emptier. For he has opened his hand to accept the judgment of another person, and lost the judgment of his own conscience. Therefore "In whose hands are iniquities: their right hand is filled with gifts."

We take meed, then, at the expense of our judgment. The bishop who tries to please both parties to a suit is taking the empty meed of human praise, and losing the meed promised by God: "He holds to the empty, he rejects the real." If he has due regard to God he must pronounce sentence for one of the parties and face the accusations of the loser. If he judges in favor of a wealthy man he will be accused of taking bribes or fearing the power of wealth; but even if he judges in favor of a poor man he will be accused of taking meed: "What meed from a poor man? 'He saw a poor man,' it will be said, 'and to avoid censure for taking part against the poor, he suppressed justice, and gave his verdict against the truth.'" The bishop must expect this sort of accusation, and remember only that he is judging before God, "who alone sees who is taking meed and who is not."[25]

Two conclusions develop from these remarks of Augustine. First, *munera*—I have translated it usually as "meed"—might mean either a just gift or reward, or an illicit bribe. The ambiguous nature of Lady Meed is already established—her royal lineage on one side, her bastard birth on the other. Secondly, Augustine interprets bribery very broadly. Anyone, it appears, who allows his judgment to be swayed from the path of truth by personal considerations is accepting some sort of illicit meed. The idea

[25] *Enarrationes in psalmos*, "In psalmum XXV," xiii. In PL, XXXVI, 195–196.

becomes a commonplace of medieval commentary. Its echoes were heard for ten centuries after the death of Augustine.

In the Rome of Jerome and Augustine, despite its Christianization, there still lingered much of the Rome of Juvenal—its wealth and luxury, its degrading system of patronage and dependency, its hollow official heritage of the forms of ancient republican and imperial greatness. It was the last flush of disease, before dissolution. One suspects that by the end of the sixth century, when Gregory the Great wrote his comments on meed, the polished and manicured, sycophantic, wheedling, meed-seeking priest was no longer the serious problem he had been two centuries earlier. The exegetical comment on the power of money becomes for some centuries relatively academic. Nevertheless Gregory picks up and elaborates Augustine's concept that the search for praise or flattery is a form of bribe-taking:

> It often happens that a hypocrite disdains to accept gold or any material goods from men, but because he does not accept them, he expects to get the greater praise from men; and perhaps he thinks that he has taken no meed, because he has refused to accept material goods. Whence it should be known that meed is offered sometimes from the hand, sometimes from the mouth. He who gives money gives meed from the hand; but he who pays words of praise offers meed from the mouth. And so the hypocrite, although he rejects material goods, perhaps suitable for worldly necessities, desires that more be given him, since, wishing to be praised beyond his merit, he is seeking meed from the mouth.

Seekers of both types of bribes, adds Gregory, are equally guilty.[26]

This idea of the multiple nature of *munera*, probably original with Augustine, seems to have been a favorite with Gregory. Elsewhere he distinguishes three types of bribe-taking: "Meed

---

[26] S. Gregorius Magnus, *Moralium libri, sive expositio in librum B. Job*, XII, liv, 62–63. In PL, LXXV, 1016.

from the heart is the pleasure received from reflection on one's good deed. Meed from the mouth is glory through applause. Meed from the hand is the price of perdition." Only the man who looks for no earthly reward is guiltless of fraud.[27] Judges who pervert justice for bribes, Gregory says elsewhere, hide their crimes not in the darkness of night, but in the shadows of the mind. The bribe-taker will not be cured until he is cured of avarice. "If perversity in judgment comes from taking bribes," he remarks, "he who accepts no bribes will not pervert judgment; and he who has extirpated the root of avarice from within his heart will reject the offered bribes lightly." [28]

Gregory's more general comments on avarice typify the commonplaces of early medieval exegesis on the subject. He is fond of quoting St. Paul on the root of all evil.[29] He describes the offspring of avarice as "prodido, fraus, fallacia, perjuria, inquietudo, violentiae, et contra misericordiam obdurationes."[30] He compares avarice to the burning fire of Job XV, 34, and, in Horace's figure, to a dropsy.[31] In Gregory's work the clichés of the medieval preacher are already taking shape.

Isidore of Seville will serve to represent the developing tradition of comment in the seventh century. More interested than Gregory in secular affairs, he sees the problem of bribery and gifts largely in terms of the perversion of civil justice. He refers

---

[27] *Moralium libri*, IX, xxxix, 53. In PL, LXXV, 888–889. Elsewhere Gregory describes the three types of bribes as "munus ab obsequio, munus a manu, munus a lingua." Cf. *XL homilarum in Evangelia libri duo*, I, iv, 4. In PL, LXXVI, 1091–1092.

[28] *In primum regum expositiones*, IV, iv, 3. In PL, LXXIX, 235–236.

[29] E.g., *Moralium libri*, XIV, liii, 65. In PL, LXXV, 1074.

[30] *Moralium libri*, XXXI, xlv, 88. In PL, LXXVI, 621.

[31] *Moralium libri*, XIV, xii, 14. In PL, LXXV, 1047. Horace, *Carmina*, II, ii, 13–16.

to it frequently, and in the *Sententiae* devotes a brief chapter "De muneribus" wholly to the subject. He who expects a reward even for a just judgment commits a fraud against God, because he is selling justice for money. He is defending justice, not for its truth, but for the love of reward. And a poor man, unable to corrupt the judges with gifts, is often oppressed even in the face of truth: "Justice is quickly violated for gold, and no criminal fears his guilt who expects to get his freedom for money." In the manner of Augustine and Gregory, Isidore outlines the threefold nature of *munera*: "the partiality of friendships, the flattery of praise, and the taking of material bribes." But material bribes corrupt the soul more than love of praise.

Isidore also lists four perverters of human judgment, which with variations became commonplace in later sermons and commentaries: fear, cupidity, hate, and love.[32] Elsewhere in the *Sententiae* he pays special attention to corrupt judges, and those who protract lawsuits for profit. They consider the gifts, he says, and not the cause, unwilling to listen but quick to condemn.[33] Likewise he castigates the venality of witnesses: "If a lie is told *gratis*, how much more likely when it is sought with money. For there will not be lacking a great crowd of liars, if only there is money at hand." [34]

Isidore's general remarks on avarice are also of interest. Spiritual warfare, he says, must begin with the defeat of cupidity, for

---

[32] S. Isidorus Hispalensis, *Libri sententiarum*, III, liv. In PL, LXXXIII, 726–727.

[33] *Libri sententiarum*, III, lii, 11. In PL, LXXXIII, 725: "Saepe judices pravi cupiditatis causa aut different, aut pervertunt judicia; nec finiunt coepta partium negotia, quousque marsupia eorum qui causantur, exhauriant. Quando enim judicant, non causam, sed dona considerant; et sicut negligentes sunt in discussione causantium, sic eorum damno solliciti sunt."

[34] *Libri sententiarum*, III, lv, 1. In PL, LXXXIII, 727.

the mind bound by earthly desires is not free to contemplate God. And the love of money is worse than other earthly loves. Quoting Ecclesiasticus X, 10, and I Timothy VI, 10, he agrees that cupidity is the mother of all crimes, causing men to lose their faith, as it once caused the sale of Christ Himself. It is the bottomless pit: "Cupidity is never satisfied. For the avaricious man is always poor; the more he gets the more he seeks; not only is he tortured by the desire for increase, but also he is afflicted by the fear of loss." This passage, reminiscent of some lines of Gregory the Great,[35] is notable also for the tag quoted from Horace: "semper avarus eget" (*Epistles*, I, ii, 56). Indeed, the tone of the passage suggests the characteristic attitudes of the Roman satirists in their own attacks on the avaricious. Isidore represents at an early stage that synthesis of Scripture, classical poetry and patristic learning from which the stuff of medieval venality-satire was drawn.

By the ninth century the tradition of commentary was well-established, widespread, conventional, impersonal and repetitive. Preachers and exegetes recited the standard comment, copied with little change from the stereotypes of earlier commentary, and leaned on iteration rather than novelty. Further analysis becomes unrewarding. Certain ninth-century homilies of the immensely influential Rabanus Maurus may be mentioned, not because they offer anything new, but because they are good examples of the early homiletic use of the venality-theme and because they carried the influence of Rabanus' name. Most of their comments on

---

[35] *Libri sententiarum*, II, xli, 1–7. In PL, LXXXIII, 645–646. Cf. Gregory, *Moralium libri*, XIX (PL, LXXV, 1093): "Bene autem subditur: Hoc est satiatus venter ejus. Venter quippe iniqui avaritia est, quia in ipsa colligitur quidquid perverso desiderio glutitur. Liquet vero quia avaritia desideratis rebus non exstinguitur, sed augetur. Nam more ignis cum ligna quae consumat acceperit, accrescit; et unde videtur ad momentum flamma comprimi, inde paulo post cernitur dilatari."

venality seem to have been repeated almost verbatim after Isidore.[36]
But Rabanus sounds one note worth particular mention. He reminds his hearers that Judas sold Christ Himself for thirty pieces
of silver, so infected was he with the disease of "phylargeria," and
that Judas has his heirs and successors: "Listen to what I say,
bretheren, because whoever sells the truth for love of money or of
worldly privilege, betrays Christ and participates in the crime of
Judas."[37] The image of the venal cleric, judge, witness, or lawyer
as the heir of Judas was destined to become a staple of later meed-
satire.

The ninth-century *Via regia* of Smaragdus also deserves passing
mention, since through it the venality-theme was transferred from
commentary and exegesis to moral advice for Louis the Pious
himself. The author's comments on meed and avarice are remote
and academic, and lean heavily on the work of Gregory the Great.[38]

There is a striking change of tone when we move from the
detached and routine commentary of the ninth century to some
of the more embattled exegesis of the twelfth. The third section
of the Pseudo-Bede's *Exegesis in librum psalmorum*, probably written
about 1150, provides an example of the "munera" theme as it was
discussed when the satirists had already been long at work. There
is a new bite in the writing. Commenting on Psalm XXV, the
author notes the false position of the venal: "What is given them
for obtaining the Kingdom of Heaven they convert to getting
earthly meed, thinking they should strive for profit where they
should for piety, as in judging and similar occasions. Which the
Psalmist means when he says: *Dextera eorum repleta est muneribus.*"

---

[36] B. Rabanus Maurus, *Homiliae de festis praecipuis, item de virtutibus*, LVIII
and LXII. In PL, CX, 108–109, 117–119.

[37] *Homiliae*, LXII. In PL, CX, 119.

[38] Smaragdus Abbas, *Via regia*, XXVI and XXVII. In PL, CII, 964–966.

When they seem to do good, they do it not for the sake of goodness, but "conquered by meed." The commentator treats the three types of *munera*, flaring into satire with his concrete references to episcopal simony and the venality of the Roman Curia:

> Meed from the hand is when money is given for anything illicitly; which bad bishops do, who give the Curia money and receive the staff of confusion. Meed from service is when any fleshly service is demanded or offered for a spiritual honor; which is manifest among the chaplains of the Curia. Meed is received from the tongue when anything which should be done solely for piety is done rather for favor and human praise; so that, in a suit between a poor man and a rich man, if the judge defends the unjust part of the poor man against the rich, wishing to be praised for his apparent justice, his hand is not innocent of taking illicit meed.[39]

The author's acid examples suggest the satiric spirit, the searching and often searing criticism which had risen from reform movements within the Church. Those movements were in part associated with the first stage of the great struggle between Papacy and Empire.

Scriptural material on venality and the power of money, then, had been subjected to a long tradition of commentary and exegesis during the first ten centuries of Christianity. Our small sampling has been sufficient to show that "munera," as well as the broader subject of "avaritia," was widely discussed; that through repeated borrowings it had come to be handled in a highly conventional manner; and that the same scriptural verses appear repeatedly in comment, as well as the same fossilized formulae (the three types

---

[39] *Beda Venerabilis, In psalmorum librum exegesis,* XXV. In PL, XCIII, 611–612. This part of the work of the Pseudo–Bede, formerly attributed to Manegold of Lautenbach, is by an unknown author. Cf. D. Van den Eynde, "Literary Note on the Earliest Scholastic *Commentarii in Psalmos," Franciscan Studies,* XIV (1954), 139–147.

of "munera," the four ways of perverting judgment, the sale of justice as the sale of Christ, etc.) The emphasis on different aspects of "munera" varied with the interests of the different commentators, though only rarely can the reader glimpse the reality—the actual problem of meed—through the formality of the exegetical prose. There is a circumscribed flatness about the comment, a lack of variety and individuality, a remoteness and abstractness of view which, though suitable to the conservator and interpreter of Scripture, could hardly alone nourish the seeds of the later satire.

With this tradition of Scripture and commentary most clerical satirists would be familiar. The learned, especially during the twelfth and thirteenth centuries, would be almost as familiar with some of the *sententiae* of the Roman poets on the subject, whether or not this knowledge had been derived from *florilegia*; certainly not every twelfth-century scholar was a John of Salisbury. But whatever its immediate source, the classical material too had become a part of the common stock of tradition.

FIVE

Verse Satire on Venality
During the Early Centuries of Christianity

During the first ten centuries of the Christian era the meed-theme was as rare in poetry as it was plentiful in scriptural commentary. The convention, common enough in Augustan satire, languished as Roman wealth was dissipated and Roman civic organization disrupted during the invasions of the early centuries. The theme must have lingered on as an exercise subject in the conservative Roman rhetorical schools, if we can judge from a single example of the fourth century—more accurately the last classical poetical

treatment of the subject than the first medieval one. An obscure
praetorian prefect in Gaul named Tiberianus has left four short
poems, obviously school exercises, but according to Raby somewhat above the usual level of such products.[40] One, which survives in a slightly defective form, is an exercise on the evils of
gold:

Aurum, quod nigri manes, quod turbida uersant
Flumina, quod duris extorsit poena metallis!
Aurum, quo pretio reserantur limina Ditis,
Quo Stygii regina poli Proserpina gaudet!
Aurum, quod penetrat thalamos rumpitque pudorem,
Qua ductus saepe inlecebra micat impius ensis!
In gremium Danaes non auro fluxit adulter
Mentitus pretio faciem fuluoque ueneno?
Altrix infelix, sub quo custode pericli
Commendas natum, cui regia pignora credis?
Fit tutor pueri, fit custos sanguinis aurum!
Inmitis nides coluber custodiet ante
Et catulos fetae poterunt seruare leanae.
Sic etiam ut Troiam popularet Dorica pubes,
Aurum causa fuit . . . .
. . . . pretium dignissima merces:
Infami probro palmam conuendit adulter.
Denique cernamus, quos aurum seruit in usus.
Auro emitur facinus, pudor almus uenditur auro
Tum patria atque parens, leges pietasque fidesque:
Omne nefas auro tegitur, fas proditur auro,
Porro hoc Pactolus, porro fluat et niger Hermus?
Aurum, res gladii, furor amens, ardo auarus,
Te celent semper uada turbida, te luta nigra,
Te tellus mersum premat infera, te sibi nasci
Tartareus cupiat Phlegethon Stygiaeque paludes!

---

[40] A. Baehrens, *Poetae latini minores* (4 vols., Leipzig, v.d.), III, 263; Raby,
Secular Latin Poetry, I, 46–47.

Inter liuentes pereat tibi fuluor arenas,
Nec post ad superos redeat faex aurea puros![41]

The material in the lacuna obviously referred to the contest for
the apple of discord and the judgment of Paris. The piece is
thoroughly pagan in imagery and inspiration, developing a stoic
and Horatian theme by the commonplace *exempla* of avarice from
mythology, in the same way that Christian commentators were
citing familiar scriptural texts. The golden bough with which
Aeneas entered Hades is there, Danäe and the shower of gold,
and the goddesses struggling for the golden apple. "Omne nefas
auro tegitur, fas proditur auro" is a sort of pagan "radix malorum."
The mannerism of the Virgilian *lachrimae rerum* is there, too, though
without the music, strength or sincerity of Virgil. There is not
a jot of satire about the poem; it is heavily moralistic with the
strong flavor of late stoicism. The spirit of Roman satire had
already departed.

Between the fourth century and the eleventh the meed-theme
almost disappears from poetry, despite the development of other
"goliardic" themes during the Carolingian renaissance.[42] Poetic
attacks on avarice, similar in tone and conventionality to the
exercise of Tiberianus, are frequent enough. Some of them reflect
similar passages in Boethius' influential *Consolation of Philosophy*,
which itself echoes the Roman poets and philosophers:

Quae iam praecipitem frena cupidinem
    Certo fine retentent,
Largis cum potius muneribus fluens

[41] Baehrens, III, 265-266. A shorter variant from a ninth-century manuscript
has been printed by A. Holder, "Mittheilungen aus Handschriften," *Neues
Archiv*, I (1876), 415.

[42] B. Jarcho, "Die Vorläufer des Golias," *Speculum*, III (1928), 523-579.
Jarcho's example of the "Romdiatribe" does not contain the specific charges
of venality which characterize the later examples.

> Sitis ardescit habendi?
> Numquam diues agit qui trepidus gemens
> Sese credit egentem.[43]

Typical of such conventional and reminiscent poetic digressions is a passage from the epic *Waltharius*, written about the third quarter of the tenth century. Deeply disturbed by King Gunther's fevered pursuit of Walther's treasure, which is about to bring death to Hagen's own nephew, Hagen utters a rhetorical apostrophe to avarice. The lines are modeled on similar passages in Virgil, Prudentius and Boethius:

> O vortex mundi, fames insatiatus habendi,
> Gurges avaritiae, cunctorum fibra malorum!
> O utinam solum glutires dira metallum
> Divitiasque alias, homines impune remittens!
> Sed tu nunc homines perverso numine perflans
> Incendis nullique suum iam sufficit. etc.[44]

But these conventional attacks on avarice lie only on the periphery of the venality theme. Hagen's complaint differs little in tone from that of Tiberianus six centuries earlier, or Virgil's "auri sacra fames" of imperial Rome. The problem of *munera* was largely academic with these poets. The fires of social satire had not yet been rekindled.

There was one considerable poem written during this long period, however, in which the author's personal experience with

---

[43] *The Consolation of Philosophy*, ed. and tr. H. Stewart and E. K. Rand (London, 1918), II, ii. We should also mention the ninth-century *Visio Wettini* of Walafrid Strabo. That rude precursor of the *Divine Comedy* depicts at some length the tortures of those damned for avarice and *munera*. Cf. PL, CXIV, esp. 1073–1074.

[44] *Ekkehards Waltharius*, ed. K. Strecker (Berlin, 1924), lines 857–862. On the models for the passage cf. Strecker's notes, p. 46, and Raby, *Secular Latin Poetry*, I, 267. Ekkehard's authorship is doubtful. Cf. M. Hélin, *A History of Medieval Latin Literature* (New York, 1949), pp. 46–47.

venality, his classical learning, scriptural knowledge and Christian piety combined to form a notable treatment of the meed-theme. It was the work of Theodulf (ca. 760-821), a Spanish Goth, Bishop of Orléans, theologian, government administrator and poet of considerable ability, one of the most important literary men of the Carolingian revival.[45] Prior to his broad experience of the world Theodulf had been trained in the classics at Spanish schools which still carried on the Roman tradition. His poetry, though without great inspiration, bears the mark of that cultivation. Most of it is in graceful Ovidian elegiacs, developed in the rhetorical descriptive tradition of the late Roman schools. Theodulf was for some time a *missus dominicus* of the court of Charles, a sort of circuit judge sent on tour into the provinces to administer justice and correct administrative or judicial abuses. Out of this appointment came a long poem, the *Contra judices*, or the *Paraenesis ad judices*. As we might expect from a man whose function was to correct abuses, Theodulf here deals frequently with bribery in the law courts. He does so with grace, perceptiveness, wit, and a rare good humor.

After some opening examples of just men drawn from the Old Testament, Theodulf remarks that he regularly sees men guilty of venality and tries to correct their faults; yet in his official capacity he is himself continually under suspicion. A description of his "praefectura" follows, in the form of a conventional *descriptio itineris*, which catalogues at length the cities of his circuit, each with an identifying feature. Wherever he and his fellow justices appear they are met by crowds of every estate, all hopefully bearing gifts, which they think will secure favorable judgments in their particular cases:

[45] On Theodulf cf. M. L. W. Laistner, *Thought and Letters in Western Europe: A. D. 500 to 900* (2d ed., London, 1957), *passim*, and Raby, *Secular Latin Poetry*, I, 180–197.

Quid moror? instanter promittit munera plebes,
  Quodque cupit, factum, si dabit, esse putat.
Hoc animi murum tormento frangere certant,
  Ariete quo tali mens male pulsa ruat.
Hic et crystallum, et gemmas promittit Eoas,
  Si faciam alterius ut potiatur agris.
Iste gravi numero nummos fert divitis auri,
  Quos Arabum sermo, sive character arat,
Aut quos argento Latius stylus imprimit albo,
  Si tamen acquirat praedia, rura, domus.[46]

Item by item, Theodulf describes the proffered bribes. Men come from all sides, in a perfect carnival of attempted bribery, offering cattle and fine cups if only they might be awarded what does not justly belong to them. They all trust in meed, and the sight causes Theodulf to curse the plague of avarice which has enslaved the whole world (PL, CV, 287C).

The gift-bearers are summarily informed that their offerings will be of no use,[47] but Theodulf out of politeness accepts a few small gifts of food and dainties. A passage of advice to judges follows, some 60 lines long, most of it condemning avarice and bribe-taking:

Aequa tibi justae sint judex pondera librae,
  Ut sua quisque libens hac tribuente ferat.
Nec sit avara lues, nec amor, zelusque, timorque,
  Quae turbent, firmus stet tibi mentis apex.
. . . .
Quattuor hae sontes, tribus est nam sontior una,
  Quae est radix cunctis dira cupido malis.
Muneris invalidas acceptio vertere mentes

---

[46] Theodulfus Aurelianus Episcopus, *Carmina*, I. In PL, CV, 286C.

[47] Both the power of these *missi dominici* and their susceptibility to bribes are suggested by a curt letter to Charles the Bald from his bishops: "We ask that the committers of crimes and despisers of apostolic discipline sent from your court as legates of proven trust be prevented from personal favoritism and from being blinded by meed." Quoted in PL, CV, 285, n.

Adsolet, a vero jusque fugare pium.
Non solum argento res haec inolescit et auro,
    Praepetis aut campos ungue cavantis equi,
Murice vel rutilo, gemmis aut syrmate pulchro,
    Aut rebus variis quas vela ferre solet.
Sed levibus verbis, paribus volantibus auris,
    Blanditiae vento mens quibus acta tumet.

. . . .

Heu scelus est ullis pro rebus linguere verum,
    Vendere seu gratis quod dare quemque decet.
                                (PL, CV, 288D-289B)

Theodulf, it will be observed, has woven into the fabric of his poem certain commonplaces of scriptural exegesis: the citation of I Timothy, the four methods of perverting judgment, the division of meed into *munus a manu* and *munus a lingua*, the attitude toward the sale of justice. All these notions appear in Isidore's *Libri sententiarum* (cf. pp. 33-34 above), with which Theodulf was almost certainly familiar. But set in the realistic background of the justice's trip, and framed by the sordid actualities which fell under his observation, they take on a vividness and reality lacking in the formal commentary. Behind the commonplaces and the conventional artifice of the rhetorical tradition is the practical administrator viewing real problems and moralizing on them, half-humorously and half-satirically, with appropriate touches of hyperbole. The poem is no masterpiece, but with all its conventionality it has the touch of life, and some of the gusto of true satire.

Theodulf's literary charge to the judges continues with descriptions of the typical faults of the law courts. Venality and avarice are as common as laziness; magistrates are late for court business, but early when there is money to be handed out (PL, CV, 290C). This sort of attack anticipates significantly the vivid (and more bitter) satires of the twelfth century. There is also a portrait of the avaricious doorkeeper, always hungry for tips:

Praemia ne quaerat moneatur janitor ipse,
  Saepe capi a populo quae veniente solent.
Est scelus a populo pretium sperare querenti
  Me miserum, scelus hoc janitor omnis amat.
Janitor omnis amat, non hoc tamen arbiter odit,
  Vix de mille unus qui horreat illud erit.
Sunt variae vires, amor est tamen unus habendi,
  Qui potius furor est, quam vocitandus amor.

(PL, CV, 291A)

The extortionist doorkeeper—especially in the person of the papal *janitor*—became a fixture of later money-satire.

A long passage on the widespread avarice of the world concludes with further advice to judges. Among other dangers that the judge must face is the possibility that his wife and family may succumb to bribes. There is an amusing picture of the wife pleading a case with her husband, full of caresses, blandishments, sighs and tears, able to think only of the promised gifts, and uttering that timeless conjugal complaint: "Whatever other women want they get, whether helpful or hurtful, but I go along with none of my wishes satisfied" (295D). The wife is seconded by a conspiracy of servants and children, who demand that the husband take pity on her. Everywhere the judge finds temptations to venality.

Theodulf pictures venality again in the person of the witness who expects rewards for his testimony—true or false. If it is a crime to sell the truth, he asks, what is it to sell falsehood?

O merces, merces, mercede nocentior omni,
  Dantem et captantem quae necat una duos.

(PL, CV, 297C)

The poet closes by urging the wealthy to refrain from oppressing the poor, of whose family they are fellow members in Christ.

The *Paraenesis ad judices*, with its portraits of the lazy, venal judge, the wheedling *janitor* and the hired witness, contains many of the elements of later satire on meed and the power of money, especially as these appear in the law courts. But Theodulf lacks the satirical cast of mind—the ruffled feelings, the jaundice, the acrid observations, the will to hurt. The half-humorous, half-satirical habit of the poet is incidental to the rhetorical-descriptive cast of the poem as a whole. It is in general quiet, episodic and digressive, without the concentration of caustic wit and raillery which were the staples of much twelfth-century satire. It was nevertheless the first considerable medieval poem—and for a long time the only one—dealing extensively with the meed-theme. Since it reflects the daily experience of the author himself, it has a liveliness —despite its rhetorical nature—often lacking in later satirists who were more intense but less experienced in the great world.

Despite, then, the plenitude of classical and scriptural sources, the theme of meed or venality is rare in the poetry of the first ten centuries. In its few appearances—Theodulf's *Paraenesis* is an exception—it tends to be merely imitative, a studied mouthing of classical or scriptural ideas in much the same language which originally expressed them. It lacks fire, animus, defined objective. The satiric tone and technique, in other words, have not reappeared. Indeed the conditions necessary for social satire had not reappeared before the eleventh century. By that time the gradual social and intellectual revival, which was to culminate in the twelfth and thirteenth centuries, began once more to produce an atmosphere favorable to satire.

There were especially pressing causes for the revival of the meed-theme in the eleventh century. Powerful reform movements within the Church and especially the papacy, the growing complexity of both the spiritual and temporal powers, the struggle between the two over investitures, and the increasing centralization of ecclesiastical authority provided material for a new satire on venality, and inspired versifiers to write it. Out of conflict came *saeva indignatio* and the cynical mockery of officialdom, both of which were to contribute to the development of venality-satire.

II

GIEZI, SIMON, ET JUDAS: THE MEDIEVAL REVIVAL
OF THE SATIRICAL THEME

ONE

PAPAL ECCLESIASTICAL REFORM IN THE ELEVENTH CENTURY

The eleventh century was a time of great men and movements, the century of Henry III and Leo IX, of William the Conqueror, Lanfranc and Anselm, of the Cardinals Humbert and Peter Damian, of Gregory VII and Henry IV. It witnessed the beginnings of a gigantic religious reform which ultimately affected all Europe. It saw the opening of the Investiture Contest and the astonishing rise of the Papacy to a position of European leadership, the results of which have been called "the culmination of medieval history."[1] It saw a large measure of religious unity restored to Western Europe, a unity spectacularly symbolized by the First Crusade. It produced Europe's first pamphlet war of propaganda, the "libelli de lite" of the Investiture Contest. The Contest developed in clergy and laity alike a consciousness of the evils of simony so strong that the corrupting power of money was reborn as a theme of satire and flourished for the rest of the Middle Ages.

The term *simony* had been applied in the primitive Church only to the sale of ordination by a bishop, but by the middle of

---

[1] G. Tellenbach, *Church, State and Christian Society at the Time of the Investiture Contest*, tr. R. F. Bennett (Oxford, 1940), p. 162.

the ninth century had come to be applied also to the sale of benefices by their controllers, whether lay or clerical. This was the
usual meaning by the beginning of the eleventh century. At
that time Abbo of Fleury stated clearly what were regarded as
the different forms of simony: the sale of sacerdotal ordination
by a bishop, the sale of episcopal consecration by a metropolitan,
and the sale of bishoprics and abbeys by secular princes. He might
also have added the sale of benefices by the lesser lords who
controlled them.[2]

It is fairly clear how simony had become one of the greatest
abuses in the Church before the eleventh century. With the social,
intellectual, and economic decline that followed the breakup of
the Carolingian Empire, a broadening feudalism had gradually
infiltrated ecclesiastical organization, though the two had little
in common. Benefices and episcopal sees fell under lay control,
and were frequently treated as purely feudal holdings.[3] The
lords who controlled such holdings tended to choose vassals for
their military, political, or other secular abilities, with little attention to their spiritual qualifications.[4]

[2] A. Fliche, *La querelle des investitures* (Paris, 1946), p. 17. All the major vol-
umes by Fliche are most useful for the study of this period. His *Etudes sur la
polémique religieuse à l'époque de Grégoire VII: Les prégrégoriens* (Paris, 1916)
gives an excellent picture of the state of the Church and the Papacy before the
Gregorian reform. His more recent *La reforme grégorienne* (Spicilegium sacrum
Lovaniense; études et documents, 6, 9, 16; Louvain, 1924–37) is invaluable.

[3] R. Rocquain, *La Cour de Rome et l'esprit de reforme avant Luther* (Paris, 1893–
97, 2 vols), I, 4.

[4] R. W. and A. J. Carlyle, *A History of Mediaeval Political Thought in the West*
(Edinburgh, v.d., 6 vols), IV, 51. I intend to sketch only very briefly those
aspects of ecclesiastical history, and especially of the Investiture Contest, which
bear on medieval satire. I make no attempt to give a complete, rounded, or
original picture of that complex struggle, nor to represent the immense bibliography of the subject.

The feudal controller of a bishopric might also decide to use it for revenue, and simply sell it to the highest bidder. The simoniac bishop in turn would be likely to recover his expenses or secure his profit by auctioning off the benefices or ordinations in his diocese. Gerbert (later Pope Sylvester II) recounts the typical defense made by such bishops, "trifling and ignorant, advanced by money, not merits":

> I was recently ordained bishop by the archbishop, and I gave a hundred pounds for him to confer the episcopal rank on me; if I had given less, I would not be bishop today. But it is better for me to diminish the gold in my chest than to lose such an office. I gave gold and I got an episcopacy; yet if I have luck, I don't despair of getting it back quickly. I ordain a priest and I receive gold; I make a deacon, and I get a large amount of silver; and likewise for every ecclesiastical rank, and for consecrating abbots and churches, I expect to get a profit in money. Behold the gold which I gave I have again, undiminished in my chest.[5]

In some areas the sale of Church offices was probably the rule rather than the exception. In France Philip I (1068-1108) remarked to a disappointed candidate for a see, who had seen his rival get the plum: "Let me make my profit out of him; then you can try to get him degraded for simony, and afterwards we can see about satisfying you."[6]

Objections to these practices are plentiful. Rodulf Glaber writes that "this pestilence rages far and wide among prelates of churches scattered throughout the whole world. They have turned the

---

[5] Sylvester II Papa, *De informatione episcoporum*. In PL, CXXXIX, 174. This passage and its context reappear in Cardinal Humbert's *Adversus simoniacos*, where they are attributed to St. Ambrose. Cf. PL, CXLIII, 1041.

[6] J. P. Whitney, "The Reform of the Church," in *Cambridge Mediaeval History* (8 vols, Cambridge, v.d.), V, 9.

free and venerable gift of almighty Christ to the increase of their own damnation through the lucre of avarice":

> Even the kings themselves, who should have appointed suitable men for holy religion, corrupted by the lavishing of meed, prefer to promote to the cure of churches or souls those from whom they hope to get the most meed. Hence they throw themselves willfully on any preferment, fearing little the sin of neglecting pastoral care, because all their trust hangs solely on chests of collected money[7].

Cardinal Humbert's testimony is similar:

> ... How abject and ignoble the bride of Christ is counted, whose injuries no one can be found to lament, whose modesty, prostituted by sacrilegious rapists, merchandised and sold, no one will defend; whom no one will ever wrest from them and restore, however stained, to her Husband . . . . From the highest rank in the Church to the lowest, no one neglects to carry on trade in things ecclesiastical. Emperors, kings, princes, magistrates, and others with wordly power, practice this above all things; and those who ought to defend ecclesiastical things with the spiritual sword, by ecclesiastical law, pursue it; and those, too, who ought to defend them with the material sword.[8]

Peter Damian's complaints are much like Humbert's.[9]

Though something must be allowed to the exaggeration common among crusaders, there is much evidence to support them. Conrad II, for example, is said to have made simony an open and important source of revenue for the German court.[10] Guifred

---

[7] Rodulfus Glabrus, *Historiarum sui temporis libri quinque*, II, vi. In PL, CXLII, 636.

[8] Humbertus Silvae Candidae, *Adversus simoniacos libri tres*, III, v. In PL, CXLIII, 1147.

[9] E.g., S. Petrus Damiani, *Epistolae*, I, xii. In PL, CXLIV, 222–223.

[10] Rocquain, I, 5; Whitney, p. 9. The regency for young Henry IV seem to have acted similarly. Cf. Carlyle, *Mediaeval Political Theory*, IV, 55.

of Cerdagne bought the archbishopric of Narbonne for 100,000 *solidi*, when only ten years old. The see of Albi was sold while still occupied, a written contract being drawn up to confirm the sale. Pluralism flourished in conjunction with simony. A noble Gascon bishop is reported to have held six episcopal sees simultaneously, and to have disposed of them in his will when he died.[11] Cardinal Humbert recounts how one simoniacal bishop was forced to pillage his own church of its marble, its statues, even its roofs, to pay for the purchase of his see.[12] A growing consciousness of the destructiveness of this sort of simony was beginning to give point to the scriptural texts and commentaries on *munera*.

By the end of the tenth century, as is frequent in such periods of spiritual decay, the vice had begun to produce a spontaneous reaction. The reforms initiated by Cluny gradually spread to the secular clergy and resulted in episcopal synods which condemned on the basis of the old decretals the major evils of the day: indiscriminate warfare and violence, the ignoring of clerical celibacy, and above all the widespread practice of simony.[13] The names of many leaders in these reforms are recorded: Nilus, Ronald of Ravenna, William of Dijon, Richard of St. Vannes, Abbot Poppo of Stablo, Rather, Burchard of Worms, and others.[14] But the reforms did not spread to the whole Church until the pious and powerful Emperor Henry III intervened to place a series of vigorous reforming popes on the throne of the Holy See.

The story of this great reform is familiar. The Church was as corrupt in Italy as elsewhere, and especially at Rome. "Indeed,"

---

[11] Examples from Whitney, pp. 10–11. Further material appears in E. Saltet, *Les réordinations* (Paris, 1907), pp. 173 ff.

[12] Humbertus, *Adversus simoniacos*, XX, xliii. In PL, CXLIII, 1131.

[13] Tellenbach, pp. 75–85; Rocquain, I, 10–11; Whitney, p. 3.

[14] Whitney, pp. 2–3.

remarks Glaber with some exaggeration, "every ecclesiastical office was then held venal, like merchandise in a worldly market place." He describes Pope Benedict IX, elected in 1045 as a mere boy about 12 years of age, "whom only money of gold and silver commended, rather than age or sanctity."[15]   The disease, added Bonitho, had spread through the Church, "so that in the whole Church scarcely one person could be found who was not illiterate or simoniacal or a keeper of concubines."[16] Though these reformers exaggerate, the picture was dark.

The resignation of Benedict IX shortly after his election produced a struggle over the papal throne which gave Henry III an opportunity to intervene.[17]   He deposed Gregory VI, who had succeeded Benedict IX, and appointed a German candidate for the See, who was elected as Clement II. But he and his German successor, Damasus II, lived only briefly after their elevations. Henry's third candidate, his relative Bruno, Bishop of Toul, who took the name of Leo IX, was learned, pious, thoroughly committed to religious reform, fearless and vigorous. Part of his success was certainly the work of the forceful and able Curia which he gathered around him, a court which contained Hildebrand, Frederick of Lorraine, Humbert of Silva Candida, Hugh the White and Boniface of Albano.

Leo's pontificate was occupied by a series of Church councils, held by the Pope in person throughout Europe, whose primary business was to destroy simony. Accused bishops who could not clear themselves were summarily deposed.[18] By this means the

---

[15] Rodulfus Glabrus, *Historia*, V, v. In PL, CXLII, 698.

[16] Bonizo Placentinus Episcopus, *Liber ad amicum*, V. In PL, CL, 819.

[17] Bonitho tells the story in his *Liber ad amicum*, but his version is not wholly trustworthy. Cf. Rocquain, I, 11–14; Tellenbach, pp. 173–117; Whitney, p. 19.

[18] Whitney, pp. 22–24.

evils of simony were widely published, and the Papacy began to resume the international character which it had virtually lost during the decadence of the tenth and early eleventh centuries. *Roma caput mundi* began to re-emerge. Leo's immediate successors—Victor II, Stephen IX, Nicholas II, and Alexander II—all continued his reform policies with varying degrees of success. Their pontificates exhibit a remarkable unity of policy, undoubtedly through the continuing influence of a Curia which contained, beside the men mentioned above, Peter Damian. The "Court of Rome" was henceforth central to the ecclesiastical life of Europe.

The aims of Leo IX and his successors can be summarized in the vague phrase used so frequently from that time onward: "the freedom of the Church." Freedom of the Papacy from Roman politics was one aspect of that liberty; but freedom here carried a much broader sense. The contemporary churchman would have expressed it as the liberation of the Bride of Christ from secular whoredom.[19] For the ecclesiastical evils of the time—simony, nicolaitism, the bearing of arms by the clergy—all tended to obscure the line which separated clergy from laity. It became clear, especially to the Curia, that simony could be prevented only if the clergy separated itself entirely from lay control; and separation from lay control meant the abolition of lay investiture as it had been practised. The ecclesiastical system could then extricate itself, at least in its spiritual capacity, from the feudal system. Insensibly, events drew toward the Investiture Contest.

Hildebrand, elected Pope Gregory VII in 1073, pressed home these papal reform policies. He continued the attack on simony with increased vigor; he attacked lay investiture directly (with little practical success), attempting to carry out rigorously principles formulated in the Curia before he had become Pope; he

---

[19] Cf., e.g., Humbertus, *Adversus simoniacos*, III, v, quoted above, p. 50.

expanded the policy of papal legates and visits *ad limina*, with particular success in France.[20] Under Gregory the Papacy itself was clearly independent and in control of its own ecclesiastical affairs, and was able at least to state and defend its claims against lay investiture. Gregory had definitively established Rome as the ecclesiastical center of Christendom. For the writers of the two centuries following Gregory VII, papal Rome was *Roma caput mundi*. It is not surprising to find her also a center of interest for later satire.

TWO

POLEMICAL PRODUCTS OF THE REFORM MOVEMENT

We have mentioned that ecclesiastical reform and the resulting Investiture Contest produced the first pamphlet war in history. Much of its writing naturally dealt with simony, and the bulk is great. If we except the work of Gerbert, Humbert and Peter Damian, sixty-nine items dealing with the controversy between 1031 and 1163 have been edited in the *Monumenta Germaniae Historica*. [21] Virtually all of these mention simony, and eight of them deal almost wholly with it. This pamphlet material was the soil out of which medieval venality-satire grew; indeed, it furnished some of the earliest examples of the revival of that theme.

The most important of these early attacks on simony were written by the two major curial publicists, whose personal influence extended from the pontificate of Leo IX to that of Gregory

[20] Z.N. Brooke, "Gregory VII and the First Contest between Empire and Papacy," *Cambr. Med. Hist.*, V, 51–85.

[21] *MGH, Libelli de lite imperatorum et pontificum*, 3 vols, Hanover and Berlin, 1891. Scholarship in Manitius, *Geschichte*, III, 21–68.

VII: Peter Damian, Cardinal Bishop of Ostia, and Humbert, Cardinal Bishop of Silva Candida. Occasionally they disagreed and engaged in controversy between themselves. Peter, for example, believed that priests ordained by simoniac bishops were canonically ordained, so long as they were not themselves guilty of simony; Humbert believed that no orders conferred by a simoniac bishop were valid—a belief, incidentally, which might have stripped the Church of half her clergy.[22]

Peter's best-known work on the subject is the *Liber gratissimus*, devoted principally to showing (as against Humbert's position) the validity of orders freely conferred by simoniac bishops.[23] But Peter's characteristic rhetoric against simony, which caught up the work of older commentators and pointed the way for later satirists, is best seen in other *opuscula*, especially the *Contra philargyriam et munerum cupiditatem* and the *Contra clericos aulicos*. The *Contra philargyriam*, addressed to the Roman Curia, begins with a warning against accepting meed for judgment:

> Among all the armies of vices roaring around you, among the heavy tempests of darts falling like hail, you must be attentively vigilant against avarice, and always oppose your shield to her arrows. For she urgently desires to inflict a lethal wound on her sufferers; primarily, however, that she may extinguish the sight not of the eye but of the heart. Whence the Wise Man says: "presents and gifts blind the eyes of judges, and make them dumb in the mouth, so that they cannot correct" (Eccli. XX, 31). For she arms clients with meed, and by this captures and blinds the hearts of those who hold a privileged place at the ears of princes—of whom our Lord complains, through Isaias, saying, "Thy princes are faithless, companions of thieves: they all love bribes, they run after rewards." (Isaias, I, 23).

[22] Whitney, p. 26; Tellenbach, p. 98.

[23] S. Petrus Damiani, *Liber qui dicitur gratissimus*. In PL, CXLV, 99–160. Scholarship in Manitius, *Geschichte*, III, 22–23.

Someone may say, "I never ask for anything, but if anything is offered freely I don't refuse it." Lo, here is described, not those who ask for bribes, but those nevertheless who love them. They are not unjustly called companions of thieves, because while they accept secret gifts, they dread being caught at it by their fellow officials and associates as if it were a secret crime. And note that it says "they run after rewards;" for however large the alms they give out of their liberality when asked, nevertheless they do not escape the stain of guilt. . . .

Clearly, the sons of Samuel were said to have no other guilt, except that they loved meed, and did not follow the example of their father's scrupulous conduct; yet they lost irrecoverably the rule over the people of Israel.

Peter's argumentative method is simple. He opens with elaborate rhetoric, draws his principles from scriptural authority, then embellishes his argument sardonically with *exempla* drawn from Scripture, massing the familiar quotations like artillery in support of his reasoning.

Peter then discusses the dangers of wealth *per se*. Wealth is permissible only if its excess is distributed to the poor. "Let the avaricious man go and build churches, let him earnestly hear sermons, join old enemies together in peace, be attentive at daily mass and remote from worldly business; yet so long as the fire of avarice is not extinguished in him, every flower of his virtue is burned up, and no one can be found more guilty than he." Avarice caused the sale of Christ Himself, and the crimes of those two scriptural types of simony, Giezi and Simon Magus. Buyers and sellers of Holy Orders are not the only simoniacs; those who sell the judgment of the synod are also guilty. If the man to whom we sell a decision is contending justly we are selling the truth; if unjustly, "we are fighting against the truth, which is Christ, with the temerity of impudent audacity."

It is not necessary that a simoniac strike a bargain for money. Those who seek rewards not bargained for are equally guilty,

like Giezi, who formed his plot after the fact. Peter finds an example
at home:

> I saw clearly when an episcopal appointment was to be made, a
> certain one of our brothers (whose name I suppress, though
> I note the vice) who jumped around, as the time for the synodi-
> cal council approached, as if the anticipated time of threshing
> or harvest were coming. For he was girding himself to collect
> meed, and to reap it he was sharpening, not a steel blade, but
> the sickle of eloquence . . . . The Old Enemy often fools the
> hopeful with this sort of gain, never giving them what he has
> promised. For just as the falconer lures the hawk with a piece
> of meat, but as soon as he holds it in his hand takes away the
> meat and binds its feet with a leather thong; so the devil promises
> lucre at first, but then withdraws it and sets the noose of sin.
> And in this way he who desires meed, like a mouse which tries
> to gnaw the bait, is strangled with the snare.

Some men promise themselves that they will not let meed affect
their just judgment. But the resolution rarely works: "Once we
have taken meed, if we wish to do something against the giver,
presently the words become soft in our mouth, the edge of our
speech is dulled, the tongue hangs as it were blushing with shame.
A mind aware that it has taken meed weakens the vigor of judicial
censure, and represses the liberty of eloquence. For if rectitude
of judgment is not entirely taken away, nevertheless the authority
of judgment is weakened." Sometimes the acceptance of apparently free gifts demands a repayment in other, unforeseen affairs.
The best advice is that of Scripture, to keep our hands from all
gifts, and so to preserve our liberty of mind. Peter's peroration
summarizes his earlier warnings:

> Let us not love bribe-taking, lest (may it not be!) in the judg-
> ment of the hidden judge, we be cast out of the priestly order
> . . . . Let us not sell the the synod, nor reduce the synodal
> decree to the quantity of a price, lest we seem to be selling the

holy spirit of the sacred council . . . . Let our money go to the hands of the poor; let our purse, which once swelled with avarice, be emptied by mercy. Let our riches and treasures be the lucre of souls, and let the precious talents of the virtues be hidden in the ark of our breast.[24]

The *Contra clericos aulicos* is an early example of that long series of assaults, stretching up through the Reformation, on churchmen whose chief employment was in the business of secular courts. Such worldly honors, says Peter, are one form of *munus*. He modifies the conventional classification of *munus a manu, ab obsequio,* and *a lingua. Munus ab obsequio,* he says, contains within itself the two other types, "for who is more clearly proven to give money to obtain honors than the man who lays out such expenses by using carriages, such sums in caring for an abundance of precious ornamented clothes?" A satirical character, in the classical manner, of the obsequious courtier follows:

> He widens his eyes, makes gestures, claims the good cheer of a serene heart. He hangs upon a nod, and awaits his lord's precept as if it were the voice of Phoebus through the Sibylline Oracle. Ordered to go, he flies; told to stay, he stands like granite. If his lord is hot this man sweats; if his lord has a fever, this man complains of the heat. But if his lord is a little cold, this man, body trembling, has to get numb. If his lord wants to sleep, the courtier gets tired; if his lord is full, the courtier must belch. And so he says nothing at all unless he thinks it will please his lord.

The work then moves to an attack on the courtier-clerk.[25] Peter Damian has more to say about venality elsewhere.[26] We shall

---

[24] S. Petrus Damiani, *Contra philargyriam et munerum cupiditatem.* In PL, CXLV, 529–542.

[25] S. Petrus Damiani, *Contra clericos aulicos, ut ad dignitates provehantur.* In PL, CXLV, 463–472. Cf. Juvenal, *Saturae,* III, 100–108.

[26] Cf., e.g., *Apologeticum de contemptu saeculi,* VI. In PL, CXLV, 256–257. Here, basing his argument on St. Paul's statement that avarice is idolatry, he

deal with some of his verse below. All his works were sufficiently popular during the century following his death to have had a strong influence on later writers.

Cardinal Humbert's fullest statement on simony is the long *Adversus simoniacos libri tres*, written about 1058 in answer to a lost piece defending simoniacal ordinations.[27] It is an elaborate work, drawing its doctrine from old papal decretals and decrees of past councils, the Church Fathers, and even a number of Roman poets. The simoniac bishops, says Humbert, are "pseudoepiscopi," like the bishops of earlier heresies, and believe outrageously that the Holy Spirit willy-nilly

> must obey their wills and their commands, and drawn by their cords of money or bound as it were by their golden chains, in the plenitude of His sanctity must participate in their cursed consecrations and cooperate in their venal works.
>
> (PL, CXLIII, 1014c)

But since they buy what they get, they do not receive free grace, and hence cannot give it. How then can their ordinations, which should be vehicles of grace, be valid? As St. Paul says, the avaricious worship idols. "Hence avaricious men, worshipping money like a strange god, consider it omnipotent, as the pagans considered their various gods; so much so that they believe money has the power to subject the Holy Spirit to itself . . . . They grow pale at

---

amuses himself with the thesis "Quod avarus nummicola verius quam Christicola nuncupetur."

[27] Manitius, *Geschichte*, III, 23–25. The work, which is printed in PL, CXLIII 1005–1094, is of great historical importance, for it represents a revolutionary denial of the sacred character of kingship, and of assertion the right of the Church to complete freedom from secular control. It suddenly brought forth in full maturity the basic ideas of the Investiture Contest. The concept of the unsale-ability of the *donum Dei*, on which much of Humbert's argument is based, is fundamentally significant. It is discussed at length below, pp. 155–158.

the sight of money, and do right and wrong at its nod, and yet think that that will be completely pleasing to God which cannot be unpleasant to themselves."

Some people claim that simoniacs are no worse than other merchants; but the merchants sell what rightfully may be bought for common necessity, and heavenly things may not be bought and sold, since both gift and price are from God:

> The seller by demanding money steals from the buyer both his faith and his money. The buyer on the other hand by offering money likewise steals faith and the grace of the Holy Spirit from the seller; and it happens wonderfully and unhappily that neither gets what he has stolen from the other, but rather each one loses what he had before and instead gets only damnation, which he did not have before. But though each of them is wretched, still the more wretched is he who has lost both his faith and his money, and also the spiritual grace which he was seeking for a price; he has stolen something from the other and has gotten nothing for himself; rather he has gotten a curse in place of a blessing.
>
> (PL, CXLIII, 1094 c)

The literature directly concerned with simony was extensive,[28] aside from the multitude of incidental references to the subject by the chroniclers, moralists and commentators. To the medieval clerical moralist there could be no more thorough subversion of Christian spirituality than the placing of a price on spiritual functions or spiritual offices. Yet, with the interpenetration of the feudal and ecclesiastical systems this had become a normal occurrence. The eleventh-century reform was an attempt to renew Christian spirituality, especially as it concerned the life of the priest-

---

[28] A few items may be mentioned: Bernoldus, *De emtione ecclesiarum* (ca. 1090); Deusdedit, *Libellus contra invasores et symoniacos* (ca. 1097); Bruno, *Libellus de symoniacis* (ca. 1108); Gerhoh of Reichersberg, *Libellus de eo quod princeps huius mundi iam iudicatus sit* (ca. 1135). All edited in *MGH, Libelli de lite.*

hood. Hence the deep significance of the whole Investiture Contest, and of the attacks on simony which formed an essential part of it. These attacks, as we have seen, were common coin by the third quarter of the eleventh century, when the characteristic literary satire on meed was beginning to make its appearance. There was much true satire, indeed, in polemics like those of Peter and Humbert.

THREE

THE REBIRTH OF VENALITY-SATIRE IN ECCLESIASTICAL REFORM

The early pamphleteering of the Investiture Contest was concurrent with a revival of interest in the Roman satirists. The study of the classical poets renewed not only the poetry of nature and of love, but also verse with a moral aim.[29] Raby has suggested that Adalbaro of Laon's *Carmen ad Rotbertum*, written in 1017 and full of reminiscences of Persius, Virgil, Horace and Juvenal, marked the return of formal satire to European literature.[30] Only a few years later, about 1025, the money-theme itself returned in the *Fecunda ratis* of Egbert of Liège, a curious potpourri of instructional material gathered by a life-long teacher.[31] Like the original ark, the *Fecunda ratis* was burdened heavily with a great variety of things, the purpose of which was to provide a store of educational ideas and principles illustrated from classical, scriptural, and contemporary sources. Egbert, who taught the trivium at Liège, had nothing to do with Church reform; but he was thoroughly familiar with Sallust, Lucan, Persius, and especially Horace

[29] Manitius, *Geschichte*, III, 964.
[30] Raby, *Secular Latin Poetry*, I, 311–312; Manitius, *Geschichte*, II, 525–531.
[31] Raby, *Secular Latin Poetry*, I, 401; Manitius, *Geschichte*, II, 535–539.

and Juvenal. The money-passages of the *Fecunda ratis* are obviously inspired by the classics:

> Dissipat hic sacros malesueda Pecunia mores;
> Rerum corruptrix regina Pecunia uincit.[32]

Egbert writes a little exercise "On Money-Worship":

> Nummorum riui, uos estis grana columbae
> Digna coli, pro relliquiis festiua beatis!
> Propter eos multis indignis fulchra parantur,
> Nobiliumque thoros ascendere sepe iubentur;
> Hos non ars sed diua Pecunia prestat honores.[33]

The echoes from the Roman satirists are obvious. A similar exercise, "On the Hunger for Gold," begins with Virgil's "Auri sacra fames."[34] And another attributes the degeneration of the Romans after their ancient greatness to corruption by *munera*.[35] Egbert's money-passages smell rather obviously of the lamp, and have none of the scornful sting found in the pamphlets of Peter Damien or Humbert. Their purpose is didactic rather than satiric, even when the vigor of the older poets vivifies Egbert's academic verse.

Horace's Queen Cash makes her appearance again in an allegorical excursus which describes the defeat of *Sophia* by *Pecunia*:

> Delibuta comas ingressa Pecunia turres
> Turritasque domos, solaria fulta columnis,
> Hinc indefensam pepulit cum uecte Sophiam,

---

[32] Egbert of Liège, *Fecunda ratis*, ed. E. Voigt (Halle, 1889), I, 669–670. Cf. Horace, *Epistulae*, I, vi, 37.

[33] *Fecunda ratis*, I, 1248–1252. The dove, according to the tradition, will not eat refuse or carrion, but always chooses the finest grain. Hence the "grana columbae" of line 1248. Cf. A. Neckham, *De naturis rerum*, LVI. For line 1252 cf. Juvenal, *Saturae*, V, 136.

[34] *Fecunda ratis*, I, 1334–1339. For line 1334 cf. Virgil, *Aeneid*, III, 57.

[35] *Fecunda ratis*, I, 1491.

Precipitem trudens, moribundam ad rudera strauit.
Quod laudant proceres, dignum dixere fere omnes:
'Haec mendica quid hic faceret sine fruge fruendi,
Que raro uel numquam nostra cupita resoluit?
Haec placet, a nobis nusquam procedat, ut absit!
Haec nos delectat magis; illa sit abdita semper,
Hinc curis confecta fameque perempta facesset,
Haec sit apud mediocres et non liberiores;
Ista suas nobis effundat tota crumenas,
Vix relique plebi uictum uestemque relinquens!'

(I, 1599-1611)

So *Pecunia* defeats the helpless *Sophia* amid the jeers of the powerful. The combat is probably the earliest medieval version of Langland's struggle between Meed and Reason, though it is hardly satire.

In mid-century, about twenty-five years after the *Fecunda ratis* was written, another poet was writing satires in imitation of Horace. Of the life of the poet who called himself by the pseudonym Sextus Amarcius Gallus Piosistratus, virtually nothing is known.[36] Internal evidence in his four books of *Sermones* suggests that he was born in the Rhineland, that he wrote in the last years of the reign of Henry III, and that he was probably a monk. He was clearly a learned man, with a knowledge not only of the Roman and early Christian poets, but also Tacitus and Pliny. Of the Romans, Horace was his particular model, and of Christian poems the *Psychomachia* of Prudentius. Though obscure, Amarcius is a true poet with a genuine feeling for satire and a firm control of his subject matter. His editor, Manitius, elsewhere calls him "the oldest of the extant great satirists of the Middle Ages."[37] The poet's feeling for satire is enlivened by a strong conception of the ills of his age, but the scholar still predominates over the satirist. "The evils of the recent period which the poet enumerates,"

[36] Manitius, *Geschichte*, II, 569–574; Raby, *Secular Latin Poetry*, I, 401–403.
[37] Manitius, *Geschichte*, II, 571.

remarks Manitius, "are drawn for the most part from the writings of the Roman satirists . . . so that he often censures Roman customs instead of Germanic; which everyone knows is a common vice among writers of the Middle Ages."[38] This habit throws a veil of conventionality and unreality over his work.

Amarcius deals with the meed-theme too in the manner of the Roman poets. In a piece "On the virtues of our forebears and the vices of their descendants," one of the sins that distinguish modern man is his slavery to money:

> Tunc qui vilis erat, quamvis centena talenta
> Palma porrigeret tremula gemmasque nitentes
> Proferret titubante vola, non ulla potestas
> Concessa est illi. Sed nunc qui vendit opellas,
> Discissos senio byrsas qui tendit olentes
> Dentibus inpressis, tereti qui lignea torno
> Vasa rotat, multo si scrinia fenore farta
> Exspolians nitidam portabit ad atria massam,
> Ille tribunus erit, quodcunque affectat habebit.
> Nemo tunc scalprum, nemo tunc scruta paterna
> Inproperat, dat gaza genus, formam, probitatem.
> Nummatis pars prima favet, laudantur amantur.[39]

The poem closes with a conventional lament on the state of the world. All is perverted, piety is destroyed, honor lost. Fraud reigns, and even the good you do is held against you. In short, the whole world is going to hell:

> Ei mihi! ad infernum totus modo cursitat orbis.
>
> (Sermones, I, i, 78)

The satire—perhaps more appropriately called an exercise—contains little that could not have been written in Imperial Rome. Despite the echo of Horace—

---

[38] In Amarcius, Sermones, ed. M. Manitius (Leipzig, 1888), p. xiv.

[39] Sermones, I, i, 51–62. For lines 61–62 cf. Horace, Epistulae, I, vi, 36–38.

> . . . dat gaza genus, formam probitatem.
> Nummatis pars prima favet, laudantur amantur—

the tone and attitude are those of Juvenal, though the lament for the fallen world is a monastic commonplace.

The second satire of Book I, "That avarice overturns laws and sanctions," is wholly devoted to the power of money. The venal magistrate is present, balancing gems against justice in the traditional scales. Amarcius versifies Saint Jerome's quotation (epist. CXXV ad Rusticum) of Saint Paul's aphorism on avarice:

> Illud pertractans animo Hieronimus inquit:
> "Omnium avaritia est mater radixque malorum."

In this satire Amarcius, an admirer of the reforming Henry III, brings the material and the spirit of the Roman satirists to bear for the first time in the Middle Ages on clerical venality and simony. The poet assails the bishop greedy for meed as well as the simoniac holder of a rural benefice who withholds the sacraments from the sick and the dying unless he receives money, and who will not preach except for money. Such a priest, he remarks, does not fear the bishop's court, for the angry bishop smiles at the sight of gold. He holds his benefice more for money than for heavenly reward (*Sermones*, I, ii, 125-152).

Amarcius returns to the theme of clerical venality in a satire on "What priests should do and what they should avoid." He pictures the venal bishop whose palm has been greased, or who has received *munera a lingua* or *munera ab obsequio*, and then utters a diatribe against the power of money, of the type which became characteristic of later money-satire:

> Nam si credendum est, quosdam, quia clam manus uncta est,
> [evil bishops] Suscipiunt, a nonnullis indebita poscunt
> Obsequia et plures humane laudis amore
> Sanctificant. . . .

.   .   .   .

Nunc quoque in ordinibus poscentes munera sacris
Indigni Christo vivunt et munera dantes.
Cur rarus nunc est sapiens? quia blanda videntur
Ocia proque libris sectatur fenora quisque,
Tractat non secum: tu tantum collige quod des.
Munera stultus amat, sapientem munera mulcent.
Iunge sales pro se, venias sine munera, nil est.
Quod si pro nichilo reputaret episcopus omnis
Munera inutilium et dignis preberet honores,
Non adeo multas satane temptatio mentes
Carperet et mundum non tantus volveret error!
Sed nunc quod non dat probitas, nummus tribuit, nunc
Dona ferens probus est, intrat, qui nil habet exit.
Attamen esse bonos aliquando videmus ineptos:
Nil dedit, ite mihi! bene me potavit, eamus.
O nummi, nummi, per vos emitur scelus omne,
Vestra presbiteri faciunt ope fasque nefasque!

(Sermones, III, vii, 887-911)

This passage, with its allusion to the three kinds of *munera* and
its reminiscences of Juvenal, is one of the earliest examples of that
meeting of classical learning and contemporary complaint which
is the heart of so much medieval venality-satire. Some of its
lines, like the generalization on *munera*,

Munera stultus amat, sapientem munera mulcent,

or that on the value of gifts in gaining entry for the bearer,

Dona ferens probus est, intrat, qui nil habet exit,

are typical of what was to follow in the twelfth century.

Satire revived in the Middle Ages with the reappearance of
classical studies, a spirit of reform, and audiences to whom the
satire could be addressed. In Amarcius these factors appear for
the first time associated with the venality-theme. Yet Amarcius
remains the distant observer rather than the embattled warrior,

more occupied with the imitation of the Roman poets than with the urgency of reform or the burning anger of social protest.[40] In the verse of Peter Damian the anger becomes more apparent.

Peter had been thoroughly trained in the classics at secular schools in Ravenna and Faenza, and was also a good poet.[41] Though most of his verse was devotional, he could use his talent for complaint. Thus he laments in a *rhythmus* the corruption of Rome under the anti-pope Cadalus:

> Heu! sedes apostolica
> Orbis olim gloria:
> Nunc, proh dolor! effeceris
> Officina Simonis.
> Terunt incudem mallei,
> Nummi sunt tartarei:
> Justo Dei judicio
> Fit ista condicio.[42]

He closes a letter to Pope Alexander II (1061-1073) with some brief advice in verse on avoiding meed: One who would keep the vigor of the Apostolic See must shun all favor and avarice. "He to whom a full purse opens its mouth with meed, poor in justice, loses his empty soul. Rome keeps the gates of heaven and holds the reins of the earth; if she wants more than these she is only seeking hell."[43] He writes other poems against avarice and the simoniacal clergy, one of them in the hymn-meter which

[40] Amarcius makes other passing references to venality. Cf., e.g., *Sermones*, III, i, and IV, iii, 203-244.

[41] On Peter Damian's training and poetic talent cf. Raby, *Secular Latin Poetry*, I, 329-374.

[42] S. Petrus Damiani, *Carmina et preces*, CLXXII. In PL, CXLV, 963-964. Peter thought well enough of the poem to include it in two of his letters (*Epistolae*, I, xx and IV, ix. In PL, CXLIV, 246-247, 313).

[43] *Epistolae*, VII, xv. In PL, CXLIV, 235.

was to become a most popular satirical vehicle in the following century:

> Mundi turba turbulenta,
> Error, et divisio,
> Haeresis Simoniana,
> Zelum, et ambitio,
> In lamentum nos compellunt
> Styli sub officio.[44]

Another *rhythmus*, offering moral advice to "all orders of all men living in the world," warns judges, witnesses and notaries (all later followers of Langland's Lady Meed) away from the attractions of *munera*:

> Pro nullo malo merito,
> Vel placitato pretio,
> Aut aliqua amicitia,
> Vertat vera judicia.
> Judex sedens in placito
> Non speret de lucratio,
> Sed Deum recte timeat,
> Et legem cito finiat.
> Testes, pro nullo munere
> Falsa loqui praesumite,
> Sed vera verba dicite
> Praesente vero Principe.
> Veraces sint notarii,

---

[44] *Carmina et preces*, CCXVIII. In PL, CXLIV, 969-970. The authorship is doubtful; it does not appear in the most authoritative MS of Peter's works. Cf. A. Wilmart, "Le recueil des poèmes et des prières de S. Pierre Damien," *Revue Bénédictine*, XLI (1929), 355. Recent investigations of O.J. Blum ("Alberic of Monte Cassino and the Hymns and Rhythms Attributed to Saint Peter Damien," *Traditio*, XII (1956), 87–148) suggest that it might possibly be attributed to Alberic of Monte Cassino, though the subject makes Peter's authorship seem more likely. For other poems by Peter on the subject cf. *Carmina et preces*, CLXXVI and CCXVII. In PL, CXLV, 964, 969.

Tenendo fidem animi:
Nec unquam pro denariis
Falsa scribant in chartulis.[45]

These rather pedestrian poems, if not satires in the fullest sense, are useful examples of the early treatment of the venality-theme in the heart of the Roman Curia, and show a willingness to voice social protest and admonition on important matters in verse. The objects of later money-satire already appear in Peter's verse: simoniac bishops and priests, corrupt judges and notaries, bought witnesses.[46]

By the end of the century satire on venality and the power of the purse was multiplying rapidly. An unusually well-written example is an attack on one Herbert of Losinga, written around 1095. In 1087 or 1088 Herbert had become through simony Abbot of Ramsey; in 1091, probably in the same way, he became Bishop of Thetford; and in the same year he bought the abbacy of Winchester for his father. This produced fifty lines of clever hexameters from the bitter pen of an unknown writer, almost undoubtedly English:[47]

Pro dolor! aecclesiae nummis panduntur et aere;
Clave symoniaca reserantur ovilia sancta.
Si presens esses, furem, Petre, nonne ferires?
Malleus argenti confringit ovilia Christi.
Quid, lex sacra, facis? quid, sancta Nicea, silescis?
Dormis an vigilas? nam cur sententia cessat?

---

[45] *Carmina et preces*, CCXXII. In PL, CXLV, 975. Authorship also doubtful. Cf. n. 44 above.

[46] The growing popularity of the venality-theme is indicated by its intrusion into such unlikely pieces as the *Carmen de bello Saxonico* (ed. O. Holder-Egger, Hanover, 1899), ca. 1076. The author attributes the capture of the castle of Heimburg to a bribed garrison, and moralizes on the effects of meed (lines 126–138).

[47] Manitius, *Geschichte*, III, 54–55.

Res nimis iniusta: fit nummis presul et abba,
Filius atque pater. Sed Spiritus almus abhorret,
Gratia furtivae quia dampnat dona monetae.
Filius est presul, pater abbas, Symon uterque.

More lines of similar complaint lead to generalizations about simony and the power of money, of the sort which soon became commonplace:

Regnat enim Symon, cum Symone pessima Mammon.
Quid non speremus, si nummos possideamus?
Omnia nummus habet; quae vult, facit, addit et aufert;
Securus regnat; obstant contraria nulla;
Distribuit leges. Quid non speretis ementes?
Si quid forte nocet, adsit modo nummulus: aufert.
Nummulus est parma; fit nummulus arcus et arma.

The peroration is an eloquent appeal to Rome:

Roma, caput mundi, tu quondam talibus ultrix,
Aut citius venias ultrices reddere poenas,
Aut, caput ut fueras, modo caudae victima fias.
Si sis venalis, quod quondam Numida risit,
Emptor non deerit; tu vendes atque peribis.
Talibus, ipse Deus, quondam cum reste minatus,
Mensas et sedes de sacris edibus arces.[48]

This effective satire, apparently well-known in England, [49] has much of the flavor and facility of the venality-verse of the next two centuries. The pointed reference to Rome and the generalizations on the power of *nummus* or *munera* are characteristic of the later verse.

But the most biting and hilarious satire of the century on meed was a prose tract written in 1099, when Bernard, Archbishop of

---

[48] *MGH, Lib. de lite*, III, 615–617.
[49] It was quoted by William of Malmesbury in his *Gesta regum anglorum*, ed. W. Stubbs (2 vols, Rolls Ser., London, 1887–89), IV, Par. 338. Cf. also Manitius, *Geschichte*, III, 55.

Toledo, visited Urban II at Rome to have his election confirmed
and to receive the legation over Aquitania. [50] The piece, usually
known as the *Tractatus Garsiae*, describes the translation of the
"relics of the precious martyrs Albinus and Rufinus" to Rome
by Archbishop "Grimoardus."

The powerful and efficacious relics of the martyrs Albinus and
Rufinus represented the white and the red, i.e., silver and gold.
By the time of the *Tractatus Garsiae* they were already widely circulated humorous euphemisms, especially among writers
against simony and the Curia, for the power of the purse. These
crudely allegorical saints must have been invented around mid-
century. Landulf, in his eleventh-century *Historia Mediolanensis*
refers to them twice, and Paul Lehmann has collected a number
of other references to them, early and late.[51] One distich was
especially common from the eleventh to the fourteenth century:

> Martyris Albini seu martyris ossa Rufini
> Romae si quis habet, vertere cuncta valet.[52]

The lines summarize well the theme of the *Tractatus Garsiae*.

The pamphlet pretends to be a description of the Archbishop
of Toledo's trip to Rome in 1099, and the events which took
place upon his arrival, written by one Garsias, canon of Toledo,
about whom nothing is known, and whose name is probably a
pseudonym.[53] The pupose of the visit is the presentation of the
relics of the two saints, newly found by Archbishop Grimoardus,
to Pope Urban, a holy man who would certainly receive them
with joy. Grimoardus wants the legation over Aquitania, which

---

[50] Manitius, *Geschichte*, III, 46. Cf. also P. Lehmann, *Die Parodie im Mittelalter*, pp. 45–50, which discusses the work and translates passages into German.

[51] Lehmann, *Parodie*, pp. 43–45.

[52] Lehmann, *Parodie*, p. 44. Note the references, p. 44, n. 1.

[53] Lehmann, *Parodie*, p. 50.

had been granted by Gregory to his predecessors. The office should not be denied to one so portly, fat, and fastidious. The wine-bibbing archbishop has a paunch so mighty that he can eat a whole salmon for breakfast. He should be the Pope's natural choice for the office, for the Pope, too, has a great paunch; and both Pope and Archbishop have risen in the Church by the same charitable activities: "proscribing the innocent, persecuting the just, deceiving the poor, violently cheating orphans out of their patrimonies . . . ."

Fortified with the precious relics, the Archbishop enters Rome, hoping to give a sermon before the Pope. His clamor at the Lateran gate is answered by the gatekeeper: "If anyone must go in to the pope, he may approach safely by the introduction of Albinus." Grimoardus finds the pontiff seated on a rich throne, surrounded by "very fat cardinals," at a banquet which turns out to be a drinking bout. The Pope is being served wine in a rich goblet and urged by his cardinals to drink deeply. He consumes toast after toast in the manner of a litany, "for the salvation of the world, for the redemption of souls, for the sick, for the fruits of the earth, for peace, for travelers, for sailors, for the prosperity of the Roman Church. . . ." In the irreverent and indecorous hands of Garsias the customary prayers of the Church have become toasts at a carouse. At the Pope's feet sits Gregory of Pavia reading from the *Anti-Cato*, or *Exterminatoreus*. The book glorifies the virtues of the saints Albinus and Rufinus:

> Oh what precious martyrs are Rufinus and Albinus, Oh how eloquent, how praiseworthy; whoever has their relics is immediately made free of sin, made heavenly instead of earthly, turned from impious to innocent. We have seen simoniac, sacrilegious prelates, wasters of their churches, who because of the aforesaid relics were purged by apostolic benediction and, entangled no more in guilt, having nothing of the old stain, returned home new and as it were reborn. Whoever, therefore,

is infected with the stain of adultery, whoever is guilty of
homicide, whoever is polluted with the crime of fornication,
whoever is pale with the stain of envy, whoever is marked by
the infamy of perjury, in sum, all the sacrilegious, disparagers,
drunkards, thieves, the avaricious, the insolent, the savage, the
betrayers, the impious, the liars, the malevolent—how many
more?—everyone detestable, proscribed, infamous, guilty, ex-
iled, condemned; finally, all who by hand, mouth or tongue
have offended God; let them delay not coming to the Lord
Pope, bearing relics of the precious martyrs, to be absolved of
everything. Otherwise their petitions will be frustrate. Come,
come, simoniac archbishops, archdeacons, abbots, deans and
priors, offer to the Roman Pontiff the two martyrs who gain
entry into the Roman Church . . . .
Ask through Albinus and you shall receive, seek through Rufinus and you shall find, knock through either martyr and it
shall be opened to you . . . .
For never-failing victory stays with these martyrs. Who will
oppose where Albinus intercedes? Who will contradict where
Albinus prays? Who will refuse where Rufinus orders? These
are the two martyrs who have bravely captured kings, emperors,
dukes, tetrarchs, princes, and other rulers of the earth; these are
the two martyrs who have triumphantly subdued bishops,
cardinals, archbishops, abbots, deans, priors, levites, priests, subdeacons, and, to end quickly, the Roman Pontiff himself. These
are the two martyrs most mighty in churches, listened to in
synagogues, triumphant in assemblies . . . .

The reading is long. What Albinus and Rufinus open, no one
closes. They exercise the power of binding and loosing at
will, for Pope Urban is completely devoted to them. He has
gone through every torment for them, "thirsting for Albinus,
burning for Rufinus. And when from various realms and distant
regions stuffed-full bishops and propped-up abbots approached
offering relics of the precious martyrs, he giving thanks received
them with great devotion of heart and compunction of soul." Yet

when the Pope's chests are full, alas, it is as if there is still nothing, such is his thirst for the relics of these two martyrs. If any son of the Church has some of their relics, let him offer all to Urban. In search of their relics the Pope has made three trips through France, and when threatened by enemies he has commended his safety to them: "Albinus is my helper: I shall not fear; what can man do to me? It is better to trust in Rufinus than to trust in man." Thus he was saved and rejoiced: "Albinus vincit, Albinus regnat," to which the cardinals answered, "Rufinus imperat."

As the reading from the *Anti-Cato* ends, the Archbishop of Toledo steps forward intoning, "Sancte Albine, ora pro nobis, Sancte Rufine, ora pro nobis." Here, remarks a cardinal, is a true son of the Church. The Pope embraces him: "And now, brother, have you found any of the relics of the blessed martyrs Albinus and Rufinus, so loved in Rome?" Grimoardus draws forth a great quantity of them, "namely of the kidneys of Albinus, of the ribs of Rufinus, of the chest, the forearm, the left shoulder; these the Roman Pontiff placed in the treasure chest of Saint Cupidity next to the shrine of the Blessed Greed, his sister, not far from the basilica of their mother, Avarice, where he buried them magnificently with his own hands, with the spices of good will and the balsam of devotion, exactly on the kalends of May." The cardinals are present, robed in white, and chanting "Feliciter, feliciter, feliciter."

The Pope delivers a sermon over the buried "relics," recounting the victories they have brought him, and praising their donors:

> Let us be consoled, let us be consoled, my people; behold Al-
> binus comes, behold the Church of Toledo brings us Rufinus.
> Behold the three Gauls make offerings; behold England, in
> which the buried entrails of Albinus are housed, sends them back
> to you. Behold the rich seat of the Flemish, where the bones
> of the martyrs lie artfully hidden, smiles on Urban . . . .

> In churches, in councils, in assemblies, in kingdoms, in cities, in territories, in palaces, in towers, on land, on sea, everywhere, we triumph, we reign, rule, entice, despoil, rape, betray, extort, deceive, defraud and cheat.

The Pope continues, praising his own powers and attributing his victories to the power of Albinus and Rufinus. Now is the time for celebration: "Consume, guzzle, devour, drink, drink, my blessed cardinals, truly blessed, for you know Albinus and Rufinus."

The Pope's drunken harangue continues at length, but finally, he seats the Archbishop. In a dialogue with the Pope, Garsias answers with deference but modifies his replies in asides, to the Pope's complete deception and confusion:

> Pope: "Brother Garsias, I know my sheep!" Garsias: "Truly you know them!" and to himself: "for you leave nothing in their purses!" Pope: "What did you say?" Garsias: "I was saying that the Rhone empties the Saone into the sea." Pope: "Brother Garsias, and mine know me." Garsias: "I agree, they know you." And to himself: "for a great robber and a swindler of high talent." Pope: "What did you say? I didn't understand." Garsias: "I was saying that Zeus and Calais were the sons of Boreas."

The scene develops into a drinking bout among the cardinals, who finally shove the drunken Archbishop in front of the Pope with the recommendation that he is a most potent potter. To which the Pope replies, "Amen, amen I say to you, the legation of Aquitania must be entered through many potations." And so the scene dissolves amid the drunken jangling of the cardinals: "John: 'It is human to drink.' Teucer: 'We are men.' And they fell asleep." Thus the satire ends.[54]

---

[54] *Tractatus Garsiae Tholetani canonici*, in *Lib. de lite*, II, 425–435. This devastating caricature seems to have had little relation to the actual character, appearance,

It is a brilliantly executed piece of work. Though its attack is blunt and its irony broad, the basic device of the precious relics is cleverly conceived and deftly handled. Paraphrase does the piece injustice. "All that can be given," remarks Lehmann, "is a scanty substitute for the Latin original, which a master of satire has written." The author achieves much of his success by making the work a *pastiche* of distorted Biblical reminiscences and fragments of liturgical formulas, of hagiographic literature and ceremonies of the Curia.[55] Aside from the element of parody, the unknown author says by way of the relics of these fiscal saints much the same thing which was to be said by the meed-satirists of the centuries to follow, whether the allegorical vehicle were *Regina Pecunia*, *Dan Denier*, Sir Penny, Lady Meed, or some other regal figure. Some of Garsias' successors may have spoken more profoundly. None spoke more wittily, or with greater verve and audacity. The technique of heavy irony, spilling over into open abuse, became a favorite device of the later satirists.

Parody plays a significant part in the *Tractatus Garsiae*, but is the essence of the famous and influential "Gospel of Mark Silver" —the *Evangelium secundum Marcas Argenti*, the earliest version of which may have appeared at this time. Composed of passages imitated or distorted from the Gospels and strung together into

---

or policy of Urban II (1088–1099), though some of the events of his pontificate appear there in distorted form. Modern historians speak of Urban as "tall and handsome, eloquent and learned. . . . It was the gentleness and moderation of his nature that won admiration; we are told that he refused at the price of men's lives to recover Rome." (Brooke, pp. 87–88). His policy was the continual development, in a quieter way, of the reforms of Gregory VII. The fat and avaricious drunkard of the *Tractatus Garsiae* seems far from the truth. One scents the disappointed office-seeker in the pamphet's background. The political caricature had come into its own.

[55] Lehmann, *Parodie*, p. 50.

a narrative, it was widely circulated until well after the Reformation.[56] The parody was frequently reworked, so that it appears in three distinct versions, the earliest of which is the briefest. This early version, from the famous Benediktbeuern Manuscript, established its pattern, and is short enough to translate here in full:

> The beginning of the Gospel according to Mark Silver: At that time the pope said to the Romans: "When the son of man shall come to the seat of our majesty, first say to him, 'Friend, whereto art thou come?' Yet if he shall continue knocking without giving you anything, cast him out into the exterior darkness." And it chanced that a certain poor man came to the court of the Lord Pope, and cried out, saying, "Have mercy on me, at least you, dispensers of the pope, because the hand of poverty hath touched me. I am needy and poor; therefore I beg that you relieve my calamity and misery." And they hearing it were moved with indignation and said: "Friend, keep thy poverty to thyself, to perish with thee. Go behind me Satan, because thou savourest not the things that are of money. Amen I say to thee, thou shalt not enter into the joy of thy lord till thou pay thy last farthing." And the poor man went his way and sold his mantle and his tunic and all that he had and gave to the cardinals and the dispensers and the treasurers. But they said: "And this, what is this among so many?" And they cast him out; and going forth he wept bitterly, and would not be consoled. But later there came to the court a certain wealthy clerk, fat and thick and gross, who in the sedition had committed murder. He first gave to the dispensers, second to the treasurers, third to the cardinals. But they thought among themselves that they should receive more. The Lord Pope, hearing that his cardinals and ministers had received many gifts, was sick, nigh unto death. But the rich man sent him a couch of gold and silver, and immediately he was made whole.

[56] Lehmann, *Parodie*, p. 54. Lehmann (pp. 54–59) discusses the work fully. There are at least 13 extant MSS, and three more can be assumed as lost originals of early prints of the piece.

Then the Lord Pope called his cardinals and ministers to him and said to them: "Bretheren, look, lest anyone deceive you with vain words. For I have given you an example: as I have grasped, so you grasp also."[57]

The piece, as its opening suggests, is set in the form of the Gospel to be read in the Mass, and was possibly once a part of a lost "missa de muneribus."[58] Its popularity must have helped inspire much of the later satire on the power of money at Rome. By Langland's time its length had tripled.[59] It is representative of the sort of mocking parody, like the drunkards' Masses and lovers' Masses, which had great vogue in the Middle Ages.

A number of other venality poems from the turn of the century are edited among the *Libelli de lite* in the *Monumenta Germaniae historica*. Most of them appear to be French in origin, and are written in the manner of Marbod of Rennes (ca. 1035-1123) and his imitators. One of the more amusing is a *rhythmus* of 90 rhymed lines:

> Sua Simon dat decreta:
> Quod si bursa sit repleta,
> Fiet presul vel propheta
> Davus, Birria vel Geta.
> Non attendit probitatem
> Neque mores nec etatem.
> Simon facit hunc primatem,
> Hunc priorem, hunc abbatem.
> Ad hoc pauper non accedit,
> Accepturum nil se credit,
> Nil habebat, nichil dedit,

---

[57] P. Lehmann, *Parodistische Texte* (Munich, 1923), pp. 7–8. Lehmann conveniently edits the three versions together in this volume.

[58] In some MSS there are additions at the beginning and end indicative of such a parody: "Dolus vobiscum et cum gemitu tuo," "Gloria tibi auro," "Laus tibi auro." Cf. Lehmann, *Parodie*, p. 58.

[59] In Lehmann, *Parodistische Texte*, pp. 10–12.

Nec in sancta sede sedit.
Simon facit hos maiores,
Hos abbates, hos priores.
Nummos quaerit et non mores,
Et nummatis dat honores.
Venter nimis incrassatus
Qualiscumqe, sed nummatus,
Aput omnes inflammatus,
Quem plus inquinat reatus,
Si offerre sit paratus,
Fiet presul et prelatus.

These pictures are becoming familiar: the avaricious merchant-prelate; the poor clerk unable to buy a benefice; the fat, wealthy and despicable simoniac. The poem attacks the wordliness of these simoniac churchmen—a herd of the swine of Epicurus, "Grex porcorum Epicuri." Having bought their places, they are interested only in the returns they can get:

Sunt tenaces, sunt avari;
Dare nolunt, immo dari.
Nummos querunt contemplari;
De favore populari
Volunt omnes gloriari.[60]

This type of *rhythmus* soon became a favorite satirical medium. Its astonishing rhythmical variety, its multiple rhymes, its compression, its adaptability to parodies of hymn and liturgy, were perfectly suited to the audacious, grimacing, punning, gymnastic type of satire which came to be called "goliardic."

Other poems of the group discuss episcopal simony, Roman avarice, the grasping papal doorkeeper, the frustrations of the poor scholar without benefice, the countries which Rome places under tribute for its wealth, the universal reign of money.[61] There are echoes of the Roman poets:

---

[60] *Lib. de lite*, III, 697–698.
[61] *Lib. de lite*, III, 698–705. The opening lines of one of the poems might

Romam vexat adhuc amor inmoderatus habendi.[62]

Almost all of the group reflect the increased activity and authority of the Papacy: "Roma caput mundi, terrarum summa potestas."[63]

These contents are characteristic. A full examination of one example will suggest the typical treatment of the venality theme at the turn of the century. This attack on the Court of Rome, written in the leonine lines which became one of the banes of medieval Latin verse, begins with the Pauline commonplace that avarice is idolatry:

> Gens Romanorum subdola antiqua colit idola,
> Argentum quondam coluit et in lucris insonuit;
> Adhuc suspirat hodie, aurum colens Arabiae.

This leads to a list of the countries from which Rome draws her wealth, and to the assertion that money is the judge at Rome, that the poor man goes unheard, and that he textortionist door-keeper awaits all visitors:

> Si das, intrabis protinus: si non, stas, stabis eminus.

Neither high birth nor eminence in learning is valued at the Court of Rome. Queen Pecunia reigns, aided by Simonia and Giesia:

> Sola regnat pecunia per terras et per maria.
> Jam regnat super cardines et angelorum ordines;
> Jam adtemptant coelestia mundi contemptibilia
> Jam regina pecunia, juncta sibi symonia

---

serve as an epigraph for the anti–Rome satire of the next two centuries:
> Ecclesiastica Roma negotia cum moderetur,
> Quaestio partibus omnis ab omnibus recitetur.
> Sola pecunia perficit omnia, nec tibi claudit
> Ianitor ostia, dona sequentia si prius audit.

[62] *Lib. de lite*, III, 703. Cf. Ovid, *Metam.*, I, 131 and *Fasti*, I, 195.
[63] *Lib. de lite*, III, 703.

Et leprosa giesia, in altiori regia,
Romae tenet concilium stans in conspectu omnium. . . .

The rest of the poem is devoted to a boast by Queen Pecunia, in which she catalogues her virtues with heavy irony:

Qui mundi quaeret gloriam et Romanorum gratiam,
Honores in ecclesia, sedes, mitras, sandalia,
Ad foras meas vigilet, me congregatim ventilet,
Me profundat latissime, obtinebit planissime
Quidquid ipse voluerit si me large prefuderit.
Distortam causam dirigo et aggravatam levigo;
Ferrum et saxa mollio, scribasque doctos lenio;
Quaecunque volo facio; ego nuptas decipio;
Ego corrumpo virgines; edomo cunctos homines;
Ego do privilegia, sed lego voluntaria.
Stant leges et judicia juxta mea consilia;
Ante me silet regula, et scripturarum formula;
Ante me silent canones; quae laudo, laudant Daemones;

She has travelled all the countries of the world and crossed all the seas, but nowhere has she found a people so dedicated to her as the Romans. Here she will make her home:

Hic erit mea requies; hic stabit mea facies;
Hic figam sedem stabilem inter plebem amabilem.[64]

Here, then, is Lady Meed, when vernacular literatures were still in their infancy. *Regina Pecunia* joins company with the saints Albinus and Rufinus. Her presence at Rome, and the generalizations she makes about her power, appear repeatedly in satire good and bad during the three centuries which follow.

---

[64] This version printed in Du Méril, *Poésies populaires latines antérieures au douzième siècle* (Paris, 1843), pp. 231-234. Also in *Lib. de lite*, III, 706-707.

FOUR

The Papacy as an Object of Venality-Satire

The revival of money-satire in the eleventh century, then, is in part a by-product of the great ecclesiastical reform movement of the period. The effect of this reform was to bring the papacy into a position of international leadership in spiritual, and often in secular, affairs. This resurgence led to the pamphlet war which characterized the Investiture Contest, where both sides made violent attacks on simony and avarice. At the same time the growing study of the Roman poets—especially Ovid and the satirists —fostered by the establishment of the cathedral schools, provided models for imitation and quotation, and inspired writers to try their hands at satire. Roman satire, along with the pertinent passages of Holy Writ, provided the new money-satirists with a language, as the spirit of reform and the sword-play of the Investiture Contest provided them with inspiration and fervor. By the close of the century their satire had developed a characteristic pattern, and conventions were already beginning to harden.

There is a paradox in these developments. Much of the money-literature is directed against the venality and avarice of the Roman Curia and even of the pope himself. This anti-Roman satire grows to an immense volume in the twelfth century. But early in the eleventh century, when the Papacy was most corrupt and degraded, it had attracted virtually no attacks. Only a reformed Papacy became the object of satire. It now seems clear that the *Romdiatribe* had its first roots in the papal Curia itself, especially among outspoken reforming cardinals like Humbert and the powerful Peter Damian. These men did not hesitate to publicize the venality which they sought to destroy; and as the struggle with the Empire developed, the imperial publicists quickly followed their lead. The early anti-Rome satire thus served both friend and foe of the Papacy; the friend as a weapon of reform, the foe as a weapon of destruction.

Nevertheless, the continued expansion of the literature on papal avarice and venality in the twelfth and thirteenth centuries requires further explanation. The longevity of this satirical theme resulted largely from the immensely expanded papal taxation necessary to support a rapidly growing institution, international in scope. By the middle of the twelfth century the Papacy had become by far the most complex organization, politically and economically, in the western world. Its tax problems—immense and complex subjects in themselves—must here be briefly sketched before we examine the venality-literature in which they resulted.

III

ROMA VORAX CAPUT: VENALITY-SATIRE, PAPAL ROME, AND THE CLERGY

ONE
DEVELOPMENTS IN PAPAL FINANCE

With the increasing activity of the Papacy throughout Europe the papal Curia grew steadily in importance and complexity. By the time of Innocent III (1198-1216), only 150 years after the rudimentary organization of Leo IX, the Court of Rome had developed a chancery, an exchequer, and a judicial division.[1] Unfortunately, little is known about the *camera*, or exchequer; documentary evidence of its methods and development before the thirteenth century, other than the broad complaints of the satirists themselves, is almost wholly lacking. But the cost of these new papal activities was obviously high. "The centralization of papal power," says Lunt, "necessitated the construction of a more efficient governmental machine. Good government, it was soon discovered, was expensive. Early in the process of transformation the Papacy began to look to its finances. Papal records were ransacked to discover all revenues which could be claimed, and demands for payment were pressed with vigor."[2]

---

[1] E. F. Jacob. "Innocent III," in *Cambr. Med. Hist.*, VI, 31-34.

[2] W. Lunt, *Financial Relations of the Papacy with England to 1327* (Cambridge, Mass., 1939), p. 31. Cf. also Lunt, "The Financial System of the Medieval

In later centuries the Crusades added to the financial burden of the Papacy.

Important studies by Lunt define the papal revenues which existed at the end of the eleventh century.[3] The most significant were the domanial incomes from the patrimonies and states of the Church, those normal feudal revenues which the Papacy had already outgrown by the middle of the eleventh century. A second source of income was the census of protected and exempt ecclesiastical foundations, which grew steadily during the centuries that followed. A third, if minor and highly irregular source, was the tribute paid by temporal rulers for papal protection. A fourth was Peter's Pence, which had begun very early in England and later spread to some other countries. Income taxes were levied irregularly on the clergy, but never for the use of the pope himself until 1228. Charitable subsidies, requested by the pope of his clergy, were also useful sources of income. Though they remained voluntary in the eleventh century, the element of choice seems to have later disappeared. An ancient source of revenue (and for some time the most profitable) was gifts and legacies to the Papacy by pious individuals. But however large this income might be, it was hardly dependable. Other sources (oblations, spoils, and fruits wrongfully received) were developed during the twelfth and thirteenth centuries, while many others (annates, fruits during vacancies, quindennia, indulgences, the sale of offices, and compositions) did not exist until the fourteenth century or later.

Papacy in the Light of Recent Literature," *Quarterly Journal of Economics*, XXIII (1909), 261–262.

[3] W. Lunt, *Papal Revenues in the Middle Ages* (2 vols., New York, 1934), esp. I, 57–136. I have dealt with satire on papal venality in "Economic Conservatism, Papal Finance, and the Medieval Satires on Rome," *Mediaeval Studies*, XXIII (1961), 334–351. Much of this chapter and some of the preceding is drawn, with changes, from that study.

The documentary evidence of these sources indicates the paucity and the irregularity of the income which they were producing at the close of the eleventh century, while the Papacy was taking its early, dramatic steps toward international leadership. Peter's Pence in England, for example, had quickly settled into a customary fixed annual sum just under 200 pounds sterling, and all of the 23 exempt foundations in England brought, as late as 1327 just over 10 pounds. This weakness forced the Papacy to depend very heavily on certain other revenues: services (*servitia*), visitation taxes, and chancery taxes. These taxes, in their rudimentary forms, are frequently at the heart of the satirists' complaints about Roman venality.

By far the most significant and profitable of these payments were those known as *servitia*. Services are defined by Lunt as "charges paid by patriarchs, archbishops, bishops, abbots and for a period by some priors on occasion of their appointment by the pope in consistory." Though these payments were not established as formal taxes, prescribed, regulated and subdivided, until late in the thirteenth century,[4] they had existed as customary gratuities from time immemorial. These gratuities (often referred to by papal sources as *servitia* long before their establishment as taxes) seem to have gradually settled into *de facto* taxes whose imposition and even amount had the force of law. The custom of paying the gratuities was well established by the time of Justinian, and was specifically recognized and accepted by Gregory the Great in 595.[5] Gregory, however, forbade outright charges for such services as ordinations and appointments. During the next four

----

[4] A. Gottlob, *Die Servitientaxe im 13. Jahrhundert: eine Studie zur Geschichte des päpstlichen Gebührenwesens* (Stuttgart, 1903), pp. 69–100, places the establishment of a formal tax in the pontificate of Alexander IV (1254–1261).

[5] *Papal Revenues*, II, 233–234.

centuries the custom of gratuities apparently hardened into a rigid convention, which probably prescribed at least the minimum gratuity for receiving the pallium from the pope. In 1027, for example, Canute complained of the high cost of these services to his bishops.[6]

Probably the amount and number of such gratuities or fees increased rapidly after the pontificate of Leo IX (1049-1055), when the great expansion of papal activity was under way, and when the number of confirmations controlled by the pope was increasing. We lack documents to show the numbers of these charges, still formally gratuities, or the amounts paid, but what was happening is clearly indicated by the satirical charges of simony, some of the earliest of which we have quoted in the last chapter. These are occasionally supported by chronicles or letters. Early in the twelfth century, for example, Bishop Ivo of Chartres replies to the papal legate, who had apparently found practices in his diocese which approached simony, that the fault lies in the example provided by Rome herself. When his deacons and cantors are accused of demanding gifts for their services, he says, they defend themselves by pointing to Rome where the officials make exorbitant demands for consecrating bishops and abbots, which they palliate under the name of "oblations," or "benedictions." The letter suggests that Roman venality was common talk: "Nec calamus nec charta gratis ibi (ut aient) habeatur."[7]

[6] *Papal Revenues*, II, 234–235.

[7] D. Ivo Carnotensis Episcopus, *Epistolae*, cxxxiii. In PL, CLXII, 141–143. Part of Bishop Ivo's attitude seems to spring from his position in the Investiture Contest; but John Bromyard's remarks (*Summa praedicantium*, Venice, 1586, "Honor," 14–19) in the fourteenth century are very similar. K. Jordan, "Zur päpstlichen Finanzgeschichte im 11. und 12. Jahrhundert," *Quellen und Forschungen*, XXV (1933–34), 61–104, deals at length with this early period of transition from gift to tax, with conclusions similar to the above. Cf. esp. pp. 80–82. He

It seems clear, then, that the *servitia* in their primitive and irregular form were the major target of the earliest anti-Rome satires; and the objections were probably the more shrill because the fees were large. Though records are lacking for the eleventh and twelfth centuries when the Rome satires first proliferated, Lunt estimates that the total expense of the consecration of a bishop cost the new prelate almost a whole year's income, which frequently had to be borrowed, and which often placed the churchman in financial difficulties for many years in the future.[8] There are thirteenth-century records of large sums being borrowed to meet the expenses of confirmation by the pope.[9] Meanwhile the noxious paradox of prescribed gratuities had raised the satirical cry of simony:

> Hoc sancivit mos Romanus,
> hoc decretum legitur:
> Non sit presul vel decanus
> is a quo nil dabitur.[10]

Visitation taxes were much lower than the *servitia* and were paid by few churchmen. The archbishops of Canterbury and

---

discusses (pp. 83–87) the one extant document which describes the early application of the *servitia*, the *Historia Compostelana*. The events described in the pertinent portion of this work took place between 1117 and 1130, and the *Historia* mentions the specific sums, which are high. Jordan's excellent summary deserves examination as a vivid account of the realities behind the satire. One is reminded of the burlesque *Tractatus Garsiae*.

[8] *Papal Revenues*, I, 87–89. The opening of one of Jacques de Vitry's *exempla* suggests the common impression of the normal state of a bishop returning from Rome:"Audivi de quodam prelato Anglico, cum a curia Romana exhaustus et sine pecunia rediret. . . ." G. Frenken, *Die Exempla des Jacob von Vitry* (Munich, 1921), p. 140.

[9] *Papal Revenues*, II, 238–239.

[10] B. Hauréau, *Notices et extraits des quelques manuscrits latins de la Bibliothèque Nationale* (6 vols, Paris, 1890–93), VI, 140. The passage is from one version of a poem attributed to Philip the Chancellor.

York, for example, paid 300 marks once every three years. The tax provided only a minor source of income to the papal *camera*; yet its existence probably helped multiply the complaints that everything at Rome had a price. To those who were hurt by these and other payments (and they could include all the clergy of a bishop's diocese) the gratuities represented the simple sale of the gifts of the Holy Spirit, the extortion of Giezi. The satire may have reflected, too, some of the opposition by growing monarchies to the export of money from their territories.

The chaotic development of the *servitia*, the haziness of its status on the borderland between gratuity and tax, and the informal nature of the Curia's whole tax structure during the period, suggest that the fees were difficult to control and to account for. They probably encouraged competition for revenue among the offices of the court, and acted as a blind for all sorts of minor extortion and tip-hunting, like that observed in the mid-eleventh century by Peter Damian—certainly an annoying and expensive practice. The custom had become so general in the thirteenth century that Innocent III was forced to recognize it publicly and in 1208 to take steps to stop the worst of it:

> We, indeed, members of the school of the bearers of the papal tiara when he visits a church in the City, and of the school of the keepers of the napery and the chaplains . . . all alike promise by taking oath that we will not in the future exact by importunity or extort by violence from any archbishop consecrated, or abbot blessed, or any one ordained, the horse or covering or any other thing, or, on account of this, impose or cause to be imposed any injury in word or deed on any one; but we will accept with an act of thanks that which shall have been given freely to us by any of the aforesaid, or that the camerarius, having been requested, shall have been able to obtain for us by way of gifts . . . .[11]

[11] Lunt, *Papal Revenues*, II, 235.

The satirists never distinguished this petty extortion from the taxes themselves. Indeed, during the eleventh and twelfth centuries there was no formally defined difference, and the complainants felt free to call their expenses simony. The complaints increased in wrath and swelled in volume as papal demands for income increased. The Church was discovering that its rejection of the early feudal ecclesiastical economy left a fiscal gap which had to be filled.[12] Viewed more broadly, the papal financial problems —like those of the rising monarchies—were significant evidence of the bursting of economic feudalism at the seams, the slow, haphazard, and painful process which transformed the dominant economy of Europe, over a period of centuries, from feudal agrarianism to a money economy. As the ecclesiastical economy, and hence papal taxation, continued to develop, so satires on Rome's venality and avarice continued to be written,[13] and Pro-

[12] On the papal financial problems cf. W. Lunt, "The Financial System of the Medieval Papacy in the Light of Recent Literature," *Quarterly Journal of Economics*, XXIII (1909), 261–262.

[13] Cf. O. Dobiache–Rojdesvensky, *Les poésies des goliards* (Paris, 1931), p. 76: "L'appareil de government du monde catholique formé peu à peu à partir du XIᵉ siècle, exigeait de grandes ressources financières. L'art de prélever l'argent, perfectionné au XIIᵉ et XIIIᵉ siècles par les agents des Innocent et des Grégoire, provoquait l'admiration des amis, les invectives des ennemis et les plaintes des contribuables. Cette fiscalité est allée en se développant sans cesse. Les étapes de la carrière ecclésiastique, les querelles des clercs, leurs procès avec les laiques traînés en Cour de Rome, les indulgences et les privilèges, les dédicaces des autels et les translations de reliques, les bénédictions et les pardons, les croisades, les pélerinages et les pénitences, les absolutions, tout servait désormais de prétexte à imposition, sans parler des dîmes, des oblations, des prémices, des cens etc. Les agents de Rome apparaissaient comme autant de tentacules pour pomper l'argent. Mais c'étaient surtout les procès *ad limina apostolorum* qui suscitaient l'animadversion: 'Gaude, mater nostra Roma . . . . Ad te trahit homines non ipsorum devotio aut pura conscientia, sed scelerum multiplicium perpetratio et litium decisio pretio comparata.'"

testant reformers who wished to turn them to their own purposes found a large body at hand.[14] Papal finance indeed had an almost revolutionary influence on the economic development of Europe.[15]

Other expenses at the Curia, poorly documented by formal records but regularly reflected in the satires, were the fees charged by the law courts. Appeals *ad limina* were encouraged to increase papal control over ecclesiastical affairs, and their cost became a regular refrain among the satirists.[16]   Some of the expenses connected with such litigation were chancery taxes; others were advocates' fees; still others were no doubt fees for the *auditores* and the petty clerks of the courts. In the absence of extant records we may surmise that these law courts were essentially self-supporting, had their own treasurers and kept their own accounts. They were clearly among the chief targets of the meed-satirists for over three centuries.

[14] Cf., e.g., the collection of one Reformation publicist, M. Flacius Illyricus *Varia doctorum piorumque virorum de corrupto ecclesiae statu poemata* (Basil, 1556), the earliest printed anthology of anti-clerical satirical verse.

[15] Lunt, "The Financial System of the Medieval Papacy." *Quarterly Journal of Economics*, XXIII (1909), 251-252: "The papacy not only organized one of the earliest and best of the medieval financial systems, but by means of its operations influenced profoundly the general economic development of Europe. . . . The Roman Church . . . with an almost modern system of taxation covering all western Europe, furnished one of the principal sources which aided the establishment of money and credit transactions on a large scale."

[16] Cf. n. 13 above.

TWO

SATIRE ON VENALITY AND THE POWER OF
MONEY AT THE COURT OF ROME

Against this background of a developing ecclesiastical economy and ever-increasing papal taxation we may consider the enormous mass of satire on the power of the purse at Rome, some early examples of which we have examined in the previous chapter. Much of it cannot be dated with accuracy. Anonymity, pseudonymity and false attributions are frequent, and style is inadequate as a means of dating the Latin poetry of the age. We can only say with assurance that virtually all the poetry to be considered was written between 1100 and 1300.

The tradition of Roman avarice was so commonplace that it achieved proverbial status, and a number of satirical tracts, verses, puns, and other devices became common property. The *Gospel according to Mark Silver* seems to have been one of these; the Rome acrostic mentioned by Walter Map is another:

> Radix
> Omnium
> Malorum
> Avaritia[17]

---

[17] W. Map, *De nugis curialium*, ed. M.R. James (Oxford, 1914), II, xvii, p. 82: "Venerunt Romani frequenter ad Offam ab imperatore missi, ditiaque ab ipso recesserunt . . . quos ut Roma uidit uestibus et auro lucidos, innata statim exarsit auaricia. Nec mirum: hoc enim nomen Roma ex auaricie sueque diffinicionis formatur principiis, fit enim ex R. et O. et M. et A. et diffinicio cum ipsa, 'radix omnium malorum auaritia.'"

There were satirical derivations of *papa* from *papare*[18] or *pavor pauperum*[19] and *Roma* from *rodo manus*.[20] This last found its way with tiresome frequency into satire, and with many variants became proverbial:

Roma manus rodit; quas rodere non valet, odit.[21]

Other puns were popular: *Marcus* and *marca* (as in *Marcas argenti*), *Luca* and *lucrum*, *libri* (of the Bible) and *libras*, *numen* and *nummus*, *reus* and *res*. The cardinals preferred a *salmonem* to *Salomonem*, and were referred to as *carpinales* or *carpidinares*.[22] Some single lines of verse or distiches became detached as metrical *sententiae*:

Curia Romana non querit ovem sine lana.[23]

[18] In the anonymous "Utar contra vitia" of the Benediktbeuern MS. Cf. A. Hilka and O. Schumann, eds., *Carmina burana* (Heidelberg, 1930, in progress), I, i, 77.

[19] I. Zingerle, "Bericht über die Sterzinger Miscellaneen-Handschrift," *K. Akademie der Wissenschaften zu Wien. Philos–hist. Klasse. Sitzungsberichte*, LIV (1866), 313:

> Papa pavor pauperum est diffinitus,
> in eo gramatice pertabatur ritus,
> nam qui fore debuit gratie dativus,
> factus est ecclesie rerum ablativus.

[20] Cf. C.-V. Langlois, "La littérature goliardique," *Revue bleue*, LI (1893), 177. Langlois mentions other "effroyables etymologies."

[21] J. Werner, ed., *Lateinische Sprichwörter und Sinnsprüche des Mittelalters* (Heidelberg, 1912), p. 86. Variants are numerous.

[22] Lehmann, *Parodie*, pp. 58–70, contains a full discussion of these puns, with many examples and references.

[23] Werner, *Sprichwörter*, p. 16. Obviously these were only "proverbial" among the learned. Other characteristic examples:

> Roma capit marcas, bursas exhaurit et archas;
> Ut tibi tu parcas, fuge papas et patriarchas!
> (Werner, *Sprichwörter*, p. 86)
> Romae Deus non est trinus, sed quattrinus.
> (*MGH, Scriptores*, VIII, 98, n. 38)

Another popular punning device consisted of plays on the Latin grammatical cases. A short poem reproduced by Lehmann, for example, characterizes the reign of the simoniac and informer in Rome in the terms *dativus* and *accusativus*: "Accusativus Romam regit atque dativus—the informer (or the plaintiff) and the briber rule Rome."[24] Some twelfth-century verses combine the two grammatical cases with the *manus rodit* cliché:

> Roma manus rodit, si podere non valet, odit.
> Dantes exaudit, nil dantibus hostia claudit,
> Accusativus si venerit ante tribunal,
> aut accuseris aut accusaberis ipse,
> proficit in neutro, si venerit absque dativo.[25]

Verses were composed of such clichés strung together like beads, without attention to form or development. The following is an excellent example, not of poetry, but of a collector's catch-all of *sententiae:*

> Praesulis Albini seu martyris ossa Ruffini
> Rome quiquis habet, vertere cuncta valet.
> Omnipotens marcus romanos conterit arcus,
> adveniente Luca fiunt decreta caduca,
> non fuit inde reus Johannes sive Matheus.
> Curia romana non petit ovem sine lana.
> Romanus rodit; quos rodere non valet, odit;
> donantes audit, non dantibus ostia claudit.
> Accusative, si Romam ceperis ire,
> proficis in nullo, si veneris absque dativo.
> Si venit ante fores bona vita, scientia, mores,
> non exauditur; si nummus, mox aperitur.
> Audito nummo, qui viso principe summo,

---

[24] Lehmann, *Parodie*, p. 76, which contains the full 18–line poem. It is something of a grammarian's *tour de force*. Lehmann cites other examples on pp. 58–70 and pp. 75–80.

[25] Lehmann, *Parodie*, pp. 78–79.

dissiliunt value, nichil auditur nisi salue,
occurrunt turbe, fit plausus magnus in urbe,
papa simul plaudit, quod nemo libentius audit.
Accipe, sume, cape verba placentia pape.
Papa, pater patrum, cur vis intrare baratrum?
te video lete nimis inclinare monete.
Papa premit multos, quos Christus mittit inultos!
Quosque deus punit, justis hos sepius unit.[26]

It is clear that most of this meed-verse is devoid of poetic value. Frequently the authors are preoccupied with puns or with epigrammatic word juggling:

Roma sitit; siciensque bibit, bibit atque bibendo
Plus bibit et sitit et bibit et sitit et siciendo
Non minuetur ei sitis immense rabiei,
Ni prius in Roma distillent aurea poma.[27]

The conventional avaricious papal doorkeeper provided the satirists with epigrammatic colloquies like the following:

Intus quis? Tu quis? Ego sum. Quid quaeris? Ut intrem.
Fers aliquid? Non. Esto foras. Fero. Quid? Satis. Intra.[28]

---

[26] I. Zingerle, "Sterzinger Miscellaneen–Handschrift," *Wiener Sitzungsberichte*, LIV (1866), 314–315. A very similar poem appears in J. Werner, *Beiträge zur Kunde der lateinischen Literatur des Mittelalters* (Aarau, 1905), p. 14.

[27] Werner, *Beiträge*, p. 55. Variant in *Beiträge*, p. 121. The ultimate source is Horace's figure (*Carmina*, II, ii, 13–16) of avarice as a dropsy, common among medieval satirists. E.g., in verses printed by J. Feifalik, "Studien zur Geschichte der altbömischen Literatur, V," *Wiener Sitzungsberichte*, XXXVI (1857), 155, the avaricious clergy, high and low, are compared to hydroptics:

Sunt velud ydropici quorum membra crescunt,
dum plus bibunt siciunt, sic magis inardescunt,
sic auari miseri nunquam requiescunt.

A similar passage is printed in E. Du Méril, *Poésies inédites du moyen âge* (Paris, 1854), pp. 314–315.

[28] H. Hagen, *Carmina medii aevi maximam partem inedita* (Berne, 1877), p. 213.

Not all the satire against Roman venality was so artistically undistinguished. Walter of Châtillon (fl. ca. 1170)—once a clerk in Henry II's chancery, a friend of John of Salisbury, a teacher at Châtillon, and a student of law at Bologna[29]—is responsible for some brilliant verse on the subject, adorned with much classical imagery. His best satire on Roman corruption is the thirty-stanza "Propter Sion non tacebo."[30]

So Walter opens, echoing Isaias. He will lament the present corruption of Rome, which is lowered to the slime, subjected to tribute, derelict, desolate and afflicted. He himself has seen the *caput mundi* become like Scylla and Charibdis. There Crassus drinks up the gold and silver of the world:

> 4. Ibi latrat Scilla rapax
> et Caribdis auri capax
> potius quam navium;
> fit concursus galearum
> et conflictus piratarum,
> id est cardinalium.

The remainder of the poem carries out more or less consistently the figure of the Homeric voyage between Scylla and Charibdis. Walter dismembers the Curia, group by group. The hounds of Scylla are the curial advocates, Charibdis the chancery:

> 11. Nunc rem sermo prosequatur:
> hic Caribdis debachatur,
> id est cancellaria;
> ibi nemo gratus gratis
> neque datur absque datis
> Gratiani gratia.

[29] Raby, *Secular Latin Poetry*, II, 190.

[30] K. Strecker, ed., *Moralisch-satirische Gedichte Walters von Chatillon* (Heidelberg, 1929), pp. 18–30.

This spate of puns, incidentally, is characteristic of Walter as well as of other "goliardic" poets. The Sirens, Walter continues, are the cardinals, who sing blandly in the poet's ear the song of friendship, and who boast their power. The poet castigates them: they are wolves, the new Nero, sellers of Christ's patrimony. Though they now rule Peter's ship, and hold his keys, these cardinals are pirates, and their leader is Pilate. The sea on which they sail is inhabited by no classical divinities:

> 22. Maris huius non est dea
> Thetis, mater Achillea,
> de qua sepe legimus,
> immo mater sterlingorum,
> sancta soror loculorum,
> quam nos bursam dicimus.

Without the protection of Purse the ship is dashed against the rocks until the traveler loses both his money and his clothes. The rocks are the doorkeepers, who admit the wealthy but, fiercer than tigers, repel the poor from the doors. The poem closes with some conventional praise of Pope Alexander as a friend of letters, and a hint that the Pope might provide a safe haven for the storm-tossed Walter.

The ideas of Walter's poem are commonplace, but the artistry is exceptional: the verbal dexterity, the skillful adaptation of the common hymn meter to satirical—almost scurrilous—effects, and the judiciously elaborated unifying imagery of the Homeric voyage (drawn mostly from Ovid) with its attendant dangers, in which the poet sets the satiric commonplaces about the Curia. In the vitriolic measures where the poet describes the suave, unctuous cardinal who addresses him at the Curia, his Latin-Italian-French jargon softened to be "sweete upon his tonge," he reaches high satire:

> 14. Dulci cantu blandiuntur
> ut Sirenes et loquuntur

> primo quedam dulcia:
> "Frare ben je te cognosco,
> certe nichil a te posco
> nam tu es de Francia.
> 15. "Terra vestra bene cepit
> et benigne nos recepit
> in portu concilii.
> Nostri estis, nostri—cuius?
> sacrosancte sedis huius
> speciales filii."

There is nothing to add to this acid-etched portrait of the unknown cardinal.

Walter retails the usual commonplaces on Roman venality elsewhere. One of the stanzas from his "Multiformis hominum" reaches the heart of the problem of ecclesiastical venality in Walter's time:

> Eligendi praesulis quotiens fit mentio,
> in primis requiritur, cum quanto marsupio
> interesse poterit Romano concilio,
> et ita de moribus ultima fit questio.[31]

So long as a bishop was likely to be a great feudal lord—and this was very frequently the case—money seemed necessary, the more so, ironically, while the Church was trying to extricate itself from secular feudalism. On the other hand, the Church was the only part of twelfth-century society in which poverty was articulate, and the relatively poor clerk had little sympathy for the problems of the wealthy bishop—unless, of course, the bishop were the clerk's means of support. The scholar and the administrator were not more likely to see eye to eye in the twelfth century than they are in the twentieth.

This eternal misunderstanding was one of the reasons that Latin verse against Roman venality had been popular in France

---

[31] Strecker, *Chatillon*, pp. 75-76.

for a half-century before Walter wrote his masterpieces. One of the earlier attacks, by Petrus Pictor, canon of St. Omer (fl. ca. 1110), will serve to exhibit the commonplaces of the type more fully, for Peter was hardly original. Like so many others, he sees Rome as a debased ecclesiastical market-place, where bishoprics and even the papacy itself are sold. All holy orders lie open to sale, and the negotiators gather together in Simon's crowd about the city. Every peddler has benefices, every gate its simonist-salesmen. Saint Peter once rejected gold; now he demands it. The common figure of the sick head and the sick members makes its appearance:

> Nec solam Romam gravat huius lesio morbi,
> Que caput est orbis, set toti iam nocet orbi.
> Nimirum capitis dolor omnia membra replevit,
> Deque malo sic principio sanies mala crevit.

Simon rages in the city. Prelates are crushing their people for love of money. The sacred chrism is sold for silver, and sacred relics like images. Even the tongues of priests are venal: to him who gives nothing the Divine Word is silent. The satire drifts off into attacks on the lesser clergy, to terminate with the striking image of the eternal Judas:

> Suspensus laqueo Iudas non totus obivit:
> Altera pars eius crepuit, pars altera vivit.
> Servus adhuc Dominum mutato nomine vendit:
> Non animum mutat, quia mutua premia prendit.
> Ergo ferat meritas Iudas cum Simone penas,
> Tartareas subeat dampnatus uterque catenas.[32]

These verses are not good poetry. Peter's techniques are merely those of irate complaint and iteration. He begins at *Roma caput*

---

[32] *Lib. de lite*, III, 708–710. On Petrus Pictor cf. Manitius, III, 877–883, and Raby, *Secular Latin Poetry*, II, 26–30.

mundi with the commonplaces about the ecclesiastical market-place, moves to the conventional contrast of Simon with Peter, and repeats the image of the head and the members. The rest of the poem is taken up with complaints in turn about the sale of each of the seven sacraments, ending with that of God Himself in the Holy Eucharist. Hence the peroration identifies the simoniac with Judas, his eternal type. Conventional as the idea was, the image of the hanged Judas is the most striking in the poem. Peter's treatment, though clumsy, is close to the conventional standard.[33]

The image of Rome as the market-place for the heirs of Judas caught the fancy of the satirists. It appears, for example, in Philip the Chancellor's sardonic "Frigescente caritatis," written, like so many of the satires, in hymn-meter. Charity, says Philip, has given way to the peddlers:

> 2. Ecce, florent venditores
> Spiritalis gratiae,
> Antichristi praecursores,

---

[33] Some lines from a long elegy on Fortune and the consolations of philosophy by Henry of Settimello (P. Leyser, *Historia poetarum et poematum medii aevi*, Halle, 1721, p. 484) will suggest the commonness of Peter's imagery and organization:

> Ipsa caput mundi venalis curia Papae
> Prostat, et infirmat caetera membra caput.
> Sacra cerne nefas, utrumque pudentius aevo,
> Venditur in turpe conditione foro.
> Crisma sacrum; sacer ordo; altaria sacra; sacrata
> Dona; quid haec ultra? Venditur ipse Deus.
> O sacra, quae sacras maculant comercia sedes!

The English Nigel Wireker (or Nigel de Longchamps; ca. 1130–ca. 1206), a better poet than Henry, worked out the idea of the head and the members somewhat more originally in his own attack on Rome. Cf. *Speculum stultorum*, ed. J. Mozley and R. Raymo (Berkeley, Calif., 1960), pp. 86–88.

> Pastores ecclesiae,
> Fures eucharistiae,
> Novi Judae successores
> Christum vendunt hodie.

Martha is busy in the market-place, seeking money; Mary is deep in the contemplation of cash (st.3). The Roman custom is that the man who gives most becomes bishop or dean. Rome, which consumes the whole world, is rightly named from "rodens manus" (st. 4). If you wish to learn how to square a circle go to Rome, where it is done regularly: the circular denarii stowed into the square purse (st. 6-7).[34]

Philip the Chancellor, a fine preacher, and one of the deftest and most brilliant satirists of his age, matched Walter of Châtillon in his love of classical imagery. In his "Bulla fulminante" he uses it to attack the venality of the Curia. The papal doorkeepers are worse than Cerberus, and even if you had the voice of Orpheus you would pray in vain for entry, unless money knocked at the door in your behalf. The court itself is Protean in its changes (st. 2). Philip closes with the exemplum of Jupiter and Danäe, from Ovid:

> 4. Iupiter dum orat
>   Danaem, frustra laborat,
>   sed eam deflorat,
>   auro dum se colorat.
>   Auro nil potencius,
>   nec gracius: nec Tullius
>   facundius perorat.
>   sed hos urit acrius
>   quos amplius honorat;

[34] G. Dreves and others, eds., *Analecta hymnica* (Leipzig, 1886–1922), XXI, 151-152. Variant in Hauréau, *Notices*, VI, 139-140. Cf. also *Analecta hymnica*, XXI, 146.

nihil iustius,
calidum Crassus dum vorat.[35]

In another satire full of classic myth Philip uses the image of the curial shipwreck, developed so successfully by Walter of Châtillon. "Unless you denude yourself," he argues, "you can hardly escape the shipwrecks of the Curia."[36]

Among the fiercest and apparently the most popular satires of the "goliardic" type against Roman venality is the brilliant and anonymous "Utar contra vitia," which appears in the famous Benediktbeuern Manuscript and many others of the period.[37] It handles the satirical commonplaces on the subject with glittering epigrammatic conciseness, as the poet announces his "rebel song" against the vices of the age. The poem is almost wholly occupied by the attack on Rome, which begins with a popular pun:

[35] O. Dobiache-Rojdesvensky, *Les poésies des goliards*, pp. 103–104.

[36] *Analecta hymnica*, XXI, 143. Variant in Flacius Illyricus, p. 41.

[37] *Carmina burana*, I, i, 76–83; commentary in II, i, 80–86. If not by Walter of Châtillon himself, this poem is by an excellent imitator. Cf. Raby, *Secular Latin Poetry*, II, 206. The Benediktbeuern MS contains among other apposite material the early version of the *Gospel of Mark Silver* (pp. 77–78 above), and a mediocre "Roma tenens morum," which, along with a number of the usual clichés (e.g., "'Accipe' 'sume' 'cape' tria sunt gratissima pape"), lumps pope and emperor together and calls a plague on both:

> Ergo non nosco   quamvis cognoscere posco,
> In quo papalis   res distet et imperialis:
> Rex capit argentum,   marcarum milia centum;
> Et facit illud idem   paparum curia pridem.
> Rex capit audenter,   sed domnus papa latenter.
> Ergo pari pena   rapientes sic aliena
> Condemnabuntur,   qui Simonis acta secuntur.

In *Carmina burana*, I, i, 87–89. Printed from other MSS by Werner, *Beiträge*, p. 16, and Wattenbach, "Bericht über eine Reise durch Stiermark im August 1876," *Neues Archiv*, II (1877), 401.

4. Roma mundi caput est,   sed nil capit mundum,
   quod pendet a capite,   totum est immundum;
   trahit enim vitium   primum in secundum,
   et de fundo redolet,   quod est iuxta fundum.

The Curia—again—is a mere market-place where laws are venal
and "a supply of money resolves contraries" (st. 5). The first
rule in consistory is that Rome denies all to him who gives nothing, and that whoever gives most pleads the best case (st. 6.). At
Rome he who asks must do so with full hands. When you ask,
you are asked; as you sow, you reap (st. 7):

8. Munus et petitio   currunt passu pari,
   opereris munere,   si vis operari;
   Tullium ne timeas,   si velit causari:
   Nummus eloquentia   gaudet singulari.
9. Nummis in hac curia   non est qui non vacet;
   crux placet, rotunditas   et albedo placet;
   et cum totum placeat   et Romanos placet,
   ubi nummus loquitur,   et lex omnis tacet.

If you grease the palm ("pascas manum") with a large gift, your
opponent will cite Justinian and the canons of the saints in vain
(st. 10). The poet erupts into angry puns:

11. Solam avaritiam   Rome nevit Parca:
    parcit danti munera,   parco non est parca,
    nummus est pro numine   et pro Marco marca,
    et est minus celebris   ara quam sit arca.

There is no place for the poor in the presence of the pope: only
the giver is favored, and if your gift is too small you will hardly
please (st. 12). Here the poet turns to the vernacular for a pun:

13. Papa, si rem tangimus,   nomen habet a re:
    quicquid habent alii,   solus vult papare,
    vel si verbum gallicum   vis apocopare,
    "paies! paies!" dist li mot   si vis impetrare.

Everything at Rome demands money: the pope, the cardinals, charters, bulls, the very doors; and if only one of them lacks his meed, the whole sea is salt, you lose your case (st. 14). Come to Rome you bloated wallets, for "at Rome, there is physic for constipated purses" (st. 15). Yet the purse there is like the liver of Prometheus, devoured only to grow again. When all has been taken, then the purse is replenished (st. 17), for the givers return home with mitres, able to extort an income from others. The poet closes with the Roman law of the scribes: "If you give to me, I will give to you." The "Utar contra vitia" is not only one of the fiercest attacks on Roman avarice; it is one of the best in literary quality. Yet the imagery is limited. Even the best of the satirists, however adept, and however skillful in the technique of versification, follow a rather well worn path.

Attacks, equally fierce and sometimes equally imaginative, appear in numerous poems from English manuscripts which went under the name of Walter Map or Golias. In the well-known *Apocalypse of Bishop Golias*, for example, the all-devouring lion of the apocalypse is the pope.[38] Another poet begins with the common device of the head and the members, then anatomizes the Curia in the manner of Walter of Châtillon and Philip the Chancellor. Like them he pictures the doorkeeper as a Cerberus. The impecunious poet observes three decrees at Rome: one, that money is necessary to get past the doorkeepers, another, that money is necessary when you go before the pope, and a third, that money is necessary for the services of the chancery. You must pay well to get a bull:

> Si plumbum aliquis Romanum emerit,
> non dans pro vendito plusquam valuerit;

[38] T. Wright, ed., *The Poems Attributed to Walter Mapes* (Camden Society, London, 1841), p. 7.

in suis subprior decretis asserit
esse falsarium qui sic evaserit.[39]

Still another satire probably of English provenance,[40] an omnibus-attack on the ills of the world, ascribes the same conventional vices to Rome, and makes use of the conventional puns:

---

[39] Wright, *Mapes*, p. 170. It is entitled in Wright's edition "De pravitate saeculi." Cf. "De diversis ordinibus hominum," also English, in *Mapes*, 229–230.

[40] T. Wright, ed., *Political Songs of England* (London, 1839), pp. 30–31 A. further example from England, though its ideas are commonplace, is among the most savage, bitter and direct attacks on Roman venality:

  1. Si quis dicit: 'Roma, vale,'
   reor illum loqui male.
   inter mala nullum tale
   tam horrendum tam mortale
    nullus est, qui noverit
    Roma leges conterit;
    Romam nichil preterit
    quod sit criminale.

After a slash at cardinals, chancellors, notaries, the poet reworks the worn picture of the poor man at the Curia:

  3. Pauper intrans ad Franconem
   nisi marcam vel mangonem
   secum ferat ad latronem,
   frustra profert accionem.
    Franco videns pauperem
    'quid huc' inquid 'facerem?
    hostes eius uberem
    habent rationem.'

The poor man, in short, is looked upon as rebel, ingrate, and lifelong sinner. For the wealthy petitioner things are different; the Thief will pray for the thief, bless him and grant his petition (st. 4–5). In W. Meyer, "Die Arundel Sammlung mittellateinischer Lieder," *K. Gesellschaft der Wissenschaften zu Göttingen. Phil.–hist. Klasse. Abhandlungen*, n. F., XI (1908–09), 46–47.

Coram cardinalibus, coram patriarcha,
Libra libros, reos res, Marcum vincit marca,
Tantumque dat gratiae lex non parco parca,
Quantum quisque sua nummorum servat in arca.[41]

The judges must be approached with cash and likewise the notaries, who will "subject the canons to its round form." Rome teaches everyone to devote heart and hand to Mammon instead of God. Once again the figure of the sick head and the sick members appears.

The theme of Roman venality likewise appears in the work of three important contemporary English prose writers: John of Salisbury (ca. 1116-1180), Giraldus Cambrensis (ca. 1147-1220), and Walter Map (ca. 1140-ca. 1209). John did not pretend to be a satirist in his *Policraticus*, and he is never unqualifiedly critical of papal taxation. Intimate with one pope and friendly with another, he always recognizes the dignity of Rome. At one point he makes an effort to explain the dilemma of the pope, who must suppress the crimes of the Romans by gifts. He cannot please his Romans without giving, and he must receive in order to give. Yet he must condemn simony, *munera*, and compensation, so that he seems to be condemning himself with his own voice.[42] John is obviously familiar with the commonplaces of the venality-satire of his day.

Giraldus Cambrensis is equally familiar with them. The strange Welshman seems to have impressed Innocent III, who compli-

---

[41] These are goliardic stanzas *cum auctoritate*, i.e., the author tries, not always successfully, to introduce a line from a classical poet as the last line of each stanza. The final line here is from Juvenal, *Saturae*, III, 143 (cf. p. 18 above). The type was popular. Walter of Châtillon wrote several examples.

[42] *Policraticus*, VIII, xxiii, ed. C. Webb (Oxford, 1909), II, 409. John here develops his own variant of Isidore's commonplace (cf. p. 33 above) four methods of perverting human judgment. John's version is "amor munerum, acceptio personarum, facilitas credendi."

mented his writing, and he in turn was strongly impressed by the Roman court. In the *Speculum ecclesiae* he deals with the Roman reputation for venality in what seems the broadest of irony. It is difficult to discover his true opinion. He notes that the charge against Rome is an ancient one and repeats Jugurtha's opinion of Roman venality (from Sallust), the story of Marcus Crassus, and the grammarians' observation that Latin possessed an ablative case, while Greek did not. The popes, he continues, have been similarly defamed, and he uses the occasion to collect a small anthology of contemporary satirical literature on Roman venality. The collection illustrates well the wide circulation of much of this material. It contains the "Roma manus rodit" epigram, two brief poems on the avarice of Alexander III, and part of "Utar contra vitia," with the famous attribution to "parasitus quidam, Golias." Giraldus repeats other satiric tags, always protesting, however, at the temerity of the satirists. The popes permit this, he says with apparent irony, because of humility, and "patiently bear everything in the name of Christ."[43] Giraldus seems in fact to have been undecided about the Roman demands for money. Clearly he enjoyed repeating the satires he had read; but the brilliant, learned and civilized court of Innocent III could hardly have failed to delight the imaginative Welshman. He seems to have been as deeply impressed by the idea of the Church Universal as John of Salisbury, and to have been merely regretful of the gap between ideal and practice created by the temporal necessities of the Church.

Walter Map is far more frankly and sharply satirical than John or Giraldus. His description of the success of the Hospitallers in a council at Rome typifies his attitude. Under attack, these men

---

[43] Giraldus Cambrensis, *Speculum ecclesiae*, IV, xiv–xvi. In *Opera*, ed. J. Brewer and J. Dimmock (8 vols, Rolls Ser., London, 1861–91), IV, 289–296.

said nothing in the council, but when it had adjourned their money began to work. "Mistress Purse opened her wrinkled lips," he says in a striking image, "who though she is not love, yet conquers all at Rome." Elsewhere Mistress Purse becomes Mother Purse. In one of his attacks on the monks he yokes a line from Psalm XXV—"their right hand is filled with gifts"—with a cynical tag from Ovid—"If you have brought nothing, Homer, you will go outdoors." In this manner he describes how the monks bought favor at Rome. He retails the Rome-acrostic (cf. p. 93 above), and describes the condemnation of Arnold of Brescia as the result of Arnold's hatred of Roman venality and avarice.[44] Unlike John and Giraldus, Walter is completely hostile to Rome. Satire delights him, and he would have been at least temperamentally capable of writing many of the scurrilous goliardic verses which long circulated as his.

The commonplace ideas of anti-Rome money-satire, then, were clothed in a great diversity of literary forms. One satirist used the rhythms of the sequences of the Church to sing a sort of *Magnificat* of Money, which treats wrathfully the policy of encouraging appeals and pilgrimages to Rome. Rome profits by her children's sins, he says, wryly anticipating the Mandevillian cynicism by some centuries:

> Gaude mater nostra Roma,
> Quoniam aperiuntur cataractae
> Thesaurorum
> In terra.
> Ut ad te confluant riui & aggeres nummorum
> In magna copia.

---

[44] Walter Map, *De nugis curialium*, ed. M. R. James, I, xxiii, p. 34; I, xxv, p. 46; xxiv, p. 40. The complaint about the monks buying favor in Rome seems clearly to be based on the papal practice of creating protected and exempt religious foundations. Cf. pp. 86–87 above.

Laetare super iniquitate filiorum hominum,
Quoniam in recompensationem tantorum malorum
Datur tibi precium.
Iocundare super adiutrice tua discordia,
Que erupit de puteo infernalis abyssi,
Ut accumulentur tibi,
Multa pecuniarum praemia. . . . .[45]

Another poet replaces Albinus and Rufinus with St. Nummulus—
little Saint Money:

Vere, Roma, nimis est; eris sitibunda,
vorax, irreplebilis, inferis secunda.
non et est? praeposterat lucri spe jocunda,
probos censet reprobos et inmunda munda.

Dudum terras domuit, domina terrarum,
colla premens plebium, tribuum, linguarum;
nunc his colla subjicit spe pecuniarum;
aeris fit idolatra dux christicolarum.

Romae, si tu reus es, vis absolvi? prome,
aes, ut sumas veniam, in os eius vome:
prece sancti Nummuli perorante pro me,
si blasphemus fuero, mox placebo Romae.

Si te Roma reputat parricidam, moechum,
Symonis apostatae cor habeto caecum;
fer argenti lilia, rosas auri tecum:
hi di sacrant reprobos, scelus reddunt aequum.

Res est et non fabula, rata res et non vana,
forum est venabulam curia Romana;
reis vendit veniam, approbans profana,
ut in forum venditur lutum sine lana.[46]

---

45 Flacius Illyricus, pp. 88–89.
46 E. Du Méril, *Poésies populaires latines du moyen âge* (Paris, 1847), pp. 89–90.

Here again the poet wrestles with the problem of rendering the clichés of the tradition—Rome's insatiable thirst, the idolatry of money-worshippers, Rome the market-place—fresh and interesting. In this he is more successful than most, with his dexterity of sound and rhythm, his direct address, and his relatively novel imagery, like St. Nummulus, the silver lilies and the golden roses, and the striking sale of the color without the cloth.

By the end of the twelfth century the convention had hardened and the satirical theme had become a stereotype. Novelty was difficult to achieve, as we can see from the examples discussed above. Some satirists leaned heavily on a rather clumsy irony. In one poem, for example, Ganfredus, fresh from Rome, lauds the city to another clerk, Aprilis, who is on his way there. He praises the city itself, the procurators, the notaries, the correctors, the judges, the vice-chancellor, the lectors, the cardinals, the pope himself and his relatives, the penitentiaries, and the bullators. The irony is poorly managed and its intent not wholly clear, until at the end the poet lamely unveils his scheme: "O miser Aprilis, haec fuit antiphrasis!"[47] It was not uncommon for writers of longer works in prose or verse to pause in their arguments for a digression on the venality of Rome. Much of Book III of Bernard of Cluny's curious *De contemptu mundi*—to take a relatively well-known example—is devoted first to simony, then to Rome and its evils. But he says nothing that we have not heard before, and he says it at great length. Other examples are likewise generally conventional and repetitious.[48]

[47] Flacius Illyricus, pp. 419–454. Discussion in K. Francke, *Zur Geschichte der lateinischen Schulpoesie des* XII *und* XIII *Jahrhunderts* (Munich, 1879), pp. 8–10.

[48] Bernard of Morval, *De contemptu mundi*, ed. H. C. Hoskier (London, 1929), III, lines 595–750. For other examples cf., e.g., Werner, *Beiträge*, pp. 12–13, 142; Flacius Illyricus, pp. 24–25, 119–121, 393–400, 416–418; T. Wright, *The Anglo-Latin Satirical Poets and Epigrammatists* (Rolls Ser., London, 1872), II,

In this manner, then, Rome became the supreme symbol of man's venality. The reactions of the satirists were almost reflexive: the mention of Rome could be expected to produce a train of moralizing on avarice and venality from any writer. The habit was as deep-rooted as the conventional satirical treatment of women. As woman was the double daughter of Eve, *dulce malum, confusio hominis*, Rome was the mother of venality, the city where money reigned, where Simon and Giezi and Judas ruled, the ecclesiastical market-place where all things were venal, where Grace was sold, where the poor, just man was always trampled. This moral-satirical stereotype persisted throughout the Middle Ages.

Certain conclusions emerge from a review of these moral-satirical attacks. Because of the financial demands caused by its expanded activities, the papal Curia found itself the leader in financial innovations which were ultimately to revolutionize the economy of Europe. The tangible instrument of these innovations was the papal system of taxation, and one of its earliest devices was the conversion of a charitable income, traditional gratuities, into a systematic tax for services. The change was gradual, perhaps not wholly intentional or even conscious, but long before it was complete it had aroused sharp reactions, voiced by the cries of the satirists. Yet while the satirists charged simony, the popes and their representatives still thought and spoke in the comfortable

---

210-212; Frenken, *Die Exempla des Jacob von Vitry*, pp. 140-141; Lunt, *Papal Revenues*, II, 241-250; Lehmann, *Parodie*, pp. 52-86; W. Wattenbach, "Kirchlich-politische Gedichte des zwölften Jahrhunderts," *Anzeiger für Kunde der deutschen Vorzeit*, XX (1873), 99-103. Many other verses, chronicles and pious treatises devote a few lines to digressions on the Roman hunger for gold, and references to it are not uncommon in the official correspondence of the day. Cf., e.g., a letter from Frederick I to the Archbishop of Trier, printed by Regierungsrath Ritz, "Mittheilungen aus dem Archiv der ehemaligen Abtai Malmedy," *Archiv d. Gesellschaft für ältere deutsche Geschichtskunde*, IV (1822), 424.

and familiar feudal categories, and in terms sanctioned by ancient Christian usage. The taxes were "gratuities," "benedictions," "subsidies," "oblations." They were not, when the satire first arose, formalized or regularized. Their purpose was undefined: they were described as applied to the personal use of the Lord Pope or the Lords Cardinals. And prelates were not "taxed"; rather they "paid their respects" with a certain amount of money.[49] Bureaucracy and the "cash nexus" had made their appearance, but their very originators knew no terms in which to speak of them, nor even the modes in which to think of them.

The satirists and moralists who bewailed the venality of Rome were clearly feudally-minded, and their work conservative in temper. However exalted or however corrupt the motives of the individual writers might be, the clerical ideal which their satire implies emerges as a rather uniform and distinct picture: a clergy freely devoted to the service of Justice and of Christ on earth, trustworthy custodians of the Patrimony of the Poor, freely dispensing the sacraments and preaching the Gospel, supported, perhaps, by domanial revenues, charitable donations, customary tithing. Significantly, most of the early clerical satire on Roman venality whose provenance can be determined was written in France, England, and the Empire—all areas where feudal organization had been strongest, and which were least touched by the commercial orientation of the Italian city states. In the incipient taxes of the Curia the satirists saw a new world of cash payments for spiritual services, of marketable talent and learning, of the justification of office by wealth. They could hardly view them with equanimity.

The immediate cause of their satire (where it was not the outcry of the self-seeking and disappointed benefice-hunter, or the imita-

49 Lunt, *Papal Revenues*, II, 236, 238.

tive treatment of a popular subject) may have been the burdens which they or their acquaintances or ecclesiastical superiors felt from papal taxation. But the intense moral animus which lay behind much of their work probably issued from the fear and dislike of an economic world new to them and alien to their modes of thought. The average sensitive and intelligent thinker had hardly adapted himself to that new world by the age of Elizabeth I. The satirists were not urging the ideal of apostolic poverty on Rome and the Curia. Most of them were too realistic. They were urging, rather, that the Papacy remain feudal, that she live on her customary revenues and refrain from the taxation which they saw as simony. As a money economy spread to the royal courts and was felt by other estates, they too fell under the condemnation of the conservative money-satirists, so that by the fourteenth century Langland's Lady Meed included among her followers all sorts of royal officials, justices and civil lawyers, mayors and merchants, as well as the clergy from the highest to the lowest.

With the simple world (real or imaginary) of agrarian stability, personal relationship, and feudal obligation dissolving around them, these writers felt sufficiently bewildered and uneasy to echo the ancient cry of the Roman satirists that *Pecunia* was indeed Queen:

> Nunc premit omnia sola pecunia, res dominatur;
> Mammona conditur, ad fora curritur, ad lucra statur.
> Stat modo Mammona, sunt onori bona, crimen honori,
> Opprobria via justiciae, pia facta pudori.[50]

But what seemed worst of all was that the walls were crumbling not at the outposts of Christendom, but at its very heart in the sacred city of Rome. It was a case of *corruptio optimi pessima.*

---

[50] Bernard of Morval, *De contemptu mundi*, II, 365-368.

The highest spiritual functions seemed measurable in terms of material wealth, and the highest representatives of Christ on earth were venal, movable only by coin, gold-idolators. In retrospect we can understand the outraged cries of simony and the Roman market-place, as well as the problems of the Papacy in attempting to create a new tax structure without any real awareness of the incipient economic revolution which it represented.

Our analysis of the mentality which produced the characteristic protests of the medieval Rome-satires is necessarily hypothetical. The nature of the evidence—the mask of objectivity and moral fervor on the part of the satirists, our ignorance about the lives or even the identities of most of them, the absence of supporting documents concerning papal taxation during the eleventh and -twelfth centuries when the outcry first arose, the conflicting interests and cross-purposes of the Investiture Contest—precludes firmly established conclusions. The uniformity of the protest remains nevertheless imposing, coming as it does from a great variety of writers: *vagantes*, secular churchmen high and low, monks, and later friars and even laymen. And the early date of its origins suggests the rigor with which gratuities for papal appointments were enforced, well before they became formalized as taxes. To this extent the anti-Rome satire becomes a significant part of ecclesiastical history.

The difficult and ambiguous nature of the problem as it appeared to the medieval man is reflected in some of the comments of John of Salisbury, certainly one of the most learned, sensible and moderate men of his day. We have already noticed (p. 107 above) John's awareness of the money-satires on Rome. Elsewhere in the *Policraticus* he recounts a conversation with his friend, the English Pope Hadrian IV (1154-1159).[51] When asked about the

---

[51] *Policraticus*, VI, xxiv. In Webb, II, 67–73.

popular reputation of the Papacy John frankly summarizes in his answer the characteristic satirical clichés about Roman avarice: "Iustitiam non tam veritati quam pretio reddunt. Omnia namque cum pretio hodie; sed nec cras aliquid sine pretio obtinebis." It would be repetitious to paraphrase them here.

When asked for his own opinion John is more circumspect; but, after remarking that he fears the Pope will hear from an imprudent friend what he does not wish to hear, he makes his own comments on the subject of Roman venality:

> Everyone praises you and you are called the father and lord of of all . . . . If, then, you are a father, why do you demand meed and remuneration from your sons? If a lord, why do you not strike your Romans with fear, repress their impudence, and recall them to the faith? But perhaps you expect to save the city for the Church by meed. Did Sylvester acquire it by meed? . . . What you have freely received, freely give. Justice is the queen of virtues, and blushes when she is sold for a price. If she is gracious, let her be gratuitous.

Hadrian laughs and thanks him, but replies with the familiar fable of the stomach and the rebellious members, who after several days of rebellion were forced to admit that their own illness arose from their failure to feed the stomach, which they had branded as lazy and voracious:

> For he from whom tribute had been withdrawn, like a public dispenser in turn withdrew support from all . . . . It is far better that he receive something to distribute than that the other members go hungry through his lack . . . . So it is, brother, he said, in the body of the commonweal where, no matter how much the magistrate hungers, he does so not so much for himself as for others. For if he is starved he is able to give nothing to the members . . . . Therefore do not measure the harshness of ourselves or of the secular princes, but pay heed to the utility of all.

The passage is a profound statement of both sides of the struggle between old feudal principle and new fiscal necessity.

These things, then, are the burden of the satire on the venality and avarice of Rome, which hardened quickly into a literary convention. Peter and Simon Magus stood opposed through centuries of satire, as the type of ideal ecclesiastical rule on the one hand and venal ecclesiastical worldliness on the other, in much the manner that Langland later opposed Holy Church to Lady Meed. Venality and avarice, the satirists knew, were by no means sins peculiar to the Roman Curia, but the twelfth century at least considered Rome their center. To the eleventh century the destructive power of the purse *par excellence* had appeared in episcopal simony; to the twelfth and thirteenth centuries it appeared in the luxury, expenditure, and taxation of the rapidly expanding Papacy. Most of the satire against these things is sub-literary, and much of the rest belongs only to the world of witticism or *jeu d'esprit*. Yet it is a significant reflection of one of the most profound medieval problems.

THREE

Satire on the Venality of Bishops and the Lesser Clergy

However concerned the satirists had become with Rome, they continued to find many targets among the bishops and the lower clergy. If the Court of Rome favored only the bearer of gifts, the moralists pointed out that the bishop also loveth a cheerful giver:

> Diligit episcopus hilarem datorem,
> Fas et nefas ausus post muneris odorem,
> Nescius resumere, post lapsum pudorem,
> Ejectum semel attrita de fronte ruborem.[52]

---

[52] Wright, *Political Songs*, p. 32. The *auctoritas* of the stanza is Juvenal, *Saturae*, XIII, 242.

Since many of the charges against Roman venality were repeated with little change against the other clergy, we can deal
with them more briefly. They are the subjects of some of Walter
of Châtillon's most brilliant efforts. The "Tanto viro locaturi,"
for example, castigates the venal clergy high and low. They do
not graze their flocks, but graze on them: their title of pastor is
derived not from *pasco* but from *pascor*. Those who have get;
the open purse prospers: "In the desert of this world no one flour-
ishes if his purse has not yet vomited."

> Bursa pregnens principatur,
> sapiensque conculcatur,
> si manus ere vacet;
> nam si pauper sit sophia,
> vilis erit. Quare? quia
> pauper ubique iacet. [53]

Walter's remarks merely transfer the anti-Rome complaints to the
courts of the bishops: nothing is without a price; the wealthy or
the briber is favored, the poor man ignored or persecuted.

Elsewhere Walter turns the familiar grammatical word-play
against the bishops. Ancient prelates were dative but modern
ones are ablative. The sighing and frustrate widow replaces the
poor clerk of the Rome-satire. She crosses the threshold of the
episcopal court in vain, "for the empty hand gets no favor." But
the man with ready meed, as at Rome, finds all sins forgiven:

> Redimunter scelera   mediante pretio,
> cuius offert dextera,   mundus abit vitio

---

[53] Strecker, *Chatillon*, pp. 5-7. The *auctoritas* is Ovid, *Fasti*, I, 218, a popular
tag in the Middle Ages. Cf. also the distich printed by Werner, *Sprichwörter*,
p. 49:

> Mos est prelatis dare prebendam trabeatis,
> Vel bene nummatis vel eorum sanguine natis.

et evadit aspera,   et expirat ultio:
sic excusant munera,   quos accusat actio.[54]

In another poem Walter includes all the clergy, from abbots to pope, in a denunciation of venality:

abbates, pontifices,   papa, patriarcha
quod non audent facinus   impetrante marca!

Albinus and Rufinus are now transformed into a god and the pope of his new cult: "The god Albus is worshipped, and Rubicundus is become a second pope, not without his liturgy."[55] And in the "Licet eger cum egrotis," Walter (or one of his imitators) warns the venal clergy that sellers of the Eucharist and prostituters of the spouse of Christ are smitten with the leprosy of Giezi:

Donum Dei non donatur,
nisi gratis conferatur;
quod qui vendit vel mercatur,
lepra Syri vulneratur.
quem sic ambit ambitus,
idolorum servitus,
templo sancti Spiritus
    non compaginatur.

"The future prelate," concludes the satirist, "makes everything smooth with gold or money."[56] Walter's attacks repeat those against the Court of Rome. Both head and members, as the poets had said, languish from the same disease. The problem of venality, wherever it might occur, seems never to have been far from Walter's mind. Even in his epic *Alexandreis* he cannot re-

---

[54] Strecker, *Chatillon*, pp. 111–112.

[55] Strecker, *Chatillon*, p. 114.

[56] *Carmina burana*, I, i, 10–11; commentary in II, i, 11–14. On the legal view of the sale of the *donum Dei* cf. below, pp. 155–158.

frain from contrasting the heroic and principled world of Alexander with the spotted and venal present. Such passages turn
the epic in places into something more like a tract for the times
than a heroic poem.[57]

The *Apocalypse of Golias* attacks the simoniac and avaricious
clergy savagely. The winged calf of the vision is the bishop,
who grazes on everything, stuffing himself with other people's
goods. The eagle is his archdeacon, a robber who lives on spoils,
and who takes what is left when the bishop finishes with his flock:
"Whatever escapes the hands of the bishop, he seizes, and tears
it with his beak and talons." One recalls the description of the
archdeacon by Chaucer's friar:

> For smale tithes and for smal offrynge
> He made the peple pitously to synge.
> For er the bisshop caughte hem with his hook,
> They weren in the erchedeknes book.
>   (*Canterbury Tales*, III, 1315-1318)

Simon is the court messenger, the archdeacon's Mercury. He sells
the Church laws, and if he can find nothing else to sell he will
sell the Church itself. He grows wealthy by extortions from
priests who keep women. Here the grammatical word-play
appears again: he orders the dean to make the genitive priest
dative. The dean is the archdeacon's hunting dog:

> Decanus canis est archidiaconi,
> cujus sunt canones latratus dissoni,
> canens de canone discors est canoni
> datis et venditis est concors Symoni.

---

[57] E.g., *Alexandreidos*, lib. VII. In PL, CCIX, 536. A variant version of
the passage is printed by Hauréau, "Notice sur un manuscrit de la Reine Christine à la Bibliothèque du Vatican," *Notices et extraits des manuscrits*, XXIX, ii
(1880), 300.

The stanza suggests how the wittier goliardic poets could make their commonplaces amusing. The cacophonous juggling of *decanus, archidiacanus, canones, canis,* and *canens* is the work of a virtuoso; and it must be admitted that sheer virtuosity is the saving grace of most of these otherwise conventional verses. The dean's chief function is to smell out money and retrieve the purses of the clergy. He will help those who "anoint his itching palms with meed," but even then his help is languid. And these officials keep ten times what they turn in to the bishop's treasury.[58]   Repeatedly the complaints of the poem suggest the summoner and his superiors in Chaucer's *Friar's Tale.*

The *Apocalypse of Golias* is an exceptionally dextrous, witty and savage poem, though full of the puns and other commonplaces of meed-satire. Few poets anatomize the ecclesiastical hierarchy as thoroughly and ruthlessly. But other works of the period, prose and verse, retail the same complaints. The most common charge was simony—the sale of prebends[59]— or accepting *munera* in the judgment of ecclesiastical cases. There was probably much fact behind the charges of episcopal simony. Although the papal campaign against that vice had been vigorously waged, its success was only relative. The idea persisted that benefices were a legitim-

---

[58] Wright, *Mapes*, pp. 7–12. Two interesting English translations from the Reformation period appear on pp. 271–292. The verses were immensely popular, and appear in over 60 extant MSS. Cf. the comments of O. Dobiache–Rojdesvensky, *Les poésies des goliards*, pp. 106–108.

[59] Cf., e.g., Wright, *Mapes*, pp. 40, 166; the "Satira communis" of Henry of Huntingdon, *Historiae liber undecimus*, in Wright, *Satirical Poets*, II, 164–166. Also Flacius Illyricus, p. 25:

> Sit Thersites, siue Dauus
> Male natus, siue ignauus,
> Si offert pecuniam,
> Mox est certus de prebenda.

ate source of feudal income. Though many of the charges were political, and though by the nature of the vice there are few records to support the claims of satirist and moralist, some cases were so flagrant that they have become recorded history. An extreme example is that of Bishop Raoul of Liège (1168-1191), who exposed the benefices of his diocese for public sale at the shop of a butcher named Udelin, where they were sold across the meat counter. A certain priest named Lambert who persisted in preaching against the bishop's outrages was summarily jailed.[60]

This is an uncommon case, but sermons of the twelfth and thirteenth centuries, couched largely in general terms, bear witness that the problem was real. Geoffrey of Troyes denounces such bishops from the pulpit: "They flatter, they seduce for extortion; they are devoured by avarice, they burn with love of possession. They are neither friends nor guardians of their churches: they are ravishers, they despoil and sell them; they sell the sacraments, they destroy justice. . . . "[61] Prévostin, Chancellor of Paris (ca. 1210), says that like Jeroboam these bishops have set up two golden calves, one in their place of judgment and one in the house of God; for they will give no judgment without gifts, nor present any prebends without a payment. For meed they sing Mass, for meed (or honors, which is worse) the theologians study.[62] Cardinal Odo de Castro Rudolfi (later Chancellor of Paris) about 1225 was preaching the same theme, calling on God to cast out the money-changers from the temple; not men changing money to buy the necessities of divine sacrifice, but men selling ecclesiastical dignities and benefices, and even episcopacies. "Today no

---

[60] L. Bourgain, *La Chaire française au XII siècle* (Paris, 1879), p. 279.

[61] Bourgain, *Chaire française*, p. 278. This study is rich with sermon material on venality, especially among the clergy. Cf. esp. pp. 270–300.

[62] Hauréau, *Notices*, III, 166.

one seems to have a place in your temple except buyers and sellers." He calls upon the papal power to crush these fiscal sinners, and to overturn the "tables of the money-changers and merchants of your court."[63]

Philip, Chancellor of Paris, attacked the same crimes in his sermons. The "pseudoepiscopi," he complains, when choosing an abbot care nothing about his worth, but only about the money they receive from him. The worthy man, if the Giezi-payment is not forthcoming, is held back.[64] Philip was equally severe in his verse. The prelates are Pilates, successors of Judas, patrons of Caiaphas.[65] Irresponsible Money is almighty in the Church:

Nummus nunquam examinat,
Quos ordinat,
  Non enim servit numini,
  Sed homini,
Nummus claudit et aperit,
Et quod non seminaverit,
  Metit in agro Domini.[66]

The English humanists of the twelfth century are similarly caustic. In the *Gemma ecclesiastica* Giraldus Cambrensis argues against temporal rewards for spiritual duties and against the accepting of meed in much the same manner as Peter Damian and Humbert in the preceding century.[67] He gathers the common scriptural texts, the pronouncements of the Church Fathers, some of the old decretals, and whatever occurs to him from the ancient poets, pagan or Christian. He favors Ovid, quoting twice a tag from the *Ars amatoria* on the power of money:

[63] Hauréau, *Notices,* VI, 204–205. On the preachers' attitude towards the state of the Church in the twelfth century cf. Bourgain, *Chaire française,* p. 272.

[64] Hauréau, *Notices,* VI, 57.

[65] *Analecta hymnica,* XXI, 128.

[66] *Analecta hymnica,* XXI, 152. Cf. XXI, 140–141.

[67] *Gemma ecclesiastica,* II, xxv–xxvi, xxviii. In *Opera,* II, 286–293, 304–311.

Aurea nunc vere sunt saecula: plurimus auro
Venit honos; auro conciliatur amor.[68]

These materials he weaves into a connected argument. His attack on venal bishops is full of *exempla*. He tells of the bishop who, having received no meed for the consecration of a certain new church, placed the church under interdict immediately after the end of the ceremonies, and of another who rejoiced in the deaths of his priests, looking forward to the sale of the vacant benefices.[69] He devotes a whole chapter to similar examples, many probably nearer to folklore than history.[70]

Folk humor sometimes attached itself to the type of the venal ecclesiastic, and occasionally appeared in the preaching of the period. Jacques de Vitry, for example, tells of Maugrinus, a wealthy and illiterate Parisian priest, and his clever bishop. Maugrinus knew no Latin, and the bishop frequently made use of the secret for blackmail. Whenever he needed money he would call Maugrinus to him and announce: "Master Maugrinus, my eyes are sore, and I'm unable to read this document; read it to me." And the illiterate priest, who knew the bishop's interests, would always read thus: "My lord, this document states that you are in sore need of money, and that I should accommodate you with ten marks." And so Maugrinus would pay the money and keep his benefice.[71]

John of Salisbury's remarks on the venality of prelates are equally strong. Deans or archdeacons, he says, are men in whose

---

[68] *Gemma ecclesiastica*, II, xxvii–xxviii, in *Opera*, II, 303, 309. The passage is from Ovid, *Ars amatoria*, II, 277–278.

[69] *Gemma ecclesiastica*, II, xxvii, in *Opera*, II, 293.

[70] *Gemma ecclesiastica*, II, xxvii, in *Opera*, II, 293–304.

[71] G. Frenken, *Die Exempla des Jacob von Vitry*, ciii, p. 148. Cf. also ci, pp. 146–147.

hands are iniquities, and their right hand is filled with gifts (Ps. XXV). Bishops thrive by taking the lion's share of the evil gains of their subordinates. This, John admits, applies only to those who serve themselves rather than God.[72] But they are too common. Unfit men creep into the Church with the help of Simon. Some fear open purchase, but like Jupiter with Danäe slip secretly into the bosom of the Church in a shower of gold. Sometimes compensation is demanded of a candidate after his appointment, in the manner of Giezi. Now any office may be bought openly, unless the seller is too modest.[73] John tells how Robert, Chancellor of Roger of Sicily, was approached by three men individually, each of them offering to buy a certain vacant bishopric. He closed the deal for its purchase with each one in the presence of witnesses, and made each give bond for payment. When the day of the election arrived, Robert disclosed the transactions to the assembled prelates, and thus the three were condemned for simony, though still forced to pay the promised bribes. A poor monk was elected in their stead.[74]

Much of the imagery, then, which we have already seen applied to the Roman Curia, also makes its appearance in connection with venal bishops. The *Marca-marcum* and *Luca-lucrum* puns, for example, are common.[75] Simon and Judas appear in connection

---

[72] *Policraticus*, V, xvi. In Webb, I, 353–354.

[73] *Policraticus*, VII, xvii. In Webb, II, 163–164.

[74] *Policraticus*, VII, xix. In Webb, II, 173–174. The story is retold almost verbatim by Nigel [Wireker] de Longchamps, *Contra curiales et officiales clericos* (Wright, *Satirical Poets*, I, 198–199). Nigel acknowledges John as his source. Further material on venal bishops and priests appears in *Policraticus*, VII, xvii–xx (Webb, II, 160–190).

[75] Cf., e.g., Wright, *Political Songs*, pp. 10–11; *Speculum stultorum*, p. 92:
　　　Praesul amat marcam plus quam distinguere Marcum
　　Plus et amat lucrum quam sapuisse Lucam.
This popular pun found its way often into sermons and moral treatises, and

with the sale of benefices by bishops, and sacraments by priests.[76]
St. Rufinus intercedes with a bishop.[77] Other charges are added.
Clerks live on "the tears and the blood of widows," often from
benefices administered by vicars.[78] Priests are interested in their
parishes only as sources of income. They sing Masses and the
canonical hours not for God but only for money:

---

has been recorded frequently elsewhere in this book. The following is from a
thirteenth century Speculum peccatorum, printed in part by Hauréau, Notices,
II, 347:

> Haec in corde suo retineat implicatus peccatis, amore mundi et
> carnis debriatus et caecatus, cui placet luxuriosi cadaveris venenosa
> voluptas quam animae suae suavitas, qui plus studet circa marcam
> quam circa Marcum. . . .

It appears also, along with the liber–libra pun in a Latin poem on the evils of
the world (love of honor, money, wine, and clothing, in that order), printed
by Wattenbach, "Lateinische Reime des Mittelalters, X," Anzeiger für Kunde
der deutschen Vorzeit, XVIII (1871), 202–203.

[76] Cf., e.g., Carmina burana, I, i, 13–14. Flacius Illyricus, p. 28, contains
an interesting apostrophe to Nummus as the cause of many ecclesiastical crimes.

[77] Speculum stultorum, p. 60:

> Praesul enim victus precibus meritisque beati
> Ruffini vota censuit esse rata.

[78] Cf., e.g., a sermon by Gautier de Château-Thierry, in Hauréau, Notices, VI,
210; also a six-stanza poem by Philip the Chancellor, Analecta hymnica, XXI,
142:

> Vae vobis, qui vivitis
>   De substantiis viduarum,
> Plebani mercenarii,
>   Praedones animarum,
> Ut corvus in cadavere
> Spem ponitis in funere,
> Pro munere
>   Sic dona datis mystica,
>   Sub specie sophistica
>   Nec vos pudet errare.

Quidem lucro prouocati,
Ad cantandum sunt parati:
Sed cum lucrum non imminet,
Tunc sunt male dispositi,
Ad cantandum praepedit.[79]

In short, venality has submerged the whole Church, from the greatest patriarch to the least vicar:

Omnes et ecclesias et prebendas prendunt,
Hi palam, nec pudor est, emunt, illi vendunt,
Munera, blanditias vel minas protendunt,
Vultures non aliter ad cadaver tendunt. [80]

[79] Flacius Illyricus, p. 96. Cf. also Wright, *Political Songs*, p. 401:

Heu! nunc mercenarii, nec veri pastores,
Rectores, vicarii, mutaverunt mores;
Ambitu denarii subeunt labores;
Tales operarii merentur moerores: etc.

Cf. also an anonymous Paris sermon, preached at the election of a bishop to the assembled clergy and candidates:

Hujusmodi enim habitacula nunqam a custodibus frequentantur nisi quando sunt fructus in vinea vel in horto; sic et plurimi clericorum raro vel nunquam frequentant ecclesias nisi propter fructus temporalis, nec vadunt ad matutinas vel anniversaria nisi quando distribuenda est ibi pecunia, quam statim ut acceperunt terga vertentes recedunt.

In Hauréau, *Notices*, VI, 160–161; another sermon in *Notices*, IV, 117, is similar. Cf. also p. 136 below.

[80] Gillebertus, *Carmina*, ed. L. Tross (Hamm, 1849), p. 26. This poet wrote in twelfth-century Flanders. As in the case of the Rome-satire, space permits only a small sampling of the immense literature on the venality of the lesser clergy, most of it of mediocre quality. In addition to the evidence cited in previous notes, cf., e.g., W. Wattenbach, "Lateinische Reime des Mittelalters, III," *Anzeiger für Kunde der deutschen Vorzeit*, XVII (1870), 87–90 (120 lines in stanzas *cum auctoritate*); C. Höfler, ed., "Carmen historicum occulti auctoris saec. XII," *Wien. Sitzungsberichte*, XXXVII (1861), 224–227; Bernard of Morval, *De contemptu mundi*, III, 261–278, III, 525–573; W. Wattenbach, *Monumenta Lubensia* (Breslau, 1861), pp. 26–29; C. Fierville, "Notices et extraits des manus-

FOUR

VENAL HEAD, VENAL MEMBERS: CLERICAL VENALITY

AND THE MEDIEVAL SATIRISTS

This, then, is the picture drawn by the Latin satirists of venality and the power of the purse among medieval churchmen. Avarice is rampant at all levels; the clergy high and low seek feverishly for *nummus*, or *munera*. The fiscal crimes are repeated at each level, in terms suited to that level. Pope and Curia sell episcopacies and abbacies, or rather the confirmation or benediction of those elected. Bishops sell the benefices in their dioceses, the consecration of their churches, and with the collusion of the dean and the archeacon the justice of their ecclesiastical courts. Priests and vicars burden the poor, withhold alms, and sell the sacraments. They sing only for money, not for the service of God. Pluralism, fostered by avarice, causes priests to live in luxury away from their benefices, while the vicars who take their places emulate the holder of the living, trying to eke out an income from the sale of their services. With money as the sole standard, learning and merit among the clergy are despised and ignored. The poor

---

crits de la Bibliothèque de Saint-Omer," *Notices et extraits des manuscrits*, XXI, i (1884), 130–132; Wright, *Mapes*, p. 43; Werner, *Beiträge*, pp. 131–132, 142; Flacius Illyricus, pp. 107, 119–120; W. Wattenbach, "Der Streit der Bauern mit dem Klerus, "*Anzeiger für Kunde der deutschen Vorzeit*, XXIV (1877), 369–372; W. Wattenbach, "Lateinische Reime des Mittelalters, XI," *Anzeiger für Kunde der deutschen Vorzeit*, XVIII (1871), 231; W. Wattenbach, "Bericht über eine Reise durch Stiermark," *Neues Archiv*, II (1877), 411–13; B. Hauréau, "Notice sur le numéro 1544 des Nouvelles Acquisitions . . . ," *Notices et extraits des manuscrits*, XXXII, i (1886), 310–311 (a lament of Christ over the vices of the clergy, almost certainly by Philip the Chancellor).

clerk will die poor, since everywhere money is required for reputation, advancement, position in the world:

> Vis decanus fieri,   presul, patriarcha?
> Auri multi tibi sit   vel argenti marca.
> Tantum habet fidei   teste manu parca,
> Quantum quisque sua nummorum servat in arca.[81]

In summation, venality at the top communicates itself irresistibly through each rank to the bottom. The sick head causes sick members; and the poor man—the widow or orphan—pays ultimately for the support of all. [82]

We have attempted to suggest the major cause of the striking and rapid development of venality-satire from its origins in the bosom of the Curia through its conversion to a weapon against the Papacy itself. Papal taxation had undoubtedly become a serious problem to churchmen; likewise on lower levels there were undoubtedly mercenary shepherds in great plenty. Yet the evaluation of this satire's relations with ecclesiastical practice is complicated and difficult. Convention developed quickly, and an examination of the satire leaves the impression that much of it sprang wholly from convention. The moral-satirical poets, writ-

---

[81] Strecker, *Chatillon*, p. 65. The *auctoritas* is Juvenal, *Saturae*, III, 143.

[82] The theme is frequent, as we have seen, in sermons as well as satire. Cf., e.g., an anonymous French sermon of the thirteenth century: "De avaritia nubes magna est; haec est nebula totam tervam tegens et obumbrans. Videtur ut de humano genere dici possit: 'a planta pedis usque ad verticem' (Job, II, 7) non est in eo claritas. Planta pedis subditi sunt, quos obnubilat avaritia foeneris et rapina. Vertex capitis sunt praelati, pupillo non iudicare, tempore necessitatis viscera misericordiae claudere, petentibus ad erogandum manus non porrigere, sed potius ad retinendum colligere." In Hauréau, *Notices*, III, 172–173.

In this discussion I have avoided satire on the avarice and luxury of monks (and later friars), which takes a somewhat different direction, however closely related. Venality, extortion, and their peripheral crimes are characteristically sins *in saeculo*.

ing on the world's evils, would easily fall into the tradition. The root of all evil, after all, was avarice. It is possible that the attack on venality even became an exercise in the cathedral schools, as it seems to have in the late Roman schools.[83] Certainly there are wide differences in attitude, as well as ability, among the venality-satirists. Some are moralistic, earnest, sorrowful, mild; others full of hatred and personal animosity. Still others, lightheartedly cynical, view clerical venality with amused contempt, spiced with the bitterness of the "have-not" toward the "have." The degree of earnestness varies from that of the preacher to that of the punster.

Nevertheless, after making allowance for the strength of the tradition, for disingenuous political and controversial maneuvering, for literary prebend-begging or benefice-hunting, and for the cries of outrage uttered by some sufferers from ecclesiastical taxation, one must conclude that medieval venality-satire gives testimony to phenomena far more significant and revolutionary than these. Through it one can glimpse a prolonged clash between two worlds, the ancient—and dying—world of personal loyalties, of feudal obligation and privilege on the one hand, and the new world—still developing, not understood or even consciously recognized—of cash payment and capital investment on the other. The satirists lacked the terms or even the categories of thought with which to deal with the monstrous new development. The ancient crimes of simony, barratry, and usury were as near as they could come in their charges. Nevertheless they recognized and resisted with all their literary power the new and frightening reign of Queen Cash. This fear and hatred become even more apparent in the long and dreary money-litanies which grew out of the

---

[83] Cf. K. Francke, *Zur Geschichte der lateinischen Schulpoesie des* XII *und* XIII *Jahrhunderts*, pp. 69–75.

venality-satire we have been discussing, but we must examine these in a later chapter.

It is one of the ironies of history that these economic changes began first to be noticed in the place where they were most shocking to the conservative moralist of the Middle Ages: the heart of the Church, and especially the Papacy. To the historian, and in retrospect, they seem the normal and necessary fiscal accompaniment of the new position of the Papacy. But at the time they were not clear even to the statesmen of the Curia, much less to the conservative moralists who regarded them from a distance. To the moralists and satirists they were simply monstrous and scandalous. Since papal activities and papal finance affected the whole Western Church, its financial methods spread to the rest of the Church with some rapidity, and complaints of the rule of Cash spread with them. Satirists began to wonder querulously, as Chaucer's Friar remarked two centuries later, whether man's soul were not in his purse.

From its beginnings, then, medieval satire on money and venality included the clergy high and low. As other professions attained dignity and importance, and as other governmental organizations expanded their tax systems, the theme broadened to include them, whether their members were clerks or laymen. Two other groups became favorite objects of satire for their venality: lawyers, and courtiers and officials of royal courts. Lawyers were especially attractive targets. The sale of justice had been the focus of venality in the Old Testament, and we have already seen that meed in papal and episcopal ecclesiastical lawsuits had attracted much attention. Satire on venal judges had been popular in classical literature, though the medieval lawyer's profession was essentially new in kind. Before discussing these groups it will be useful to glance at the work of some of the moralists who helped mould the intellectual milieu of the twelfth-century satirists.

IV

NUMMUS VINCIT, NUMMUS REGNAT:

THE FLOWERING OF THE VENALITY-THEME

IN LATIN SATIRE

ONE

The Meed-Theme in the Moral Treatises

The systematic moral treatises of the twelfth and thirteenth centuries dealt with the venality theme at considerable length, often in tones which differed little from those of the satirist. A characteristic example is the *De consideratione* of St. Bernard of Clairvaux, the most mature treatise of one of the giants of the twelfth century, addressed to Pope Eugenius III, an old pupil of Bernard. In it Bernard expresses himself freely and vigorously on abuses in the Church. He attacks ecclesiastical lawyers in several chapters. The substance of the attack is that the poor man can find no defense in a lawsuit; that the lawyers devote themselves not to the defense of truth but to the perversion of law and the subversion of justice; and that all this is done for the sake of money. He advises the pope to hold the whip over such men, as Christ did to the money-changers.[1] He warns him

---

[1] S. Bernardus Abbas Clarae–Vallensis, *De consideratione libri quinque ad Eugenium Tertium*, I, x–xii. In PL, CLXXXII, 740–742.

of the dangers from the officials who surround him, whose riot and luxury might corrupt the pope himself.[2] Finally, in a passage later cited by John of Salisbury, he commends to the pope the examples of men who have abstained from *munera* in the face of temptation.[3]

Bernard was probably the most influential writer of his time on the subject, but it received far fuller treatment in the *Verbum abbreviatum* of Peter Cantor. Peter, who died in 1197, was a man of high reputation, associated with the episcopal church of Paris, and widely known for his biblical exegesis.[4] He devotes much space in the *Verbum abbreviatum* to bribes and gifts, superfluous wealth, temporal rewards for spiritual services, simony, and related problems. Peter was a practical and lively moralist, a thorough humanist who knew how to wield a caustic satirical pen. The Roman poets, though not so frequently quoted as Scripture, are equally at home in his work.

In his chapter "Contra acceptores munerum," Peter collects scriptural *exempla* against venality: Abraham's shunning of gifts of all kinds, Esau's error in accepting gifts from his brother, Moses' hatred of *munera*, and many others.[5] He divides "acceptio munerum" into six types: (1) accepting permissible gifts for no unjust cause, "dangerous nevertheless, because by that we sell our liberty"; (2) accepting gifts for justice done (Giezitical) or to be done, or omitted, or hastened (Simoniacal) or for doing injustice; (3) gain from hidden or open robbery by force, usury, theft, or extortion; (4) accepting gifts for the performance of spiritual offices; (5) accepting rewards for entertainments, or taking unneeded

---

[2] *De consideratione*, IV, ii. In PL, CLXXXII, 775.

[3] *De consideratione*, IV, v. In PL, CLXXXII, 782–784.

[4] P.C. Spicq, *Esquisse d'une histoire de l'exegèse latine au moyen âge* (Paris, 1944), pp. 134–135.

[5] Petrus Cantor, *Verbum abbreviatum*, xxii. In PL, CCV, 78–82.

gifts; (6) accepting gifts from illicitly acquired wealth, for use in pious works.[6] All these are wrong. Against the second type he amasses a formidable array of authorities: Scripture, the Church Fathers, Propertius, Arator, Claudianus, and Cicero.

He lashes clerical avarice and the strategems of prelates, "by which they empty the purses of the poor, and become fishers of money, not of souls." Peter cites Ovid and the Scriptures, but gives the impression that he is leaning less on authority than on experience. His attack is witty and biting. It reads, indeed, much like the "Apocalypse of Golias." Some prelates, he continues, "not content with their incomes, through henchmen and officials spread their nets to catch money, sending their nets into the deep (that is, into the depths of cash), saying to their henchmen: 'Make a draft, make a draft, all the way to the bottom of their purses.'" The greatest banes are the bishop's confessor, the summoner, the archpriest, and the archdeacon. Peter adds an *exemplum*: A certain clerk, when he had lost at dice all he owned except five pounds, began to blaspheme God, and promised his last five pounds to the man who would teach him how most to offend God. The winner by consent of all advised him thus: "If you wish to offend God more than any other sinner, become an official or a quaestor in the palace of a bishop." Peter's attack on the extortion and fiscal crimes of the lesser diocesan administrators is even more detailed than that of the "Apocalypse of Golias."[7]

He turns his attention to other priests who seek mere temporal benefits from their spiritual calling, with the story of the clerks hurrying from a dice game to church when they hear that the offerings are to be distributed to them before the singing of vespers. And there are other *exempla*:

[6] *Verbum abbreviatum*, xxiii. In PL, CCV, 82–83.
[7] *Verbum abbreviatum*, xxiv. In PL, CCV, 90–95.

A prelate sought to have a choir in church to sing hymns and canticles on the double feast of St. Stephen, but did not succeed until he promised them a yearly dinner and refreshment, and also the duplication of their matin money in the evening: so that they were celebrating rather the feast of Doubled Money than the feast of St. Stephen. Item: the *exemplum* of the Lombard mourners who weep and lament at funerals of the dead only for a price. But they are similar to those who sing in church for a price, of whom it may be said:

O money, money, to you he pays the honor.
(Juvenal, *Satires*, V, 136)

Brothers, money is their discipline, money their dean, and even their god. They are idolators, adoring money before God; not singing to God, except for money.[8]

Peter then attacks the sale of the sacraments, especially the eucharist, ending with a variation of the usual comparison with Judas: "We sell Christ more shamefully than Judas did, and are more evil than he. For he sold what he thought was merely a man, when his family was in need: but we sell one whom we know to be true God and man. He for thirty pieces of silver, we for pennies and vile pittances." "When all the other vices tremble and flee from the holy places," he concludes, "simony has invaded the altars themselves."

Peter makes similar attacks on venality in saying masses, on pluralism (he compares the pluralist to Geryon and Briareus) and on "exterior simony," the sale of Church offices. He analyzes the types of simony after Gregory (*a manu, a lingua, ab obsequio*), attacks the acceptance of illicitly acquired wealth and of unneeded gifts, and finally laments the venality of lawyers and judges.[9]

In these sections of the *Verbum abbreviatum* Peter Cantor has developed an almost complete handbook for the venality-satirist,

---

[8] *Verbum abbreviatum*, xxvi. In PL, CCV, 98.
[9] *Verbum abbreviatum*, xxvii–li. In PL, CCV, 102–161.

furnished with the appropriate classical quotations and allusions. One wonders how many of the versifiers were familiar with his book, as his reputation in his own age was great. He was, says de Ghellinck, a "personnalité spécialement en vue comme théologien moraliste, et prédicateur écouté; loué unanimement par tous les chroniqueurs même en Angleterre, très estimé par ses contemporains. . . ."[10] With such a reputation, with a style more sprightly and attractive than those of most of his contemporaries, and with a vigorous and practical approach to moral problems, he might well have influenced a number of satirists.

The *De contemptu mundi* of Innocent III is sufficiently familiar from the fame of its author and from its literary influence. Despite its dramatic possibilities it is, as de Ghellinck has said, didactic, rather than eloquent.[11] Its very mediocrity and conventionality, however, make it a useful summation of the moral commonplaces of the age, and its fame makes it a likely source of influence on the writers who followed Innocent. But the work itself is little more than the usual earnest bead-stringing of Biblical texts.

Innocent deals with the sins associated with avarice in the first part of Book II. Love of wealth is the worst of the desires which plague mankind; and avarice is truly the root of all evils:

> It commits sacrileges and thefts, practices rapine and spoil, wages wars and commits homicides; it buys and sells simoniacally, seeks and receives unjustly; it pursues with deceits and threatens with frauds; it dissolves agreements and violates oaths; it corrupts testimony and perverts judgment.

[10] De Ghellinck, *Littérature latine*, p. 80. De Ghellinck notes that Peter's quotations include material from Seneca, Cicero, Suetonius, Aulus Gellius, Quintillian, Prudentius, Arator, Terrence, Horace, Ovid, Virgil, Juvenal, Lucan, and Martial; also, notably, writers of the generation just past: Hildebert, Gilbert de la Porée, and St. Bernard. In the passages we have examined he also quotes Claudian and Propertius.

[11] De Ghellinck, *Littérature latine*, p. 157.

The short chapter "De iniquis muneribus" is a tissue of quotations on meed from Isaias, Ezechiel, Michaeas, and Deuteronomy. Innocent comments on Isaias's accusation (I, 21-23) that everyone is hunting for bribes and payments: "O unfaithful rulers, companions of thieves, who love bribes and run after rewards, you will never tear your hand away from meed unless you first drive cupidity from your breast." He closes the chapter with a spate of the familiar Biblical quotations.

Innocent follows with an attack on the sale of justice, also heavy with scriptural quotation. Unjust judges, he says, "do not hear the merits of the case, but the merits of the persons; not law, but *munera*; not justice, but money; not what reason dictates, but what the will affects; not what the law sanctions, but what the mind wishes." They sell justice, which was freely given to man, and defer judgment in order to heap up payments from the litigants. These remarks lead to a chapter on the insatiability of avarice, based on Ecclesiastes (V, 9) and Juvenal (XIV, 139): "Crescit amor nummi, quantum ipsa pecunia crescit." He repeats St. Paul's identification of avarice as idol-worship. The pagan fears the mutilation of an image, the avaricious man the diminution of his wealth.[12] The discussion ends with a portrait of Avarice, not unlike many other "characters" of sins and sinners scattered so freely through the Christian literature of the Middle Ages

---

[12] This concept of St. Paul's is worked over tirelessly by the commentators. Cf., e.g., Petrus Lombardus, *Collectanea in epistolas D. Pauli* (PL, CXCII, 209), "In ep. ad Ephes.," V, 1–6: "Sed attende quod dicens, *avarus*, adjunxit, *quod est idolorum servitus*, aequans avaritiam idololatriae, quia illum avarum significat, cujus Deus nummus. Vel ideo avaritia equata est idololatriae, quia sicut idololatra Dei honorificentiam usurpat et sibi vindicat, ita avarus res Dei quas vult servari indigentibus, usurpat sibi et recondit." A similar passage appears in his commentary "In Ep. ad Colos.," III. Cf. also Hugo de S. Victore, *Quaestiones et decisiones in epistolas d. Pauli* (PL, CLXXV, 584–585), VII, xiv.

and the Renaissance: "The avaricious man is prompt in seeking, slow in giving, shameless in refusing. If he spends anything he loses all, is sad, querulous and morose, sighs uneasily and worries; etc."[13]

Though it all leans heavily on moral commonplace, there is something of a new spirit in the writing of men like Bernard, Peter Cantor, and Innocent on venality. Their ideas, attitudes, and authorities can be paralleled as far back as the Fathers, but their exposition tends to be more concrete, vigorous and animated. Their ideas on *munera* and the power of money do not seem so detached from the world of affairs as those of the earlier moralists. They write less to their parchments and more to their contemporaries. Their clerical audience, though small, is highly educated, humanistic in its outlook as well as Christian, an audience well able to enjoy the Roman poets with whom Peter Cantor, and sometimes Innocent, spice their writings. Even the ascetic St. Bernard was not unaffected.

One new theme appears in the works of these moralists: the venality of lawyers. Venal judges had been a subject of satire from the days of ancient Israel, but the new lawyer class was largely a product of the twelfth century. Though ecclesiastical advocates appeared earlier than secular lawyers, both attracted attention, and the moralists frequently attack them in the same breath with the judges.[14] The charge against them is virtually always the same. Lawyers do not care whether justice is done but will defend anyone, just or unjust, who provides them with money. The poor, widows and orphans, however righteous their

---

[13] Innocentius III. *De contemptu mundi*, II, ii–xiii. In PL, CCXVII, 717–722.

[14] For examples of such attacks cf. Adamus Abbas Persenae, *Epistolae*, xxiv (PL, CCXI, 666–668); S. Bernardus, *De consideratione*, I, x–xi, II, xiv (PL, CLXXXII, 740–742, 757–758); Petrus Cantor, *Verbum abbreviatum*, li (PL, CCV, 159–161).

causes, are ignored and oppressed because they have no money.[15] As the simoniac sells the free gifts of the Holy Spirit, so the evil advocate sells the talent of his knowledge and eloquence, which he has freely received from God. He makes his tongue venal.[16] Lawyers are learned in the service of falsehood against justice, wise to do evil, eloquent to obscure the truth.[17] They twist and

[15] Cf. Adamus Abbas Persenae, *Epistolae*, xxiv (PL, CCXI, 667): "Judex saeculorum ubique injuriam patitur, nec de jurisperitis invenies aliquem, qui se in coelesti jam exhibeat advocatum. Omnes si dederint, etiam in injustis causis multos advocatos inveniunt: solus Christus, licet sit dator omnium, cum sit causa ejus justissima, habere aliquem non meretur. Ubique sponsa ejus opprimitur, blasphematur ipse ab omnibus, pauperes, orphani, viduae, praeda divitum facti sunt, nec illis, aut juris nostri peritia, aut legum subvenit disciplina, de inflante scientia soli inservitur quaestui, solumque ventosa loquacitas requirit commodum pecuniae vel honoris. . . . Verborum cavillationibus potentes sunt, et docti ad subversionem judicii, aut impium justificare pro muneribus, aut de injustitia convincere innocentem. " Also Petrus Cantor, *Verbum abbreviatum* li (PL CCV, 160): "Vidi morbum incurabilem, ad quem curandum non inveniebatur medicus, quia de salute aegrotantis desperabatur; sed nunquam vidi causam adeo perditam vel injustam, pro qua tuenda non inveniretur advocatus." The widow-and-orphan theme, no doubt derived from Isaias I, 23, and many other old Testament passages, is a common part of the attacks on lawyers and judges.

[16] Petrus Cantor, *Verbum abbreviatum*, li (PL, CCV, 159–160): ". . . advocatus gratis talentum naturae, talentum scientiae et gratiae a Deo accipit, et nullum gratis solvit, sed linguam venalem facit, licet sit modicum membrum in udo situm, et de facili labile." If the advocate is in need, Peter continues, he is worthy of his hire, and may charge a reasonable amount for his services, if the client is able to pay; but not otherwise. The avaricious lawyer makes himself as vile as the petty servants of a household: "Sicut enim pugiles, cursores, praecones et hujusmodi alii officiales viles erant et abjecti, ita et advocati; nec fiebat aliquis advocatus, nisi in paupertatis suae remedium, ut officio cibum quaeritaret."

[17] S. Bernardus, *De consideratione*, I, x (PL, CLXXXII, 740): "Hi sunt [advocati] qui docuerunt linguas suas loqui mendacium, diserti adversus justitiam, eruditi pro falsitate. Sapientes sunt ut faciant malum, eloquentes ut impugnent verum. . . ."

distort the technicalities of law, protracting litigation for profit. At the sight of gold, says Peter Cantor, they have "the eyes of Argus, the claws of the Sphynx, the hands of Briareus, the perjuries of Laomedon, the subtlety of Ulysses, the deceits of Sinon, the faith of Polymnestor, the piety of Pygmalion, the counsel of Achitophel, and the kisses of Absalom."[18]

The venal tongue became a central image in the attacks of the moralists, the very symbol of the evil lawyer. Thus Jacques de Vitry tells the *exemplum* of the venal lawyer whose tongue, after his death, stuck out as a sign of great opprobrium.[19] Caesarius of Heisterbach (ca. 1230) tells of another who in death was found to have no tongue. "And he deserved to lose his tongue when he died," remarked a priest, "for he had often sold it when alive."[20]

---

[18] Petrus Cantor, *Verbum abbreviatum*, li. In PL, CCV, 160–161. Peter is elegantly rhetorical: "Hi sunt, qui causas morantur admissi, impediunt praetermissi, fastidiunt admoniti, obliviscuntur potati, dedignantur locupletati. Hi sunt qui emunt lites, vendunt intercessiones, judicanda dictant, dictata convellunt, attrahunt litigaturos, pertrahunt audiendos, trahunt addictos, retrahunt transigentes, retractant transactiones. . . . . Hi sunt in exactionibus harpyae, in collationibus statuae, in quaestionibus bestiae; ad intelligendum sapei, ad judicandum lignei, ad succendendum flammei, ad ignoscendum ferrei, ad fallendum vulpes, ad irascendum tigres, ad saeviendum tauri, ad consumendum minotauri. Quorum si nares afflaverit uspiam rubiginosi aura marsupii, quod si dolosi species refulgeat nummi, mox videbis et oculos Argi, et Sphingum ungues, et Briarii manus, et perjuria Laomedontis, et Ulyssis argutias, et Sinonis fallacias, et fidem Polymnestoris, et pietatem Pygmalionis, at Achitophel consilia, et Absalonis oscula."

[19] Frenken, *Die Exempla des Jacob von Vitry*, pp. 102–103.

[20] Caesarius of Heisterbach, *The Dialogue of Miracles*, tr. H. Scott and E. Bland (2 vols., London, 1929), II, 275. *Exempla* of venal or avaricious lawyers, and especially of the horrid fates of these men after death, were popular during the Middle Ages. Cf., e. g., *Anecdotes historiques, légendes et apologues tirés du recueil inédit d'Etienne de Bourbon*, ed. A. Lecoy de Marche (Paris, 1877), pp. 366–

Alain de Lille, who gives an excellent summary in one of his sermons of the faults popularly attributed to lawyers, also emphasizes the venal tongue and the sale of the talent freely received from God.[21]

The humanistic Peter of Blois (ca. 1135-ca. 1205) summarizes fully in one of his letters the bitter complaints of the moralists of his age against the venality of advocates:

> Today lawyers argue cases out of avarice alone, and that once venerable name and glorious profession of advocate is now debased by notorious venality, and sells its miserable and abandoned tongue, buys litigation, dissolves legitimate marriages, breaks friendships, revives the ashes of sleeping disputes, violates contracts, calls settlements into question, shatters legal traditions, and in setting its nets and snares for the capture of money destroys all justice. . . The lawyer should give freely of what he has freely received, should plead for the orphan and widow, for the good of the commonwealth, for the liberty of the Church, demanding nothing, undertaking obligations voluntarily, "delivering the poor

---

367, 379–380; *Liber exemplorum ad usum praedicantium*, ed. A. Little (Aberdeen, 1908), pp. 40–43. For a widely diffused *exemplum* in a lighter vein, frequently associated with lawyers, cf. pp. 196–197 below.

[21] Alanus de Insulis, *Summa de arte praedicatoria*, xli. In PL, CCX, 187: "Non avaritia incurvet animum, non injustitia deducat in invium, non lingua venetur pecuniam, non lepore verborum popularem captet auram, sed orationis finem constituat rectum, sermonis terminum faciat honestum. Non prostituat linguam, non venalem exponat loquelam, non vendat Dei donum, non locet gratuitum Dei beneficium. Quod accepit de solo munere gratiae, non prosternat venditione. O quam exsecrabilis simonia est, vendere patrimonium pauperis, locare subsidium inopis." Odo of Cheriton is the author of similar remarks, printed by Hauréau, *Notices*, III, 33–34: "Quam gloriosa lingua, quam fructosa scientia lex Tarpiliana, lex Aquilina, quae in modice hora plus lucratur quam lingua sacerdotis qui de Christo et operibus ejus per anni circulum cantilenas, missis et cetera officia clamabit."

from the hand of them that are stronger than he; the needy and the poor from them that strip him" (Psalm XXXIV).[22]

The letter is of special interest, as it was written to dissuade a friend from deserting theology for the study of civil (Roman) law, a pursuit which Peter considered unsuited to the clergy. Clearly, civil lawyers were already under attack before the close of the twelfth century.

TWO

MEED AND THE JURISTS

The revival of the study of law in Western Europe and the reappearance of the lawyer took place in the twelfth century with the renewed study of Roman and canon law.[23] The study of canon law developed first, brought about largely by Church reform, the exigencies of the Investiture Contest, and the growing complexity of ecclesiastical organization. The Investiture Contest led to the careful study of old decretals and canons, to support arguments on both sides. As Church organization became more centralized, the frequency and complexity of the legal problems brought to Rome increased immensely, so that the help of specialists in the canon law became necessary at the Curia. Since the popes were encouraging appeals *ad limina*, the legal structure grew rapidly. Well before the end of the twelfth century the Curia had cardinals especially trained in canon law to act as *auditores* of cases and as standing counsel. The study of the canon law was immensely aided by Gratian's compilation of his *Decretum*, which

[22] Petrus Blessensis, *Epistolae*, XXVI. In PL, CCVII, 91–92.
[23] Whitney, pp. 13–22.

helped reduce the chaotic ecclesiastical laws to the beginnings of order.[24]

The profession of civil law developed somewhat later in the twelfth century, under the influence of the great law school at Bologna, and of the jurist Irnarius (ca. 1060–ca. 1130). The study, though at first (like all learned disciplines of the Middle Ages) conducted by and for the clergy, was later revolutionary in producing the first large group of learned laymen in Christendom, at a time when the Church was beginning to discourage the participation by the clergy in the business of secular government. "It was a great advantage to European royalty," remarks Haskins, "that, just when the clergy began to fail it, a class of educated laymen began to appear, trained in law as well as letters, from whom the expert administrators and agents of the future could be taken. With the growth of bureaucracy even the Church leaned more heavily on its lawyers, and it was natural that kings should turn to the lay jurist or legist. For good and ill, the lawyer had come as an active element in the world's government, and he had come to stay."[25]

We do not know when the first civil lawyers made their appearance in the courtroom, but their coming undoubtedly partly depended on the introduction of the original writ, probably first used in the twelfth century, though not made compulsory until later. "Written documents in any affairs," says Cohen, "may require interpreters, and in important matters expert interpreters. Yet we do not know when written pleadings were first intro-

[24] C.H. Haskins, *The Renaissance of the Twelfth Century* (Cambridge, Mass., 1928), pp. 214–215. Haskins' chapter (pp. 193–223) on "The Revival of Jurisprudence" provides a most convenient short summary of the twelfth-century history of the subject. Also brief and useful is H.D. Hazeltine, "Roman and Canon Law in the Middle Ages," in *Cambr. Med. Hist.*, V, 697–764.

[25] Haskins, *Renaissance*, p. 222.

duced; probably they came gradually, and with them, assuredly, specialist composers. But the writ alone, with its long history, would account for the rise of a specialist class; form was the very essence of a writ."[26]

The complaint was common in the twelfth century that clerks were forsaking theology to study law, leaving piety for profit.[27] Versifiers lamented that everywhere they saw the clergy scurrying to reap the returns of the new profession:

> Videsne cum senibus iuvenes studere,
> Quali modo valeant multa possidere,
> Nullum modo studium dulcius est acre,
> Aere dulcis labor est loculos implere.

> Properes ulterius, non hic pedem sistas,
> Sed magistros aspice, respice legistas,
> Divinos doctiloquos atque decretistas,
> Hi non curant loculos implere, sed cistas.[28]

A widely-circulated distich pointed up the unhappy lot of the literary man in competition with the professions of law and medicine:

> Esto causidicus, medicus, si munera queris;
> Gramaticus, logicus: pauper, egenus eris.[29]

---

[26] H. Cohen, *A History of the English Bar and Attornatus* (London, 1929), p. 125. There is of course a marked distinction between the lawyer of the English common law and the continental legist of the Roman law, and the circumstances of their appearance obviously differed. On the continent there was no dichotomy between (Roman) law and legal practice.

[27] Haskins, *Renaissance*, p. 216. Cf. also Peter of Blois, p. 142 above, and Prévostin, Chancellor of Paris (ca. 1210), in Hauréau, *Notices*, III, 166.

[28] Gillebertus, *Carmina*, p. 25.

[29] Werner, *Sprichwörter*, p. 29. A similar distich is quoted by G.G. Coulton, *Medieval Panorama* (Cambridge, 1938), p. 410:

> Dat Galenus opes; dat Justinianus honores:

Other poets sang the same song in their own manners:

> Non pro justitia multi discunt modo jura,
> sed quia avaritia bona volunt acquirere plura.
> Des iuriste confundantur rogo, Christe;
> non sunt psalmiste, sed sunt sathane cithariste.
> Causidicus, medicus, meretrix semper meditantur,
> si quis plus tribuat, illum fallendo sequantur.[30]

> Sed Genus et Species cogitur ire pedes.

Among others, Peter Cantor laments the abandonment of the liberal arts and theology for law, because of lucre. Cf. *Verbum abbreviatum*, li (PL, CCV, 160): "Hodie autem hoc genus hominum maxime reprehendendum est, de cupiditate et negligentia sui. Omissis enim artibus liberalibus, coelestibusque disciplinis, omnes codicem legunt, et forensia quaerunt ut foris et in exterioribus appareant, sicque gloriam et lucrum mendicent."

[30] I. Zingerle, "Bericht über die Sterzinger Miscellaneen-Handschrift," *Wiener Sitzungsberichte*, LIV (1866), 310. Cf. also a stanza from a thirteenth century English "song of the times," in Wright, *Political Songs*, p. 47:

> Jam nil valet aliquis ni sciat litigare,
> Nisi sciat cautius causis cavillare,
> Nisi sciat simplices dolis impugnare,
> Nisi sciat plenius nummos adunare.

Similar ideas appear in a fabliau printed by A. Montaiglon and G. Renaud, *Recueil général et complet des fabliaux. . .*, II, 266–267. A couplet printed in *Anzeiger für Kunde der deutschen Vorzeit*, XXV (1878), 348, may also be quoted:

> Qui nec causidici nec usure vel amici
> Indiget aut medici, felix poteri bene dici.

Cf. also f.n. 21 above. Lawyers are not uncommonly bracketed with usurers, as in the couplet quoted above. Cf., e.g., a sermon printed by Hauréau, *Notices*, IV, 277–278: "Bona temporali debemus sic ordinare ut non acquiramus male, sed tantum secundum Dominum. Quod non faciunt multi, ut avari, usurarii et advocati. Isti enim sunt similes perdici, quae nutrit aliquandos pullos alienos; cum autem vident pulli jam adulti perdicem non esse matrem suam, eam statim deserunt."

The judge and the law-court had existed in one form or another from time immemorial, but the development of a special lawyer class was slow—a product, as we have seen, of the increased complexity of the law and the increased formalism necessary in legal procedure. "*A priori*," says Cohen, "we should expect that a visible increase of verbal formalism would beget in mere spectators a suspicion that the proceedings were a sort of organized tricks conventionally played by the actors of both sides, that the words used had more weight with the judge than the facts of the case, and, indeed, very early we find that the lay mind took this view. . . ."[31] The satirists attacked the lawyers as soon as they achieved importance.

Satire on venality in the law courts followed much the same pattern as the development of the legal profession itself. Attacks on venal judges are as old as literature, as the denunciations in the Old Testament bear witness. Similarly, Latin satire on the venality of justice in the twelfth and thirteenth centuries most frequently took the form of attacks on judges who perverted their judgment for bribes. There were attacks on lawyers, but they were almost always concerned with the lawyers of the ecclesiastical courts, where the profession of *advocatus* or *causidicus* was already well-developed. Jubinal has pointed out that attacks on lawyers are far rarer in French satire of the twelfth and thirteenth centuries than those on the clergy. It was not until the fourteenth century, "quand le gouvernment fût tombé aux mains des légistes—ces hardis démolisseurs qui respondaient à un procès fait au roi par un procès fait au pape," that satire on the lawyers came into its own.[32]

---

[31] Cohen, p. 112.

[32] In Rutebuf, *Oeuvres complètes*, ed. A. Jubinal, Nouv. Ed., 3 vols (Paris, 1874–75), II, 19–20, n. 2.

When the satirists deal with judges they frequently cite the four methods of perverting human judgment set forth by Isidore of Seville and numerous later commentators. These were reduced to a single line of verse:

Livor, amor, terror, munus sunt iudicis error.[33]

Or memorized as a couplet:

Quatuor ista: timor, odium, dilectio, census
Sepe solent hominum rectos pervertere sensus.[34]

The satirists found *munus* or *census* the most dangerous of the four.

John of Salisbury provides a convenient introduction to twelfth-century attacks on venality in the law courts. He knew the courts well, both ecclesiastical and secular, and was fond of describing their faults.[35] His remarks in the *Policraticus* are typical of the age. To sell justice, he begins, is evil; to sell injustice insane. Both buyer and seller of justice are evil, but of the two the worse is the seller, "who drags the ruler and queen of his office, by which faith serves, like goods out into the marketplace, and like an unfaithful servant sells his master." For every magistrate is the servant of Justice. And the seller, though he loses justice by his sale, does not convey it to the buyer; for the buyer receives only iniquity. Hence the only man who can sell justice is the one who does not have it. The man who sells justice makes venal not justice, but his own soul.[36]

John's reasoning here parallels precisely the arguments of the earlier moralists against the sale of Church livings. It is especially similar to that of Cardinal Humbert in his *Adversus simoniacos* (cf. pp. 59–60 above), both in language and development. John

[33] Werner, *Sprichwörter*, p. 46.
[34] Werner, *Sprichwörter*, p. 76.
[35] Cf. Cohen, pp. 116–120.
[36] *Policraticus*, V, xi. In Webb, I, 332–333.

probably knew Humbert's arguments, but even if he did not, the similarity indicates a profound and highly instructive unity in medieval thought about the nature of venality. The venal men of the satirists were always the custodians of some special gift of God to man, a gift which in the eyes of medieval thinkers belonged by its nature to all mankind, which could not be measured in terms of material wealth, and which must perforce be rendered freely by its custodians. There was no real difference between the simonist and the venal judge or lawyer, between the merchandising of Grace, or of Justice, Talent and Learning. The simonist sold or bought Grace in the form of Church offices, themselves vehicles of Grace, or in the form of the sacraments. The venal judge sold Justice, like Grace a gift of God. And the lawyer sold Talent and Learning, likewise gifts of God to be placed in the service of Justice, not in the service of lucre. All were in the deepest sense simonists, traffickers in divine authority. Hence it seems that the horror of the moralists and the outrage of the satirists at human venality were rooted in the heart of theology itself, in the doctrine of Grace. The venal official or prelate, in the final analysis, was arrogating to himself a power which belonged to God alone, the control over the free gifts of God. The creature, for the sake of material wealth—the lowest of goods —was attempting pitifully to dispossess the Creator. Langland for good reason opposed Lady Meed to Holy Church.

Walter Map, at one time an itinerant justice himself, makes a lively attack on venal judges. Some of our judges, he says, like the judges of Pluto will declare a guilty man innocent if he "considers" (*respicere*) them, or an innocent man guilty if he fails to do so. "To consider," he explains, is to be glossed in the manner of our Lord Pope; that is, "to give." These judges are rigorous champions of justice unless Mother Purse opens her lips. For she is mistress of all, the prime mover who remains firm and causes all else to be moved.[37] Alexander Neckham deals with them similarly, quoting the usual scriptural examples and citing a Justinian law on advocates who take money: "If advocates take lucre and money, they will be numbered among the lowest, as vile and degenerate." But the vice, adds the moralist, is worse in a judge; for the venal advocate sells only his tongue, but the judge sells Justice itself. And while both sides try to sway him with gifts, the venal judge swings like a sensitive balance with the weight of the bribes.[38]

The poets repeat the cry. Today, says Walter of Châtillon, law is bought, and any legal action must be accompanied by *munera*. The widow without meed to offer prays in vain, and enters court like a fool; but for a price any crime can be redeemed.[39]   A popular distich echoes Walter's complaint:

[37] Walter Map, *De nugis curialium*, pp. 252–253: "Habemus et nos censores sub serenissimo iudice, quorum iusticiam domini sui iustitia remordet, quia iurati coram ipso quod equitate seruata censebunt, ut predicti tres Plutonis arguti iudices, si respexerit eos reus, iustus est; si non respexerit iustus, reus est. Hoc autem respicere glossatur more domini pape, qui dicit, 'Nec in persona propria neque per nuncium uisitauit nos neque respexit,' id est, non dedit.

"Hi sortes in urnam mittere uidentur, id est, causarum casus in inuolucrum, obuolentes calumpniis ydiotas, districto culpas examine censentes, quarum nulla ueniam consequitur, nisi pro qua mater ore rugato loquitur bursa. Hoc est illa cunctorum hera, que culpas ignoscit, 'iustificat impium' et 'non uult mortem peccatorum,' nec sine causa 'eicit uenientem ad se,'
'stabilisque manens dat cuncta moueri.'"
(Boeth. *Consol. Phil.*, III, met. 9, 3)

[38] Alexander Neckham, *De naturis rerum*, ed. T. Wright (Rolls Ser., London, 1863), pp. 332–33.

[39] Strecker, *Chatillon*, p. 112:
Hodie ius emitur   magno quidem pretio,
iudici tribuitur   totique collegio;

Iudicium iustum iudex pro munere mutat,
Absolvitque reum, iustum pro munere dampnat.[40]

A late thirteenth-century poet, probably English, treats the
theme more spaciously. Many souls, he laments, are now en-
dangered by their worldliness, and "this comes from money
which almost the whole court has now taken to wife." The crimes
of judges make them the devil's servants, violators of the natural
law:

Nam jubet lex naturae,
Quod judex in judicio
Nec prece nec pretio
acceptor sit personae;
quid, Jhesu ergo bone,
Fiet de judicibus,
Qui prece vel muneribus
cedunt a ratione?

Judges, the poet reveals, have messengers who go secretly to a
litigant and arrange the case to his satisfaction—if they receive
enough money. And at court sit the clerks, waiting for gifts.
The man who does not offer must face a long delay. A beautiful

tamen haut perficitur   ius sine dispendio,
nisi rursus sequitur   muneris oblatio.

Frustra gemens vidua   preces fundit hodie,
nisi doni congrua   condiantur specie;
ferens nil ut fatua   limen intrat curie,
manus enim vacua   nichil habet gratie.

Redimuntur scelera   mediante pretio,
cuius offert dextera,   mundus abit vitio
et evadit aspera,   et expirat ultio:
sic excusant munera,   quos accusat actio.

[40] Werner, *Sprichwörter*, p. 44.

woman with hair dressed in the latest fashion ("cum capite cornuto")
and bound with gold, gets her business done without a word;
but the poor woman, without bribes, beauty or family, will go
home without accomplishing anything. The prosecutors, doorkeepers, sheriffs and court clerks are to a man extortioners or gapers
after gifts.[41] The writer is circumstantial enough to leave the
impression that he was inspired by bitter experience.

Other poets provide the same kind of evidence. Hugo, cantor
and archdeacon of York, calls the venal judges Satan's sons,[42]
and Bernard of Cluny devotes a violent passage to them in his
De contemptu mundi. Venal judges, he complains, let all evils
flood the world, and money conquers all—"Aes domat omnia,
res piat impia, lex silet aere." Judges care nothing for the Theo-
dosian law, but only for money. Mammon sets the law of life.[43]

[41] Wright, *Political Songs*, pp. 224–230.

[42] Wright, *Satirical Poets*, II, 226–227.

[43] Bernard of Morval, *De contemptu mundi*, II, 331–368. Some of the passage
deserves quotation:

> Ad lucra supplicat, et male judicat ob lucra judex.
> Te scelus impedit, aureus expedit aere silet lex.
> Aes domat omnia, res piat impia, lex silet aere.
> Vim lupus ingeris, agnus habeberis, offer habere.
> Per tua munera tangis et aethera, lege cremandus.
> . . . .
> Proh furor! aspice quam cito judice lucra tenente,
> Stent mala, jus ruat, haec levet, haec spuat ille triente.
> Quam sine judice judicet, aspice, quam sine jure;
> Quippe pecunia, non Theodosia lex sibi curae.
> . . . .
> Nunc premit omnia sola pecunia, res dominatur;
> Mammona conditur, ad fora curritur, ad lucra statur.
> Stat modo Mammona, sunt oneri bona, crimen honori.
> Opprobri via justiciae, pia facta pudori.

Bernard is rarely capable of moderation. His poetry lives on the extremes of

The lawyers—*legistes, advocati, causidici, jurisperiti, juridici*—receive their share of attention, though in these early centuries it is less than the judges receive. They all turn aside after money, says one poet, and pervert the laws, giving their kiss to cash.[44] They sell their lips, complains Philip the Chancellor in conventional fashion, and pay more attention to the quantity of their rewards than the quality of their cases. "Nummis obligati," the canon lawyers pervert the sacred laws of the ancient decretals.[45] The Flemish poet Gilbertus tells the same story. In their practices the jurists follow the princes, the bishops, the patriarchs; they rarely make any of their wealth available to the poor, "but as the price of their tongues add marks to marks." They are ready in great numbers to speak for the wealthy, but they shame the poor man in his poverty. These advocates love the wealthy as a prudent man loves a fruitful tree. But the poor man has the choice of speaking ineffectually for himself or remaining silent; he is barren ground. The advocate knows how to follow the

---

emotion—either raptures of delight or paroxysms of fury.
Cf. also *Carmina burana*, I, i, 1 ff. and Hauréau *Notices*, II, 183–184, where an unknown poet contrasts God, the highest judge, with venal earthly judges.

[44] Flacius Illyricus, p. 23.

[45] *Analecta hymnica*, XXI, 203. Cf. also the digression of an unnamed poet in Flacius Illyricus, p. 227, on the "doctores decretorum":

> Non ingreditur ad eos
> Causa uidualis;
> Sine nummo facit reos
> Quorum Decretalis.
> Pro tam uili precio
> Iura uendunt tales,
> O qualis discretio?
> Quantum habes, tantum uales.

rich just as a hunter knows where to spread his nets, or a fowler in what bushes he will take the most birds.[46]

Many of the charges made against the lawyers would be accounted grave violations of professional ethics in any age. The profession was in its infancy, with no code of ethics as a guide and no governmental or professional organization to assume the functions of watchdog, so that such practices as the deliberate protracting of litigation or the jumping from client to client for higher fees could be carried on with impunity. But modern readers may find it strange that the mere practice of law—the simple acceptance of fees for legal counsel—subjected the lawyer to attack as a venal person, even a sort of simonist. The basic cause of this attitude was the old view of the lawyer as the custodian of special divine gifts. In the ideal at least—and it was to this that the satirist habitually turned—the lawyer, whether cleric or layman, was the servant of the Truth of God; the service expected of him was heroic—and gratis.

---

[46] Gillebertus, *Carmina*, p. 26:

> Pauperem pauperies, non crimen, infamat,
> Solus pro se loquitur, solus pro se clamat;
> Quare pro divitibus quilibet declamat?
> Fructuosam arborem quivis prudens amat.

> Defensare pauperem nullus est qui vacet,
> Pauper inutiliter loquitur aut tacet;
> Pauper cur despicitur? cur ubique iacet?
> Infecundi cespitis ager nulli placet.

> Scit quare causidicus divitem defendat;
> Cur eum tantopere iuvat et commendat?
> Scit venator retia cervis ubi tendat,
> Scit auceps quo frutice plures aves prendat.

Note the reminiscence of Ovid (*Fasti*, I, 218) in line 3 of the second stanza quoted.

Professors Post, Giocarnis and Kay have described in detail
the development of this tradition of the obligations of teachers
and jurists in both canon and civil law during the Middle Ages.[47]
The tradition in canon law had its roots in Christ's admonition
(Matth., X, 8; Luke, IX, 1-7) to his apostles when he sent them
forth to teach: "Gratis accipisti, gratis date." The canonist Johan-
nes Teutonicus, commenting (ca. 1215-17) on the *Decretum* and
observing that twelfth-century decrees forbade masters in the
cathedral schools to receive fees from the clergy or the poor,
set forth the principle generally accepted throughout the Middle
Ages, that learning like Grace was a gift of God and could not
be sold: "scientia donum Dei est, unde vendi non potest. . . ."
The commentators on both canon and civil laws consistently
held this ideal before the eyes of philosophers, teachers, jurists,
all the learned men of the Middle Ages. The concept implied—it
was sometimes expressly stated—the priesthood of the learned,
and hence implied the possibility of the simony of the learned:
the man who sold a *donum Dei* was a simonist, whatever the gift
he marketed. The civil lawyers, agreeing with the canonists,
traced their tradition back to the foundations of Roman law.
Ulpian (d. 228), indeed, had called jurists the *sacerdotes* of Justice
and his glossators agreed, as Post has pointed out, that "like priests
they administer *sacra*, and just as the priest in ordering penance
'ius suum cuique tribuit,' so does the judge or jurist in judging."[48]

Nor was this attitude confined to the thinking of the legists
and canonists. Saint Thomas Aquinas, in the tradition of the
canonists, also establishes that it is simoniacal to receive money
"pro spiritalibus actibus," even those not specifically functions

---

[47] G. Post, K. Giocarnis, and R. Kay, "The Medieval Heritage of a Humanistic
Idea: 'Scientia Donum Dei Est, Unde Vendi non Potest,'" *Traditio*, XI (1955),
195–234. The paragraphs which follow lean heavily on this useful study.

[48] Post, Giocarnis, and Kay, p. 206.

of the priesthood. The man with knowledge whose office commits him to the use of that knowledge for the benefit of others,
says Thomas, is guilty of a dangerous sin if he accepts fees for
his services. This principle expressed so clearly in canon and
civil law does much to clarify statements which we have examined
earlier in this chapter, the moral-satirical attacks on the legists
by men like Saint Bernard, Peter Cantor, Innocent III, Alain
of Lille, Peter of Blois, and John of Salisbury.

The canonists and legists had not, however, abandoned the
teacher and jurist in this uncomfortable position, for Christ had
ended his charge to the apostles with the remark that the laborer
was worthy of his hire: "dignus enim est operarius mercede sua"
(Luke, IX, 17; in Matth., X, 10: *cibo suo*). Hence the glossators
distinguished between the learned man's accepting money for
learning considered as mere goods and his accepting money as
the price of his labor. The teacher or lawyer could accept money
within limitations, as the price of his labor; he was worthy of
his hire. Generally speaking, then, the canonists arrived at a
compromise between the clearly stated ideal and the demands
of practical necessity by deciding that a beneficed teacher or jurist
could demand no fees, though he might receive honorable gifts.
Those without livings could demand fees as the price of their
hire from all but the poor. As the priest had the fundamental
right to live by the altar, the man of learning had the right to
live by his labors in *scientia*. Saint Thomas agreed that the scholar
with no beneficed office was entitled to subsist on fees.

This principle of canonists, legists and philosophers was near
the heart of much medieval venality-satire, especially that directed
against the lawyers. It is, I believe, one of the most significant
of medieval social attitudes, and reminds us forcefully of the
ambivalence of the medieval Second Estate: a priesthood on the
one hand, a learned class on the other. Setting aside the priestly

function, the greatest single obligation of this learned class to society was to conserve and transmit to mankind the divine gift of *scientia*. The priest-scholar, then, was the custodian of two analogous gifts of God by virtue of his orders and his learning: divine Grace, whose channel was the priestly administration of the sacraments, and knowledge, whose channel was the the teaching of the clerk, or perhaps his service as a jurist. To sell either of these gifts was equally simony. It was on this principle that the moralists and venality-satirists leaned most heavily. In their angrier moods they tended to concentrate wholly on the scriptural admonition to give freely what was freely received, and to ignore its complement, that the laborer is worthy of his hire. This obviously one-sided development of the argument seems to have proceeded from the unspoken assumption that the income of the learned, like that of the other estates, should come from the land—through ecclesiastical benefices or endowments, usually—in the customary feudal manner. Thus the views of these venality-satirists appear as a peculiar blend of conservative feudal assumptions with a broadly sacramental view of the world. The class of lawyers seemed peculiarly repugnant to these views. Most satirists were undoubtedly quite conscious of the theoretical justification of their attacks against lawyers on the principle of the *donum Dei*. At least one versifier, probably of the thirteenth century, took pains to echo the legal language of the principle:

> Profitentur quidam leges,
> Legis tamen sunt exleges
>   Dum vendunt scienciam:
> Donum dei spiritale,
> Quod exponunt ut venale,
>   Venandi pecuniam.
>
> Isti vendunt veritatem
> Et defendunt falsitatem

Amore pecunie.
Aput istos nil perorat,
Nisi nummus, quem adorat
Servus avaricie.[49]

The evil which medieval moralists and satirists found in lawyers
was compounded by the lawyer's seeming willingness to support
either side of a law case if he were paid a fee. Few men of the
time recognized any necessity for this specialist class in dealing
with highly technical points of law. Much of the satire represents
the non-specialist's suspicion of the subtle, the technical, and
the obscure. The strange formalism of the courtroom, where
Tongue seemed balanced against Truth, certainly produced much
hostility. Ironically, the moralists who objected so bitterly to
lawyers who pleaded the causes of guilty parties were unconscious-
ly subverting all process of law themselves, assuming the defendant's guilt before the trial. But this passed unnoticed in the
ethical orientation of the arguments.

The ancient ideal of the lawyer which had flourished in the
age of Cicero died a lingering death. The lawyer of Cicero's
age was ideally a man of senatorial or equestrian rank—hence
of independent wealth—who pleaded cases without thought of
fees, as part of the obligation owed the state by one who had entered on the steps of public office. He was a *sacerdos*, as Ulpian said
later, of Justice and a follower of *vera philosophia*. His knowledge
of the sacred laws was not measurable by coin, and he could not
think in terms of fees. The actuality died early; Justinian's codifications recognized the lawfulness of payments to lawyers, and
some medieval thinkers were aware of this.[50] But many moralists

---

[49] W. Wattenbach,"Lateinische Reime des Mittelalters, XI," *Anzeiger für
Kunde der deutschen Vorzeit*, XVII (1871), 231. Cf. also Walter of Châtillon's
remarks in his "Licet eger cum egrotis," p. 119 above.

[50] E.g., John of Salisbury, *Policraticus*, V, xiii. In Webb, I, 340. Cf. also

remained suspicious, though thoughtful men like Peter Cantor and Peter of Blois admitted the righteousness of moderate fees. The Ciceronian idea of public service persisted and fused with the concept of the lawyer as Christian clerk and servant of Truth, custodian of the *donum Dei*. Judged by this ideal the lawyer who served a guilty party seemed the worst sort of simonist, selling not justice but the service of injustice; and all lawyers, if not clearly simonists, were defective in charity, for they reserved their services to those able to pay. The poor, the widows and the orphans—those special spiritual wards of the Church from its earliest days—suffered for lack of legal counsel.

In summary, then, the corrupt judge was a fairly familiar figure in literature through the centuries, and the satirists' treatment of him tends to be conventional, composed largely of echoes of the Old Testament. Only in the hands of men like Walter Map, who had observed working judges closely, does the satire come to life as much as that in Theodulf's *Paraenesis*. The new science of law, which brought formalism, technicality, and hence the lawyer, into the courtroom, produced a more lively reaction, and distilled more venom. The unintelligible processes of the courtroom could hardly have failed to arouse hostility in the minds of callow and conservative observers. But the venality of lawyers, judges and the civil courts in general does not reach its greatest popularity as a satirical theme until the fourteenth century.[51]

Petrus Cantor, *Verbum abbreviatum*, li (in PL, CCV, 160): "Si eges, 'dignus est operarius mercede sua,' moderata tamen, non superflua."

[51] I have dealt briefly with the medieval satire on lawyers in "The Venal Tongue: Lawyers and the Medieval Satirists," *American Bar Association Journal*, XLVI (1960), 267–270. Part of this discussion has been drawn from that account.

THREE

VENALITY IN THE ROYAL COURTS AND ELSEWHERE

The Latin venality-satirists of the twelfth and thirteenth centuries were largely concerned, then, with the fiscal vices of the clergy and ecclesiastical jurists. Nowhere else had the functions of organization and management assumed such complexity as in the Church. This complexity was especially great in the bureaucratically organized Roman Curia, but was in some measure also present in the diocesan organization of the clergy, and showed itself in small ways in the operation of every parish. Bureaucracy communicated itself, like the disease in the satirists' figure, from head to members. The expenses of administering spiritual services scandalized the satirist, seeming to fly in the face of Christ's admonition: "Gratis accepisti, gratis date." The triangular contrasts involving this ideal of Apostolic poverty, the feudal ideal with its fixed rents and payments, and the new economy which the Church was perforce helping to create, angered and embittered the satirist. They also confused him, for he did not understand the full significance of the activities he attacked. Like most men faced with novelty he rejected the new economy and all its works, seeking refuge in ideas more comfortably traditional. He provides a remarkable example of the truism that in economics one generation's tyranny is another generation's order, one generation's extortion another's tax. Caught between the (for most men) terrifying marriage to Lady Poverty and the morally repulsive marriage to Lady Meed, he tended to retreat to a spiritual alliance with feudalism, and from its standards to criticize the phenomena of the new economy. Yet, ironically, it was the penetration of the feudal system into ecclesiastical organization which first gave scandal. Now, when the costs of clerical functions were exceeding the incomes from clerical fiefs and demanding their own incomes, he began to speak of Giezi, Simon and Judas. The paradox was clearly insoluble by the old standards.

One must recall that the learned Latin literature of this time was a clerical literature, occupied almost exclusively with clerical interests—often, in more trivial pieces, with what can only be called ecclesiastical shop-talk. The layman's world attracted the writer's interest only incidentally. The new bourgeois, though traditionally grasping, was in no position to market spiritual gifts or (except in Italy) secular offices, and hence was largely exempt from charges of venality. The financial organization of the courts of most kings and great nobles remained rudimentary in contrast with that of the Curia, and hence was slow to attract the satirists' attention. When royal courts reached that complexity, and royal taxes that urgency, they too came under the scrutiny of satire, as we know from the episode of Lady Meed.

Probably the best satire of the time on venality at a royal court is that of John of Salisbury. John, closely associated with the highly advanced court of Henry II (he dedicated his *Policraticus* to Thomas Becket while Thomas was Chancellor of England), warns the courtier not to believe "that justice, or truth, or piety are at home with those among whom you see that everything is venal." "Those who do everything for a price and nothing free are fleeing from grace and driving it away." If sentences are to be executed, cases examined, if a bond is to be accomplished, money sets everything in motion; truth is blind, piety lame. John turns to Juvenal to point up his attack:

> quantum quisque sua nummorum seruat in arca,
> tantum habet et fidei.

Contemnere fulmina pauper
creditur atque deos, diis ignoscentibus ipsis.
(*Saturae*, III, 143-146)

The more corrupt a man is and the more he corrupts others with meed, the more highly he is esteemed. If you have business at court you must first escape the hands of the prince; but after that the road is still difficult:

> Cossus gets your documents ready. If you can greet him, it will be well for you. If you do not bring a passport, you approach in vain. But if you have one, it is useless, nor will he agree to soil his noble hand with the dirt of the parchment. In short, you must buy some of his, since he will give you neither his services nor the juice of sepia or the black cuttlefish unless you buy them. . . . If by chance you have a fine belt or a useful plat-ter, or any other pretty baubles, consider them his unless you wish to lose your labor and expense. For unless your liberality forestalls it, they will be extorted from you by requests. . . . Now you may leave Cossus, but the fires of purgatory still threaten you, for Vegeto remains, whom you will solicit with much insistence and a very elaborate arrangement of prayers and gifts, just for him to look at you without opening his mouth. . . . Unless you have already softened him, he will object that the order of your account is not faithfully observed, or the style is barbarous, or the kindness or negligence of the law on the part of the notary or scribe has departed from the accepted form; and there is always some knot which money must loosen.[52]

These men are harsher than Charon, who demands only a small coin; they demand pounds, multiplied over. At court even the non-existent, the very lack of things, is venal. You must pay not only for words and deeds, but for silence: "silentium namque res uenalis est." For the tongues of courtiers are lethal unless tied by silver cords. Nor can you escape by bribing only a single

[52] *Policraticus*, V, x. In Webb, I, 323-324.

official; you must pay them all, for if you buy the favor of one you excite the envy of the others. And the most dangerous are those who seem most suave, elegant and learned.

The court official, continues John, may indeed accept gifts honorably if they flow freely from the liberality of the giver. He should never accept the gifts of unjust men, however, and thus obligate himself to unjust judgments. "But," says John, "the dishonesty of courtiers is so notorious that a man trusts in vain in the testimony of his own conscience, the grace of his conduct, the odor of his reputation, the soundness of his case, or the flow of his eloquence, unless meed intervenes." He draws a familiar epigram from Ovid:

> Ipse licet uenias Musis comitatus Omere,
>   si nichil attuleris, ibis Omere foras.
>   (*Ars Amatoria*, II, 279-280)

Though you are Orpheus or Arion or Amphion, you will get nothing from the courtiers "unless you soften their leaden hearts with a golden or silver hammer on the anvil of vanity or avarice." Though Hades has only one Cerberus, at court a Cerberus fills each cubicle, his appetite insatiable. Their chests are filled, but their avarice never diminishes. There is an old proverb, says John, "A petition with empty hands is rash." And among physicians and courtiers the rule is, "For mere words we use mountain herbs; for precious things we use fine pigments and spices." Since evil example produces evil subordinates, the prince must restrain the avarice of his courtiers, and pay them enough so that there will be no extortion. Otherwise the court will continue to corrupt men.[53]

Despite the brilliance of John's rhetoric, he says nothing on the venality of courtiers which we have not found before directed

---

[53] *Policraticus*, V, x. In Webb, I, 324-329.

against the officials of the Curia. He duly applies the doctrine of the Fathers on *munera*. He repeats the old image of the court as hell, with its associated mythological figures—Cerberus, Orpheus and Charon—the same tags from Juvenal and Ovid, the same attacks on notaries and other petty court officials, the same complaints of omnipresent venality. These were the common complaints about Rome, and John probably patterned his satire on the *Romdiatribe*, with which he he was familiar (cf. pp. 115-116 above). Secular venality did not differ from clerical venality, though it was perhaps less shocking to the moralist. The satire developed with the courts themselves.

John makes one practical suggestion not usually found in such satire: let the officials be paid well enough so that they are not driven to extortion. One is reminded that this satire provides vivid and picturesque insights into the growing pains of governmental organizations, pains resulting from the attempts to operate a new bureaucracy on the worn assumptions of feudal government: the creation of offices without the creation of commensurate salaries, hence the swarms of petty officials subsisting almost wholly on extorted gifts; taxation by enforced gratuities rather than by statute, hence the complete obscuring of the line between taxation and barratry or simony. These were characteristic medieval economic maladies and the characteristic medieval venality-satire is at least partly the protest against them. In the progressive court of the kings of England John's attacks on the "follies of courtiers" signalize the revival of the satirical theme in secular clothing.

Walter Map's *De nugis curialium* reflects similar ideas in a more caustic spirit. The court is once again compared to hell, avarice is "dominatrix curie cupiditas," and Charon, the grasping boatman obsequious for a promised bribe, is a symbol of court venality.[54]

---

[54] *De nugis curialium*, I, i, p. 2, and V, vii, p. 250.

Walter, apparently drawing on his own experience, also discusses some of the royal officials who roam beyond the confines of the court. The itinerant justices, sheriffs, and beadles are like the night birds which fly out of hell to prey on corpses, to rob and to slander. They punish innocence while greed escapes unharmed. Despite their oaths they are perverted by gifts to tear the fleece from the lamb but leave the foxes unharmed; for the foxes are recommended by silver, knowing that "res est ingeniosa dare."[55]

An English Latin poem which we have already discussed for its attack on venal officials of the law courts (cf. p. 151 above) also treats sheriffs with indignation. The poor who cannot give are subjected to all kinds of indignities, and punished at the assizes. When sheriffs are comfortably entertained at a house or an abbey, they and their whole train must receive gifts, and robes must be sent to their wives. Otherwise they will rob the manor and imprison the owner until they receive double their original demands.[56]

Nigel Wireker finds in meed the greatest source of tyranny: "Meed makes a destructive tyrant of a king, and turns his hands against his own members." He draws a brief picture of the misery of a kingdom when its ruler has turned tyrant through *munera*.[57] Here the English satirist was probably influenced by

---

[55] *De nugis curialium*, I, x, p. 6. The last phrase is from Ovid, *Amores*, I, vii, 62.

[56] Wright, *Political Songs*, pp. 228–229. Cf. also p. 100, where a poem written just after the Battle of Lewes (1264) suggests causes for the venality of the court of Henry III. The king is surrounded by lying flatterers, says the poet, so that no one can obtain justice without giving generous gifts:

> Quod nullus justitiam posset optinere,
> Nisi qui superbiam talium fovere
> Vellet, per pecuniam largiter collatam.

[57] *Speculum stultorum*, p. 90. Cf. Werner, *Sprichwörter*, p. 63.

the *Policraticus*. Nigel's *Contra curiales et officiales clericos*, a long
prose tract with a verse introduction, reflects John of Salisbury's
ideas, and quotes directly from the *Policraticus*.[58]

Though few secular courts were sufficiently complex to inspire
the sort of venality-satire which was being written in England,
we occasionally find brief anatomies of their venality in other
countries. Philip the Chancellor furnishes perhaps the most entertaining example:

> Ab aula principis,
>   Si nihil habeas,
>   Oportet abeas,
> Spem vanam concipis,
>   Tenuis fortuna,
>   Omnimoda
>   Ad commoda
>   Hominum mens una;
> A quo nihil emungitur,
>   Opus perdit et operam,
> Quod habenti dabitur,
>   Tenent omnes ad literam.[59]

Princes and their courts, then, were virtually the only secular
targets of venality-satire at this time. Among the poor only the
avaricious minor court officials, and the humble pastor or vicar

---

[58] *Contra Curiales*: in Wright, *Satirical Poets*, I, 149-150:
> Curia curat opes, inopum fastidit amores,
>   Nausea divitibus pauper amicus adest.
> Curia suspendit tales in poste salutes,
>   Quae vacuis manibus nil nisi verba ferunt. . . .
> Plurima si dederis, modicum tibi forte refundet,
>   Colligat ut rursum fertiliore manu. . . .
> Curia, crede mihi, sine munere nescit amicum,
>   Munera si dederis hostis, amicus eris, etc.

[59] *Analecta hymnica*, XXI, 151. Cf. also the couplet printed by Werner,
Beiträge, p. 169.

who sold the sacraments and sang masses for money, could be extortionists. There were general attacks, to be sure, on the scramble for money among all classes, high and low. Verses and prose tracts *de contemptu mundi* frequently contain such passages. One *Cursus mundi*, for example, describes, profession by profession, the search for lucre in which all estates are indulging. The poem does not idealize the plowman. He tills his fields, as the tailor makes clothes and the merchant scours the seas,[60] only for money. The carpenter, the thresher, the cook, all follow the penny "sicut carnem canes"—as dogs follow meat. Nor do artists and craftsmen live and work for art's sake:

> Faber per fabrilia,
> Sculptor per sculptilia
>   Nummum consequuntur,
> Quem cum apprehenderint
> Antequam expenderint
>   Forte moriuntur.

And so—ending on St. Paul's note—"All men are money-worshippers; few are worshippers of God, except by lip-service":

> Omnes sunt nummicolae
> Pauci sunt deicolae
>   Nisi voce tantum.[61]

The picture is one of a great many rudimentary forerunners of Langland's "faire felde ful of folke," occupied with getting and spending and forgetful of spiritual ends. The literary transformation wrought later by the vernacular allegories brought the theme to the stage of Langland's vision on the Malvern Hills.

---

[60] An interesting "dissuasio navigationis ob lucrum," (Wright, *Satirical Poets*, II, 159; also Hagen, *Carmina medii aevi*, p. 171) by Godfrey of Cambrai, obviously inspired by Horace, attacks the scouring of the seas in search of wealth.

[61] *Analecta hymnica*, XV, 263–266.

Attacks on venality among other groups were usually submerged in broader generalizations (treated below) on the power of money. There is an occasional reference to the omnipotence of Gold in giving power to the merchants,[62] but these are rare. Physicians receive some attention. One recalls that Chaucer's fourteenth-century Doctour of Phisik "kepte that he wan in pestilence," and was a special lover of that cordial, gold (*Canterbury Tales*, I, 441-444). He had his precursors in the Latin satire, whose most successful cures, as one sardonic versifier remarked, were cures for their own poverty:

> Quidam morbes arte curant,
> Dum curare sese curant
> A morbo penurie:
> Quos paupertas non excusat,
> Amor nummi quos excusat,
> Et sitis pecunie.

> Sepe curant paupertatem,
> Sed infirmo sanitatem
> Raro valent reddere.
> Ventrem movent os ut fomat
> Et ut nummi bursa promat
> Bursam cogunt promere.[63]

---

[62] Cf., e.g., C. Höfler, "Carmen historicum occulti auctoris saec. XII," *Wiener Sitzungsberichte*, XXXXVII (1861), 239:
> Sed mercatores sunt militibus pociores
> Nam qui mercantur bene mille viri memorantur
> Est tibi multorum locus officiumque fabrorum
> Precipui quorum sunt fabri denariorum
> Nam cum rex summus sit in isto tempore nummus.

[63] W. Wattenbach, "Lateinische Reime des Mittelalters, X," *Anzeiger für Kunde der deutschen Vorzeit*, XVIII (1871), 203. There remain occasional attacks on the venality of the other, less significant groups. At least one Paris preacher, Jacques de Lausanne, scored the gratuity–grubbing beadles of the schools for

There is, finally, the venality of women, for venality was—as all readers of medieval anti-feminist literature know—one of the numberless failings of that disingenuous sex. It is alluded to repeatedly by the versifiers and has produced a modest body of verse, mostly inspired by Ovid, entirely devoted to the theme. Spurius, the wily slave in William of Blois' *Alda*, for example, instructs the lover in the necessities of a campaign of love, in lines obviously reminiscent of Ovid:

> Nam sicut nequeunt sine munere numina flecti,
>   Sic sine muneribus nulla puella capi;
> Exemplumque mali dociles imitantur, amorque
>   Muneris, ut uendit cetera, uendit eas.
> Non genus aut formam moresque requirit amantis
>   Femina; de precio est questio prima suo.
> Non dantem, sed munus amat; metitur amorem
>   Ex dono; quantum donat, amatur amans.[64]

There is even a debate between *Amor* and *Nummus*.[65] But these attacks on female venality are more properly a part of the *femina*

---

this vice: "Utinam non servetur ordo in ecclesia sicut in scola, ubi bedellus saepe situat scolares non secundum merita, sed secundum dona; unde nobiles, dantes bedellis vestes et pecunias, ante omnes situantur." In Hauréau, *Notices*, VI, 125. But this is merely an early portrait of the Eternal Headwaiter.

[64] G. Cohen, ed., *La "comédie" latine en France au XIIe siècle* (Paris, 1931), I, 139-140. Note the Ovidian elegiacs. Cf. Werner, *Beiträge*, p. 177:

> Femina, donare si cessas, cessat amare;
> Femina pro dote nummorum dicit: amo te!

Cf. also Werner, *Sprichwörter*, no. 42, p. 100. Henry of Settimello, too, in his *De diversitate Fortunae*, III, 215-220 (In Leyser, p. 485), decries feminine venality. Today, he says, even those classical paragons of chastity, Lucretia and Penelope, would listen to the sound of money.

[65] In W. Wattenbach, "Mittheilungen aus zwei Handschriften der k. Hof- und Staatsbibliothek," *Bayerische Akademie der Wissenschaften. Philos.–philol. und hist. Classe. Sitzungsberichte*, III (1873), 704–707. Cf. p. 176 below.

dulce malum theme than satire on the power of the purse. Their function is incidental rather than central.

FOUR

THE SATIRICAL GENERALIZATION ON THE POWER OF MONEY

From attacks on venality at Rome, or among clergy and lawyers, satirists slipped easily into broad generalizations on the power of wealth in this world, frequently aided by loose personifications of money or meed. Such generalizations became one of the most obvious and wearisome commonplaces of the satirical theme. We have seen the tendency repeatedly in the satires we have examined. The personifications are usually no more elaborate or imaginative than our "Almighty Dollar," but they were given full rein in the generalizations on *Nummus* and *Munera*. Satirists exhausted their wits by ringing changes on the power of money. Much of their product is the simplest form of litany. It is rarely good verse, and often exceptionally bad, but its sardonic epigrammatic quality and the nature of its subject seemed to appeal widely to medieval tastes. The most popular of these medieval money-litanies appears in the Benediktbeuern and at least 43 other manuscripts, with innumerable variations:

> In terra summus   rex est hoc tempore Nummus.
> Nummum mirantur   reges et ei famulantur.
> Nummo venalis   favet ordo pontificalis.
> Nummus in abbatum   cameris retinet dominatum.
> Nummum nigrorum   veneratur turba priorum.
> Nummus magnorum   fit iudex conciliorum.

The poem contains fifty leonine lines, most of them beginning with *Nummus*. *Nummus* wages wars, makes peace, carries on lawsuits. When *Nummus* speaks, the poor man is silenced; *Nummus* kills the hearts and blinds the eyes of the wise; it procures beautiful and expensive clothes, captures towns, cures the sick, smoothes the rough, celebrates Mass and sings both versicle and response, brings honor, gives probity to the infamous: "Behold it is clear to everyone that *Nummus* reigns everywhere."[66]

This is the unimposing pattern of most satirical generalizations on the power of money in twelfth and thirteenth century Latin poetry. Versifiers rarely conceived their personifications of the money-power in any truly dramatic manner. Instead they strained to achieve the witty, the striking, the epigrammatic, and the paradoxical. The Benediktbeuern poem is only a moderate effort. The most ambitious *Nummus*-litany was probably written by Godfrey of Cambrai, Prior of St. Swythin's at Winchester, in the early twelfth century. It is composed in the familiar baneful leonines. A 38-line prologue announcing the theme—the description and praise of Money in verse—leads to 866 leonines which begin with *Nummus*, running in turn through all the grammatical cases. It is a monotonous *reductio ad absurdum*, at a very early date, of the *Nummus*-litany:

> Nummus honor fidus,   lux praevia, dux, via, sidus.
> Nummus ad ipsa citus   discrimina, navita litus.
> Nummus mendicus,   nunquam comes, omnis amicus.
> Nummus habet ritus,   dat, tollit, ubique peritus.
> Nummus agit causas   et vult a lite repausas.

---

[66] *Carmina burana*, I, i. 15–16. For variants cf. the editors' notes, pp. 16–29. The technique is used in a rather lighter poem of seven lines printed by J. Feifalik, "Studien zur Geschichte der altbömischen Literatur, V," *Wiener Sitzungsberichte*, XXXVI (1860), 175, beginning:

> Lex datur a summo,   quod nullus bibat sine nummo.

C. Höfler, "Carmen historicum occulti auctoris saec. XIII," *Wiener Sitzungsberichte*, XXXVII (1861), 248, and Werner, *Sprichwörter*, pp. 7, 15, also print lines which make clear that *sine nummo* there is no *vinum*.

The author is tireless. *Nummus* is orator and conciliator, creator and destroyer of peace, giver of true and false, gentle and severe. It is the dispenser of honors and the touchstone of truth, it softens enemies, is the "dux populorum," the server of food and wine, the king of kings, the creator of thieves and liars, the setter of all standards, the arbiter of all customs and manners.[67] The poem is far too long to pursue in detail, and reaches its end more from the author's exhaustion than from a preconceived plan. Its only organization is a systematic progress through the grammatical cases of *nummus*, and the poet's lone virtues are dexterity and an occasional felicity of phrasing; but the monotony of theme and form submerges these sparse epigrammatic pleasures. The author achieves one noteworthy conclusion, however: he precedes Langland by centuries in recognizing the complexity of the influence of wealth, and the ambivalence of *nummus* itself. In his long pursuit of the theme Godfrey finds much to say about the power of *nummus* for good, though this is far outweighed by its power for evil, and Godfrey is clearly exasperated that it has any power at all over the souls of men. Occasionally, then, like Langland, he seems able to separate money as mere economic instrument from Money as baneful symbol of human worldliness. But one thing seems certain: nothing new is said in the Middle Ages about the power of wealth after Godfrey of Cambrai. Later novelty is wholly novelty of expression or application.

This then is the sort of litany on the power of the purse which became a satirical staple. Occasionally "nummus" was replaced by "munera," meed. Thus Nigel Wireker's Burnellus, recounting his woes, interrupts his laments with a long monologue on the powers of meed:

[67] J. A. Yunck, "The *De Nummo* of Godfrey of Cambrai," *Duquesne Studies Annuale Mediaevale*, II (1961), 72–103.

> Munera conturbant reges rursusque serenant,
> Munera dant pacem, munera bella parant.
> Munera pontifices subvertunt, munera reges,
> Munera jus statuunt destituuntque simul.[68]

Burnèllus holds forth in this style for sixty lines. Meed makes learned the tongues of fools; when meed speaks others are silent; meed perverts laws and refutes decretals, and so on. The ideas were already threadbare by Nigel's time, but his verse, however devoid of originality, is superior to the exercise of Godfrey of Cambrai, partly because it avoids Godfrey's unfortunate leonine rhymes and escapes his obscurity of diction and syntax. But the passage is merely a conventional interruption of Nigel's narrative, as commonplace and perhaps as meaningless as some of the long descriptive passages in the later romances. It becomes difficult to distinguish the satirist's indignation from the student's exercise or from the rhetorician's commonplace.

Such money passages had indeed become, even before Nigel's time, a sort of decalcomania fresco, easily transferred from one context to another for rhetorical-moralistic decoration. A characteristic example appears in prose in the *De planctu naturae* of Alain de Lille, where nature describes the vice of *Nummulatria*, one of the offspring of *Idolatria*:

> This is the evil through which money is deified in the souls of men and the authority for divine veneration is given to cash, through which when money speaks, the trump of Ciceronian eloquence is hoarse; when a coin goes to war, the lightnings of Hector's warfare cease; when money battles, the strength of Hercules is subdued. For if one is armed with money as with a silver

---

[68] *Speculum stultorum,* 2593–2596. The same sort of litany appears in some of Nigel's unpublished poems, especially a *Passio Sancti Laurenti martyris*; cf. J. Mozley, "The Unprinted Poems of Nigel Wireker," *Speculum,* VII (1932), 398–423.

breastplate, the rush of the Ciceronian torrent, the splendor of the onset of Hector, the might and bravery of Hercules, the cunning craft of Ulysses, count only for light trifles. For to such a degree has the hunger for possession enflamed men that the subtlety of dialectic is silent, the culture of rhetoric languishes....

Money would have bought the eloquence of Cicero, the chastity of Lucretia and Penelope, the honor of Hippolytus; it would have defeated the lyre of Orpheus, the song of Amphion, the muse of Virgil. Money is our patriarch, our archbishop, our bishop. But we can hasten over the passage, with its familiar images: "Quid plura? nummus vincit, nummus regit, nummus imperat universis."[69] Despite its worn contents and its facile rhetoric, the authority of Alain de Lille's name must have made it influential.

In Hildebert's poem against women, avarice and ambition, another famous name was attached to the tradition. The saint of Hildebert's money-litany was not *Nummus* or *Munera*, but *Aurum*,[70]

---

[69] Alanus de Insulis, *De planctu naturae*, Prosa VI. In Wright, *Satirical Poets*, II, 488–89. Cf. also Metrum VII, pp. 491–494. Most of its imagery, and some of its language, we can find elsewhere. The parody, in the final line, of the *Laudes regiae* is obvious and popular. The lines also have many similarities to a long passage in the *Miles gloriosus* (G. Cohen, *"Comédie" latine*, I, 199) on the power of money. Fragments of this passage are scattered throughout medieval MSS as *sententiae*. Cf., e.g., Werner, *Sprichwörter*, p. 51:

> Munera rethoricos penitus novere colores;
> Nummus ubi loquitur, Tullius ipse silet.
> Dulci gaza sono citharizat in aure potentum:
> Nescit tam placitum musica tota sonum.

Also Hauréau, *Notices*, VI, 327. Similar commonplaces are printed by Werner, *Sprichwörter*, pp. 12, 16, 36, 50, 55, 72, 79, 100.

[70] Hildebertus Cenomansis Episcopus, *Carmina miscellanea*, cx. In PL, CLXXI, 1429. Also printed by Werner, *Beiträge*, p. 32, and Hauréau, "Notice sur les mélanges poétiques d'Hildebert de Lavardin," *Notices et extraits*, XXVIII (1878), 367.

though its virtues are the same. An unknown poet provides another variation:

> Dum cano 'si dedero,' protinus mea commoda quaero.
> Si dedero, decus accipiam flatumque favoris:
> Ni dedero, nil percipiam, spem perdo laboris;
> Si dedero, genus accumulo famamque potentis;
> Ni dedero, clauso loculo parit ars sapientis; etc.[71]

The variations are almost countless. A satirist of the reign of Frederick II of Sicily writes an inferior imitation of the *Gospel of Mark Silver* in the form of an *Epistola notabilis de pecunia*, a parody of an Imperial letter. Like the money-gospel it is a cento of scriptural texts, though its attack is not confined to the clergy.[72] Another satirist makes his contribution in a parody of the medieval grammatical catechisms:

> What is the mood of *nummus*? Infinitive. Why? Because there is no end to the active and operative quality of its power. —Compare it. *Nummus*? No. Why? Because *Nummus* by itself disposes of (*comparat*) kings, princes, knights, barons, commoners, manors, kingdoms and empires. etc.[73]

Yet elsewhere *Mammonia* becomes a great worker of miracles.[74] And still another poet treats the theme in an elaborate and prayerful elegy to *Denarii*:

> Denarii salvete mei, per vos ego regno,
>   Terrarum per vos impero principibus;
> Quod probor et veneror; quod diligor atque frequentor,
>   Gratia vestra facit que michi magna facit.
> Per vos imperium Caesar tenet, et sine vobis

---

[71] T. Wright and J. Halliwell, *Reliquae antiquae* (London, 1845), II, 6.

[72] Printed in Haskins, *Studies in Medieval Culture* (Oxford, 1929), pp. 138–139.

[73] Lehmann, *Parodistische Texte*, pp. 15–16.

[74] Du Méril, *Poésies inédites du moyen âge*, p. 315.

Imperium nullus Caesar habere potest,
Denique quidquid agant reges terraque marique
Certent sive gerant praelia, vos facitis. etc.[75]

The only surviving Latin debate on the subject pits *Nummus* against the god *Amor*. In the argument over their relative might, *Nummus* boasts most frequently of his power over the clergy: "Every clerk enslaves himself to me, nor does he remember that he ought to have any master beside me; and the pope, rejoicing, saves me and accumulates me." People flock to the formal debate from all over the world. *Amor* is surrounded by elegant ladies, entertainers, and music, *Nummus* by a troop of usurers; but the end of the debate is lacking.[76] Though poor poetry, the work is an interesting fusion of the satirical theme with the love-theme and the allegorical romance. The background—the castle, the assembling audience, and the entourages of the contestants—is courtly in flavor. The descriptions of the trains of the contestants especially bring the theme a step nearer to the allegory of Lady Meed and the rout who surround her.

Narrow as the device was, the money-litany was sometimes handled with considerable felicity. The "Manus ferens munera" of the *Carmina burana*, for example, with its description of the baneful effects of *nummus* on justice, is incisive, dextrously phrased, entertaining, and not so long (60 lines) that it wearies the reader:

Manus ferens munera
pium facit impium;

[75] Jules de Saint–Genois, "Notice sur le *Liber Floridus Lamberti Canonici*," PL, CLXIII, 1014–1015. The editor there ascribes it to Peter [Pictor?], "Chanoine de St.-Omer."

[76] W. Wattenbach, "Mittheilungen aus zwei Handschriften der k. Hof–und Staatsbibliothek," *Bayerische Sitzungsberichte*, III (1873), 704–707. The MS is badly defective near the end. Wattenbach gives only extracts from the text. I have relied on his summary for the remainder of the narrative.

nummus iungit federa,
nummus dat consilium;
nummus lenit aspera,
nummus sedat prelium.
   nummus in prelatis
   est pro iure satis;
   nummo locum datis
   vos, qui iudicatis.[77]

A similarly attractive poem from an English manuscript uses a vivid device—the cross which appeared on the back of every penny—to symbolize the power of money in the world. Behind this striking figure of the Cross of Silver appear the old commonplaces, versified artfully:

Crux est denarii potens in saeculo;
   regem et principem facit de servulo;
   mendicum servulum facit de regulo;
   rectorem, praesulem de parvo famulo.
Virtutem continet nummus mirabilem;
   iratum judicem reddit placabilem;
   oditum nimium facit amabilem;
   plenum criminibus clamat laudabilem.

The poem continues for 100 lines, describing the power of the *crux denarii* in consistory, in battle, in palace, in courtroom. This cross is honored by all estates and can change guilt to innocence, fraud to justice; can obtain absolution, can make a John the Baptist out of the worst Herod. The poor sinner finds no friend in the consistory court, but the rich one, by offering the cross, saves himself:

nummus purificat quicquid commiserit;
   est crux amabilis, cum culpas operit.

---

[77] *Carmina burana,* I, i. 1.

In the courtroom the denarius makes the invisible visible, the movable immovable. A full purse wins any case, for it blinds the eye of any judge.[78]

Walter of Châtillon used the device in some of his best verse. In his "Missus sum in vineam," goliardic stanzas *cum auctoritate*, he successfully weaves the familiar money-tags of Roman satire into his stanzas:

> Qui virtutes appetit,   labitur in imum,
> querens sapientiam   irruit in limum;
> imitemur igitur   hec dicentem mimum:
> o cives, cives, querenda pecunia primum.
>
> Hec est, que in sinodis   confidendo tonat,
> in electionibus   prima grande sonat;
> intronizat presules,   dites impersonat:
> et genus et formam regina pecunia donat.
>
> Adora pecuniam,   qui deos adoras:
> cur struis armaria,   cur libros honoras?
> Longas fac Parisius   vel Athenis moras:
> si nichil attuleris, ibis, Homere, foras.[79]

---

[78] Wright, *Mapes*, pp. 223–226. This striking figure of the cross on the coin appears elsewhere with some frequency. Cf., e.g., *Piers Plowman*, XV, 500–509. An equally well executed, but graver and more sober, attack on the power of money is probably the work of Philip the Chancellor. The poem is moralistic rather than cynical, *Nummus* a villain rather than a hero: If the world were without money we would live in peace and concord; but avarice has planted conflict, hatreds and discord among us. Now money gives what it pleases, softens all harshness. No one who offers *munera* asks in vain, but requests which come empty-handed are useless, and learning does not help them. On the contrary, there is no one so hateful and depraved that money will not make him decent and likeable. Meanwhile, the poor man suffers: "Pauper jacet vilis." In *Analecta hymnica*, XXI, 149–150.

[79] Strecker, *Chatillon*, pp. 83–84. The *auctoritates* of the quoted stanzas are

Walter's theme is commonplace and his quotations trite, but as usual he has the touch of the master. His work always has a fluency rare in verse satire of the type, and he treats the theme with great variety. In his "Captivata largitas," on the same subject, the power of money becomes a sort of triumphal refrain at the end of each stanza, in a phrase parodying the *Laudes regiae* and often echoed by other writers:

> Nummus vincit, nummus regnat,   nummus cunctis imperat,
> reos solvit, iustos ligat,   impedit et liberat.[80]

Another poet builds his verse on Juvenal's idea of an altar to *Nummus* (*Saturae*, I, 113-114; cf. p. 17 above), and from this beginning moves to the Christian image of the beatification or canonization of *Nummus*, a figure already familiar from the popular Saints Albinus and Rufinus, and Saint Nummulus:

> Et si nondum ara nummo
>   Fabricata sit in summo,
>   Tamen plus Diis colitur.
> Si nondum canonizatus
>   Nummus sit, neque beatus,
>   Ipse genu flectitur.

Horace, *Epistulae*, I, i. 53; I, vi, 37; and Ovid, *Ars amatoria*, II, 280, respectively. An interesting parallel treatment of the uselessness of liberal studies in a money-mad world is Petrus Pictor's "Cur ultra studeam." Cf. Werner, *Beiträge*, pp. 139–140. The final lines of Nigel Wireker's verses "Ad Dominum Guliemum Eliensem" (Wright, *Satirical Poets*, I, 238–289) also treat the same subject. Walter's "Fallax est et mobilis" (Strecker, *Chatillon*, pp. 101–103), though ignoring the liberal-studies theme, is otherwise similar in tone to the "Missus sum in vineam."

[80] Strecker, *Chatillon*, pp. 110–112. This refrain is echoed, e.g., at the end of the passage from Alain's *De planctu naturae* quoted p. 174 above. Walter's "Stulti cum prudentibus" (pp. 63–70) and his "Multiformis hominum" (pp. 73–79) are both pertinent to the theme.

> Quanta numme operaris
> Quod plus quam Deus amaris
> A clero & a laicis.[81]

In order to suggest how thoroughly static and stereotyped the theme had become in the verse of the period, I have deferred until last a discussion of two of the earliest and most influential writers of these satirical generalizations: Marbod, Bishop of Rennes, and Hildebert, the great Archbishop of Tours, both important poets and humanists writing at the close of the eleventh century, and both products of the flourishing French cathedral schools.[82] These churchmen were very famous, Hildebert exceeding in reputation only slightly the elder (and lesser) Marbod, and they were good friends, both torn unwillingly from the schools to be made prelates. Their fame undoubtedly did much to establish any subject on which they wrote as suitable material for later poets. Well before the close of the eleventh century Marbod had written two poems on the dangerous power of *Nummus*. Perhaps his perverse preference for leonines helped establish that ungracious verse form as a popular medium for Latin venality-satire. The verse, like most of Marbod's work, is undistinguished, but is good evidence of the early development of the commonplaces of conventional money-satire:

> Cum nummo detur decus a multis, et ametur,
> Fallit honorantes fallax, et fallit amantes.
> Princeps, praeiatus, monachi, populique senatus,
> Clericus et miles, mulier, sexusque viriles,
> Nummo laetantur, jussique suis famulantur.

---

[81] Flacius Illyricus, pp. 23–27.

[82] Both poets are fully discussed by Raby, *Secular Latin Poetry*, I, 317–337. They were contemporaries, and perhaps acquaintances, of Godfrey of Cambrai, whose *De nummo* is discussed above, pp. 171–172. Cf. Yunck, "The *De Nummo* of Godfrey of Cambrai," *Duquesne Studies Annuale Mediaevale*, II (1961), 75.

Omnis ei plaudit. Si quid jubit impiger audit.
Quod placet impletur, quod displicit hoc prohibetur.
Dum nummus loquitur, cunctorum vox sepelitur.
Justo praefertur, dum plurima causa refertur. etc.[83]

Hildebert touched on the subject a number of times in his shorter poems. We have mentioned one in which he deplores the power of gold (p. 174 above). His *De perfida amica*[84] likewise deals with this evil power of gold, especially as it concerns the frailty of women. And elsewhere he treats briefly that favorite theme of Walter of Châtillon, the uselessness of learning without money.[85] But Hildebert's best and longest satire is a poem usually entitled *De nummo, seu satyra adversus avaritiam*. The title is misleading, for its 1190 lines are in fact a sort of miniature *speculum de naturis rerum*, developed with some inspiration and great poetic charm. Above all it is the work of a humanist; every section is rich with classical allusion, and every moral bolstered by classical example. One should add that in recent years the attribution of this poem, long counted among Hildebert's best verse, has been called into question on the basis of new manuscript evidence. The poem

[83] Marbodus Redonensis Episcopus, *Carmina varia*, xxxvii; in PL, CLXXI, 1727. The other poem, on the self-deceit of those who live for money, is less central to our theme. Cf. *Carmina varia*, xxxix; in PL, CLXXI, 1728.

[84] Hauréau, "Notice sur les mélanges poétiques d'Hildebert de Lavardin," *Notices et extraits*, XXVIII, ii, 415–417.

[85] Hildebertus, *Carmina miscellanea: Supplementum*, ix. In PL, CLXXI, 1456–1458. Hauréau, *Les mélanges poétiques d'Hildebert de Lavardin* (Paris, 1882), pp. 56–57, provides a better text of this poem *Ad Odonem*. In his commentary (pp. 57–58) Hauréau draws parallels with Petrus Pictor, Matthew of Vendôme, and Vital of Blois. Lines from Vital are characteristic:

Vincit amor census et nummi carmina cedunt;
Multa licet sapias, re sine nullus eris.

The tradition seems in large part inspired by Ovid (esp. *Ars amatoria*, II, 274–280 and *Amores*, III).

has been attributed to Theodoric of Saint-Trond, a contemporary of Hildebert.[86] Should the new attribution prove correct it will not affect our speculation about the poem's influence, for the *De nummo* began to pass as Hildebert's almost immediately after its composition and continued to pass as his throughout the Middle Ages. The manuscript tradition is so strong, indeed, that it has succeeded in surviving the careful scrutiny of Hauréau and others.

We are concerned only with the hundred lines which the poet devotes to money and its power.[87] They follow a long introduction lamenting the state of the world, where piety and friendship are dead and every man lives wholly for himself. The ancient virtues have been killed by inexhaustible avarice. This thought leads to the usual ironic glorification of *nummus*:

> Jus, fas, majestas regni, curule, tribunal,
>   Nummo cesserunt; omnia solus erit.
> Publica spes nummus; nunc rege potentior erit
>   Extollit praesens, dejicit aufugiens.
> Nummus nobilitas, nummus sapientia, quae nunc
>   Praetendens superat; pauper ubique jacet.
> . . . .
> Piscis aquae, mel api debetur, vitibus uva,
>   Caseus et lacti; gloria, numme, tibi.
> Umbra, jubar solis, nummi jubar, umbra decorem

---

[86] A. Boutemy, "Hildebert dépossédé une fois de plus," *Moyen âge*, LII (1946), 146–147, and Boutemy, "Le patrimoine poétique de l'abbaye de Saint-Trond," *Moyen âge*, LIV (1948), 393–395.

[87] This was clearly the most popular part of the poem, judging from the frequency of its appearance in MSS detached from the main body of the work. Cf. PL, CLXXI, 1402–1405; Wattenbach, "Mittheilungen aus zwei Handschriften der K. Hof–und Staatsbibliothek," *Bayerische Sitzungsberichte*, III (1873), 742–744; A. Jubinal, *Nouveau recueil de contes, dits, fabliaux et autres pièces*, II, 427. The full poem, published in F. Otto, *Comentarii critici in codices bibliothecae academicae Gissensis graecos et latinos* (Giessen, 1842), pp. 163–198, was copied only rarely.

> Assequitur: non sit nummus, et umbra perit.
> Solus nunc nummus virtutis habetur alumnus,
>   Solus diligitur, solus adhuc colitur.
> Stipatur multo tua curia, numme, senatu;
>   Incurvare genu quem pudet, alme, tibi !
> Si nummi nondum templi surrexerit ara,
>   Divina colitur religione tamen.
> Si non per nummum juratur, quis tamen horret
>   Nunc causa nummi sacrilegus fieri?
> Olim philosophi fuerat lucra spernere nummum:
>   Nunc nisi nummatus Plato foret fatuus. etc.[88]

The influence of this poem, and especially of the detached money passages which appeared so frequently in manuscripts, must have been enormous. At least one money poem by another author was attracted to the famous name of Hildebert.[89] The archbishop's literary reputation was so great that he was probably partly responsible for the frequent choice of meed as a subject by later poets.

Hildebert's education at the cathedral school of Le Mans, and Marbod's at the cathedral school of Angers, may remind the reader of the large number of identifiable venality-satirists who were products of the French cathedral schools or the early University of Paris. Walter of Châtillon was a product of Reims and Paris, John of Salisbury of Chartres and Paris, Philip the Chancellor and Walter Map of Paris, Petrus Cantor of Reims, Peter of Blois of Tours and Paris, Alain of Lille probably of Paris. Certainly this circumstance partly explains their common humanism and their identity of interests. It explains also why their reader often observes in them the unity of a school of thought, despite their

---

[88] Hildebertus, *Carmina miscellanea*, 1. In PL, CLXXI, 1404–1405.

[89] Cf. Yunck, "The *De Nummo* of Godfrey of Cambrai," *Duquesne Studies Annuale Mediaevale*, II (1961), 74–75.

diverse ranks, literary techniques, and views of life. Further, one may speculate that satires on the power of money, the decline of the liberal arts, and pelf-ridden professionalism were regular exercises at these schools. Certainly many of the poorer verses we have examined are marked by that conventional learnedness and lack of poetic substance which usually characterize school-poetry. The general uniformity and wide diffusion of the venality-theme in the Latin verse of this period may be taken, indeed, as another indication of the deep influence of the cathedral schools on the medieval revival of learning.

Perhaps the clearest conclusion to be drawn from these relatively early venality verses of Marbod and Hildebert is that in the Latin verse between the end of the eleventh and the end of the thirteenth century the satirical theme underwent virtually no change or development. In fact Hildebert treats the powers of *Nummus* with greater fluency and grace, and with higher thought-density, than most of his successors, Walter of Châtillon and a few others excepted. However genuine the problems with which the satirists were grappling, the theme had solidified into an almost inflexible convention, part of the enormous amount of fluting, gargoyle-work, and drollery which went into medieval verse, perhaps more often decorative than meaningful.[90]

FIVE

THE SENSE OF THE SATIRE

The weight of convention and the odor of the school-exercise make it difficult to assess the significance of these Latin generaliza-

[90] For other generalizations on the power of wealth cf. C. Fierville, "Notices et extraits des manuscrits de la bibliothèque de Saint–Omer," *Notices et extraits*

tions on the power of money. The most striking thing about them is probably their abundance. Hardly another subject of satire—not even woman—was so attractive to writers; and it must be admitted that hardly another subject offered such an easy theme, such a well-staked-out area, for the mediocre satirist. Yet conventionality or insipidity do not preclude sincerity or even fervor in the threadbare repetition of these versifiers. Literary conventions do not endure for centuries without roots in reality. On the other hand, it is neither accurate nor fruitful to take the satirists at their hyperbolic word, as did the early Reformers, and thus dismiss the whole age as hypocritical, venal and simoniac. Hauréau once described concisely the care with which they must be interpreted. "Les satires ne méritent pas sans doute une entière confiance," he remarked, "mais il y a toujours plus ou moins de vérités. Si vous les prenez à la lettre, elles vous trompent; si vous en dégagez ce que la passion y a mis de trop, elles vous instruisent."[91] However conventional the writers, they could see in their convention the reflection of harsh economic realities—realities which upset ideals and habits of thought established centuries earlier by the regressive economics of the Dark Ages. The student of

---

XXXI, i, 124–125, 152; John de Hanville, *Architrenius*, in Wright, *Satirical Poets*, I, 295, 303, 316–319, 335–338; A. Wilmart, "Poèmes de Gautier de Châtillon dans un manuscrit de Charleville," *Revue Bénédictine*, XLIX (1937), 327–330; Godfrey of Cambrai, *Epigrammata*, clxxix, in Wright, *Satirical Poets*, II, 133; *Miles gloriosus*, 79–124, and *Alda*, 211–238, both in G. Cohen, *"Comédie" latine*, I, 199–200, and 138–139; M. Esposito, "A Thirteenth-Century Rhythmus," *English Historical Review*, XXXII (1917), 400–405; O. Kernstock, "Mittelalterliche Liedercompositionen," *Anzeiger für Kunde der deutschen Vorzeit*, XXIV (1877), 68–73; T. Wright, *A Selection of Latin Stories* (London, 1843), pp. 70–71; Hauréau, *Notices*, VI, 327.

[91] B. Hauréau, "Notice sur le numéro 1544 des Nouvelles Acquisitions (Fonds Latin) à la Bibliothèque Nationale," *Notices et extraits*, XXXII, ii (1886), 312.

this satire will be wise to return repeatedly to John of Salisbury's interview with his pope (cf. pp. 115-116 above), and recall that medieval society—especially in the medieval Church—was learning its lessons in economics through hard and jarring experience.

The theme came naturally to the clerical poet, for it was one of the most obvious points of contrast between ideal and reality. Christ had said, "Ask, and you shall receive," remarked one mendicant preacher, but our modern princes and prelates say, not "Ask," but "Give to us, or we will take it away from you."[92] The horror of the contrast was here most apparent. Through their venality-satires these clerks were characterizing, in their various ways, the Fair Field Full of Folk, and like Langland expressing their chagrin at finding large numbers

> Of alle maner of men   the mene and the riche,
> Worchyng and wandryng   as the worlde asketh.
> (*Piers Plowman*, Prol., 18-19)

The ideal reflected in this satire, then, when it can be recognized, is a sort of reactionary utopianism. It differs little from the Roman utopianism of the Golden Age, reflected in the Latin satirists who were the literary models for so much medieval satire. This arch-conservatism of reform runs through the medieval venality-satire from its beginnings past Langland's Lady Meed. Though the theme is obviously associated with the change from a "natural" (agrarian) economy to a money economy, we know far too few details about the economic history of the times or about the identities and attitudes of most of the writers to relate specific satires to specific economic developments. The meaning of these developments was often only dimly recognizable to the satirists themselves.

Nevertheless, the most striking aspect of this satire, besides its bulk and general mediocrity, is its lack of development, its stability

[92] Hauréau, *Notices*, III, 66.

and homogeneity. Most poets were content to repeat the recognized clichés in the usual way, using their subject as often
for poetic and moralistic filigree-work as for social reform. It
is difficult to separate the public moralist from the rhetorician.
By the end of the eleventh century writers had said everything
there was to say—to their limited clerical audience—on the theme.
The rest was repetition, the ringing of changes and the variation
of imagery on an old subject. Indeed, fostered by the scholarly
humanism of many of the satirists, a sort of neo-classicism developed
in the satire, a preoccupation with form, with polish, with mythological decoration, with the witty tricks of the trade, at the
expense of earnest devotion to content. Much of this disappears
in the cruder but more ingenuous verse of later vernacular satirists, usually addressed to a broader and less learned audience.

Since the Latin satire was the literature of a priestly class with
a strong conception of sacerdotal dignity, it centers on the special
fiscal vices of that class, vices which seemed especially to outrage
that dignity. Though the other estates were at first largely ignored,
the attacks on clerical venality led easily to the characteristic,
conventional satirical generalizations on the power of the purse
throughout society which flooded the collections of *sententiae* and
provided convenient rhetorical digressions for long poems. Yet
with all their conventionality the complaints were meaningful
to both writers and audiences. *Nummus*, or *munera*, was the great
toe-hold of Mammon in the City of God. "Men aim at three
things most," lamented Innocent III, "opes, voluptates, honores."[93]
As the medieval anti-feminist satire attacked *voluptates*, so the
satire on venality attacked *opes*. Later, Langland's Lady Meed
episode did likewise; for unbridled and misdirected *munera* was
the great public vice, as unbridled and misdirected *concupiscentia*
was the great vice of the secret heart.

[93] *De contemptu mundi*, ii. In PL, CCXVII, 717.

V

L'AMOUR DE DAN DENIER:

THE VENALITY-THEME IN THE VERNACULAR

ONE

FRENCH SATIRICAL ATTACKS ON BRIBERY AND VENALITY

Vernacular satire on venality and the power of the purse was plentiful in the Middle Ages, though its volume falls short of the great bulk of the Latin satire. The extant literature in English, indeed, is silent on the subject through the first part of the fourteenth century; but the theme begins to appear in French in the last quarter of the twelfth century and is common during the thirteenth. Relatively rare in both literatures are the short, "lyric" venality-satires, of the type written in Latin by so many obscure goliards and moralists, as well as by famous authors like Walter of Châtillon and Philip the Chancellor. Such Latin verse had usually been addressed, as its tone, imagery and attitudes suggest, to a small, learned group of clergy. In the vernacular, especially in French, the theme usually appears in sections or digressions of long, moral-didactic verse treatises written by the clergy for the instruction of lay audiences. Such works of instruction multiplied during the thirteenth century as a result of the decrees of the Fourth Lateran Council, and much of the early French venality-satire is to be found in them. The didactic context modifies the tone of the satire considerably.

The clerical authors of this vernacular satire were obviously familiar with the Latin satire on the subject, some of them possibly writers of it. Occasional puns have clearly been translated out of the Latin. The *manus rodit* etymology of *Roma*, for example, appears as *ronge mains*.[1] The French writers approach the commonplaces of Latin satire so frequently that it is impossible to doubt the influence of the *genre* as a whole. In one case we have a French translation of a Latin original, far more popular in the vernacular than in the Latin.[2] But for the most part the French satire merely reflects loosely the ideas and imagery of the Latin writers. Since this vernacular literature was largely intended for a lay audience, it is not surprising that the bulk of the French venality-satire is relatively small. Bribery and venality, as we have noted, were usually matters of concern only in ecclesiastical and court circles during the twelfth and thirteenth centuries. Popularizers concerned with the vices of their lay readers were unlikely to deal with simony, barratry, and the sale of justice.

The vernacular satire attacked the same groups as the Latin satire: the pope and his curia, bishops and the lesser clergy, judges and lawyers, and, rarely, other groups. We shall consider French venality-satire through 1350 as it applies to each of these groups, and summarize briefly the little English material on the subject during the period. For though much French satire on venality was probably Anglo-Norman, there is virtually none in English before 1350.

French vernacular satire on the Papacy and the Roman Curia differed little in theme from the Latin. The charge remained

---

[1] E.g., in Rutebuf, *Œuvres complètes*, II, 224.

[2] The *Lamenta* of Matheolus (ca. 1290) was translated into French (ca. 1370) by Jehan le Fevre. Both versions are edited by A.G. Van Hamel, *Les lamentations de Matheolus et le livre de leesce*, Paris, 1892. On their popularity cf. M. Wood, *The Spirit of Protest in Old French Literature* (New York, 1917), p. 7.

the unlimited hunger for money, which bred simony. That charge
appears in French as early as 1175 in the *Livre des manières* of
Etienne de Fougères, Bishop of Rennes, a man well acquainted
with English court circles.[3] He avoids a direct attack on the
pope himself, and concentrates his attention on the Curia—especially its courts and its administration of justice. The cardinals
are warned against taking meed—"loier:"

> Vilanie est de loier prendre
> Et justise por deniers vendre.

The thirst for meed may seduce them from rendering true justice.[4]
The warning to the Curia is brief, as might be expected in a work
of popularization addressed to an audience for whom Rome
was only a name. And Bishop Stephen is more interested in
the problems and duties of bishops. His tone is that of the preacher-
moralist rather than of the satirist.

Roman venality again comes under attack about 1195 in the
Vers de la mort of Hélinant, that curious and extremely popular[5]
early example of the *danse macabre* motif, written by a severe
monastic ascetic. Again the treatment is brief, though the author
is not so careful as Etienne of the person of the Pope. The cardinals nevertheless bear the brunt of the assault, which here has
a true satirical flavor, not the restrained, sermonizing character
of Etienne's writing. The author bids death greet Rome,

---

[3] Wood, pp. 3–4.

[4] Etienne de Fougères, *Livre des manières*, ed. J. Kremer (Ausg. u. Abh.
aus dem Gebiete der romanischen Philologie, xxxix; Marburg, 1887), pp. 127–
128.

[5] Hélinant, *Vers de la mort*, ed. F. Wulff and E. Walberg (SATF, Paris, 1905),
pp. vii–xxvii, xxxiv. Hélinant was the author of a sizable body of extant work
in Latin, including a chronicle, sermons, and brief moral treatises. The sermons
especially are rich in quotations from the Roman poets. The meed–theme
also appears in these works. Cf., e.g., PL, CCXII, 689–90, 741–42.

Qui de rongier a droit se nomme,
Car les os ronge et le cuir poile,
Et fait a simoniaus voile
De chardonal et d'apostoile:
Romme est li mauz qui tot asomme,
Romme nos fait de siu chandoille. . . .

He urges death to mount the cardinals on his horses, the cardinals (*chardonal*) who stick tighter than burrs (*chardon*) to beautiful and costly gifts. Rome, he continues, uses (symbolically) many false deniers, silvered over so that you cannot tell the good from the bad.[6] Here, then, is the familiar atmosphere—even to the puns—of the Latin satire of the two preceding centuries.

No more than a decade later, around the turn of the century, the unknown Norman author of the *Roman des romans* is making—cautiously—the same complaints about the Curia. Like Etienne and Hélinant he spends little time on Rome. Ecclesiastical misgovernment nearer to home is of more interest to him, and a few stanzas suffice. "Some men have told us," he remarks, "but they are surely liars—that he who wishes to have his case well handled at Rome, will be able to have his cares relieved better if he carries red deniers with him."[7] At almost the same time, Guiot de Provins attacks the Curia far more harshly in his *Bible Guiot*. Guiot, a jongleur turned monk, does not fail to include the pope in his censures, and even suggests that the civil powers rise up and destroy Roman presumption. Rome, says Guiot, is like a father who slays his children; but it slays them daily. When the cardinals arrive on the scene all is lost:

Tout est alei tout est perdu
quant li chardenal sont venu,
qui vienent sai tuit alumei

---

[6] *Vers de la mort*, pp. 12–14.
[7] *Roman des romans*, ed. I. Le Compte (Paris, 1923), p. 19.

de covoitise, et embrasé.
Sa viennent plain de simonie
et comble de malvaise vie,
sa viennent sens nulle raison,
sans foi, et sens religion,
car il vendent Deu et sa meire
et traïssent nos et lor peire.

What do they do with the gold and silver? They build no roads, hospitals, or bridges with it. And in Rome they live worse than pagans. The pope, too, has part of their gain; so Guiot has heard. And the deceitful legates of the pope carry off all our goods. The civil lords should destroy such corruption.[8] Few satirists go as far in their recommendations as Guiot. Incidentally, both Guiot and Hélinant mention the avarice of the legates, little noticed in the Latin satire. The papal policy of maintaining ecclesiastical control by means of legates was carried out with greater concentration and greater success in France, where the central political power was weak, than elsewhere, where power was more concentrated. It met with the most successful opposition in England. In either country the legates were likely to draw the attention of the satirists.

Around 1226 the learned Guillaume le Clerc (de Normandie) wrote a lengthy work entitled *Le besant de Dieu*. It is moral rather than satirical, and its attacks on the characteristic vices of the various orders of society are relatively restrained and judicious. Nevertheless Guillaume comments sharply on the venality of Rome. He compares the Church to a ship whose captain, the pope, though himself good, is surrounded by the covetous, who make his ship go astray. The mariners closest to the master, the cardinals who should be his helpers, love the red deniers too

---

[8] *Bible Guiot*, 660–780; in *Les oeuvres de Guiot de Provins*, ed. J. Orr (Manchester, 1915), pp. 30–34.

much. "There is no one, feverish, hydroptic, or leprous, who drinks as freely as they take deniers":

> Onques uncore nul fevros
> Ne ydropiqe ne lepros
> Ne but autresi volentiers
> Com cil prenent les deniers.

The usual attendants of the pope are under attack:

> . . . ses collaterals,
> Ses boteillers, ses senescals,
> Ses diacres, ses chapelains,

"who are always opening their hands and baring their claws to pluck those whom they should be carrying over the sea." The pope himself is innocent, but his servants betray their trust, especially the cardinals and legates, who are sent into France and England. They love white money much, and red money more— "E plus icele qui rogeie"—and are so much more covetous than the others that they leave poverty in their tracks.[9] All this we have heard before, in both Latin and French.

Absent from this early French satire is the dexterity, wit, and sparkling versification of the better Latin treatments of the theme. Guillaume's figure of the Church as a ship in rough seas, for example, is pale in contrast with the Homeric voyage through the Curia in Walter of Châtillon's "Propter Sion non tacebo." This is understandable. Not only are the sinews of the young language less flexible, but the satiric attacks themselves are mere episodes in long moral-satirical works, designed for popular instruction. The poet-moralist, with hundreds of hortatory verses to be written and the necessity of saying things simply and clearly, had to

---

[9] Guillaume le Clerc (de Normandie), *Le besant de Dieu*, ed. E. Martin (Halle, 1869), pp. 65–68.

plod his way quietly. He could not afford the intellectual and metrical acrobatics of a Philip the Chancellor, for example, or a Walter of Châtillon. Nevertheless, when his purpose is considered, he gained something toward his end from his very pedestrianism, for the gloss of neo-classical artifice is absent from his verse, as it was never absent from the more finished Latin verse of the period. The formal sleekness of the Latin verse surprises and pleases, but its very dexterity stands in the way of the moralist. The veil of technique falls between poet and audience. No such excellence troubles the reader of most of the long, laboriously versified French treatises. If we fail to find poetry, we frequently do discover a feeling of great moral earnestness, and occasionally even of fervor. Perhaps the poet-popularizers would have been most satisfied with that.

The *Romans de carité*, written in the first quarter of the thirteenth century, contains an especially interesting treatment of Roman venality. The poem is a long, moral-satirical account of the author's attempts to find the home of a personified Charity. Its method is essentially that of the *cursor mundi*. Its interest to the student of *Piers Plowman* is its simple framework: that of a pilgrimage to Charity similar to the one which Langland makes the heart of his poem. Finding that Charity has apparently disappeared from the earth, the poet begins his futile search for her at the Roman Curia, for he feels certain to find her in those exalted circles. But she has been thrust from the Curia by *Covoitise*, "the bursar, who does not fear to commit treason, so dear does he hold money." Most of the next 150 lines are devoted to the conventional satire on Roman avarice and venality. The details are familiar: the poor cannot gain entry, for the doorkeeper awaits his bribe; *Covoitise* rules everywhere; the cardinals are merchants; the very doors are venal. At the courts both counsel and judges are likewise venal:

Mais je vi k'il sont dessené,
Tant aiment et l'or et l'argent;
Une fois font lor jugement
Estroit, autre fois largement.
Chil sont de conseil assené
Ki font a lor mains oignement;
Et chil ki nes oignent noient
Chil sont dou tout desassené.

From this point in the poem, *oignement* and the greased palm become symbols of Rome. The author tells the story—extremely popular for the next two centuries[10]—of the ignorant old lady,

[10] The "greased palm" motive appears repeatedly in *exempla* of the time, though usually applied to the judges and lawyers of lesser courts than that of Rome. It appeared, for example, almost at the same time as the *Romans de carité* in a sermon of Odo of Sherington. Cf. L. Hervieux, ed. *Les fabulistes latins* (Paris, 1884–99), IV, 301. A brief but typical example is that printed by T. Wright, *A Selection of Latin Stories* (London, Percy Society, 1843), p. 43, "De muliere ungente manus judicis:"

> Audivi de quodam iudice venali, quod cum paupercula muliercula ab ipso jus suum obtinere non valeret, dixit quidam mulieri, 'Judex illi talis est, quod nisi manus ejus ungantur, non obtinebis jus coram ipso.' Mulier haec verba simpliciter et ad literam intelligens, cum sagimine procino ad consistorium judicis accedens, cunctis videntibus manus ejus ungere coepit. Judex dixit, 'Mulier, quid facis?' Respondit, 'Domine, dictum est mihi quod nisi manus vestras unxissem justitiam a vobis assequi non possem' Judex suum confusus judicium emendavit in melius.

An almost identical version appears in Herolt, *Promptuarium exemplorum* (Speier, 1483), I, xliii, and a similar one in Bromyard, *Summa praedicantium*, "Judices," Par. 20. The thirteenth-century Dominican, Etienne de Bourbon, applies the tale to a venal bishop (*Anecdotes historiques*, p. 378), and an unknown writer of fabliaux applies it to an extortionist knight (Montaiglon and Renaud, V, 157-159, "De la vielle qui oint la palme au chevalier"). The tale appears in other vernaculars, e.g., *El libro de los enxemplos*, No. 24 (ed. P. de Gayengos, *Biblioteca de autores Españoles*, LI, Madrid, 1952, 453). For further examples cf. the note in Wright, *Latin Stories*, p. 225, and that in Etienne de Bourbon, *Anecdotes historiques*, p. 378.

unfamiliar with the ways of the Roman courts, who had a case to be tried. A lawyer whom she begged for help ignored her, and a stranger suggested that the lawyer needed his palm greased. She took the suggestion literally, explaining to the enraged and embarrassed lawyer that "the man said you would help me if I anointed your palm." The attack continues along conventional lines: Rome measures a man by the size of his purse; the Roman tongue cannot talk without being greased; and to get into the court you must anoint the door. Everywhere you must apply "grease":

> Quant plus est d'oint d'argent emplus
> Li Romains, tant seke il plus.
> Romains fu fius d'une ordre ointiere.

More fully, the Romans are descended from *Covoitise* and a grease merchant; but in their hot hands the necessary grease disappears in an instant. Thus the author ends his search for Charity in Rome, and resumes the hopeless pilgrimage in other directions.[11]

After the middle of the thirteenth century Rutebuf wrote satire on the avarice and venality of Rome, some of it obviously the result of his defense of the University of Paris against the Dominicans, who were supported by Pope Alexander IV. His satire is the usual contrast of the charitable ideal with the venal reality.

---

[11] Li Renclus de Moiliens, *Romans de carité*, ed. A. G. Van Hamel (Paris, 1885), vii–xx, pp. 5–12. P. Meyer, "Mélanges de poésie Anglo-Normande," *Romania*, IV (1875), 388–391, prints an Anglo-Norman poem on the estates of the world from about the same period which contains similar material:

> Veez l'apostolie de Rume,
> Plus est cuvoitus que altre hume:
> Qui cinc cenz mars d'argent li nume
> Tost li charra del dos grant sume.
>   Ja n'ert grevez
> Pur nul forfet qui les diners dune a plenté. etc.

Rome, which should be the foundation of our faith, has become the home of avarice and simony, the shame of the world. The man who gives money gets prebends. They are not given as God commanded; for at Rome only *dare* is followed by *impetrare*:

> On set bien dire à Rome: "Si voille empêtrer: *da*,
> Et si non voille *dare*, enda la voie, enda !"[12]

The more elaborate and sharp "Lections d'Ypocrisie et d'Umilitei" is a dream vision in which Rutebuf goes to Rome, where his host is a certain "Cortois" (apparently the new Pope, Clement IV), whose wife is "Bele-Chiere," the perfect Christian. Cortois tells Rutebuf about the Curia, where all justice is venal: "If you have, you will get, but if you do not have, you will fare like a goose on the ice. . . ." Rutebuf, too, is familiar with *Roma manus rodit*:

> Mains ruungent & vuident borces,
> Et faillent quant elz sont rebources,
> Ne ne vuelent nelui entendre
> C'il n'i puéent runger & prendre,
> Car de reungier mains est dite
> La citeiz qui n'est pas petite.

Those who go to Rome return as poor beggars, for there Avarice is mistress:

> Avarisce est de la cort dame
> A cui il sunt de cors & d'âme,
> Et ele en doit par droit dame estre,
> Qu'il sunt estrait de son ancestre,
> Et ele est dou mieulz de la vile;
> Ne cuidiez pas que ce soit guile,
> Car ele en est née & estraite,
> Et Covoitise la seurfaite,
> Qui est sa couzine germainne;

---

[12] Rutebuf, *Œuvres complètes*, II, 32.

Par ces ii. se conduit & mainne
Toute la cours entièrement.[13]

By the time these lines were written the heyday of the allegorical
dream-vision had begun, through the enormous popularity of
the *Roman de la rose*. In Rutebuf's brief satire are all the essentials
of Langland's later Lady Meed episode: the dream vision, the
court (here the papal rather than the royal court), the rule of
Covoitise, personified as a fine lady. *Bele-Chiere* is even a rudimentary form of Langland's Holy Church. Rutebuf's picture of the
reign of *Covoitise* at Rome was probably suggested by the *Romans
de carité*, and the charges against Rome are the common ones.
Nor is Rutebuf here at his best. But his combination of poetic
devices looks to the future as well as the past.

Papal venality remained a popular theme during the fourteenth
century, as the following blast at Pope Clement V suggests:

La loy saint Pere
Comme vrais pere
Garder devroies;
Par charité
En amité
La gent commune;
Cou ne fais mie,
Tu n'as amie
Fors la pecune.[14]

---

[13] Rutebuf, *Œuvres complètes*, II, 223–225.

[14] "Dou Pape, dou roy et des monnoies," *Société de l'histoire de la France.
Bulletin*, II, ii (1835), 221–224. Cf. also the passing reference to Roman venality
added by Jehan le Fevre (ca. 1370) to his translation of *Les lamentations de Matheolus*, p. 277, and an Anglo–Norman song (ca. 1256) directed against both king
and pope for collusion in taxing the clergy. In Wright, *Political Songs*, pp.
42–44, and P. Meyer, "Mélanges de poésie Anglo–Normande," *Romania*, IV
(1875), 397.

The Provençal anti-Rome satire, much of which sprang from the hatreds engendered during the Albigensian Crusade, should also be mentioned. A typical example is the satire of Guilhem Figuerra, based on the idea that the Crusade was inspired by Roman avarice rather than love of orthodoxy. Only late in the poem does the author reach his main theme: "Rome, for money you commit many crimes and many misdeeds and many villainies." Mistress *Covoitise* is transformed to the leader *Don Cobeitatz*:

> Roma, 'l glorios
> Que sufri mort e pena
> En la crotz per nos,
> Vos don la mala estrenha;
> Quar totas sazos
> Portatz la borsa plena,
> Roma, d'avol for;
> Quar tot vostre cor
> Avetz en tezor;
> Don cobeitatz vos mena
> El foc que non mor.[15]

These same anti-Rome satirists are also responsible for much of the satire in French on the venality of bishops and the lesser clergy, for the common pattern of medieval French satire is that of the *cursor mundi* or the sermon "sur les états du monde," in which the writer begins with the faults of *Roma Caput Mundi* and continues down the social ladder until he has anatomized the vices of the peasant. Evil clerks, says Etienne de Fougères, know well how to get money, either by fines or bribes, until even the rich are impoverished. The guilt lies mostly with the bishops, who permit such corruption in their subordinates, taking bribes themselves for their silence. It is disgraceful to sell benefices, yet these

---

[15] M. Raynouard, *Choix des poésies originales des troubadours* (Paris, 1819), IV 311–317. Cf. also Raynouard, IV, 271–280.

bishops will only give when they can get. Etienne then turns to the complaints so common in the Latin satire, the helplessness of learning and piety in competition with cash:

> Si bon clierc est de bon tesmoing
> Et n'a deniers plus de plein poig
> N'aura mostier ne pres ne loig,
> Si enz la paume ne li oig.
> Escience n'i vaut ne leitre,
> Ne bien feire, ne mal demestre;
> Si en iglise te velz meitre,
> Prente au doner, lei le premeitre.

Nor should the bishop take anything for maintaining justice. To sell justice is to sell Christ, and the venal bishop is the successor of Judas:

> Vendre justice est Jhesum vendre,
> Per a Judas seit entendre
> Qui de Jhesu velt deniers prendre,
> Peis se corut au scür pendre.[16]

Etienne says little about the venality of the lower clergy. The aged bishop in his last work was most concerned with the duties of his own office.

There is good reason for the multiplication at this time of the long, sermonizing vernacular poems on the estates of the world. From 1225 onward a powerful religious revival swept both clergy and laity, under the influence of the friars, especially the Franciscans. The remarkable successes of the preaching orders, at least during their earlier years, produced a strong spiritual reaction among the laity and did much to awaken the secular clergy to the significance of their pastoral duties. But the basis of this revival was a force even more powerful than the mendicant orders,

---

[16] *Livre des manières*, 217–220, 253–313.

the canons of the Fourth Lateran Council (1215-1216), calling for fundamental changes in three specific directions: administrative reform, moral and intellectual reform of the clergy, and instruction of the mass of the faithful.[17] From these canons the numerous reforming councils and diocesan "constitutions" of the thirteenth century were derived, and the same canons were probably the ultimate inspiration of the religious handbooks, the "manuels des péchés," of the thirteenth and fourteenth centuries. All major religious writing of the period was touched by the sweeping reform movement.

The new universities, too, contributed to this religious revival. The combination of these three powerful forces—episcopal directives inspired by the Fourth Lateran Council, the mendicant orders, and the universities—as Arnould points out, inspired virtually all the known religious verse of the period. Nor was this revival wholly a phenomenon of the thirteenth century. It seems clear that the Fourth Lateran Council, held under Innocent III, was the culmination of the papal reform efforts begun almost two centuries earlier under Gregory VII and his predecessors.

It can hardly be doubted that Guillaume le Clerc in his *Besant de Dieu* was strongly affected by the ideas of the Council. He attacks clerical love of luxury and affinity for money: he has seen wealthy clerks rise high in the Church through simony and has seen them thinking of nothing but deniers after they have become bishops. Greedier than a dog with a bone, they heap up wealth, never giving to the poor. But, promises Guillaume, they will suffer for it on the Last Day, for such bishops are far from salvation. And the officials of the diocesan courts are equally bad:

> Arcediacres et diens
> E officiaus e les maiens

---

[17] E. Arnould, *Le manuel des péchés* (Paris, 1940), p. 11. In this and the following paragraphs I lean heavily on Chapter I (pp. 1-59) of Arnould's work.

> Qui as chapitres sont les sires,
> Qui consentent les avoltires,
> Les causes jugent e terminent
> E as loiers prendre s'enclinent,
> Les fornicacions cunsentent,
> Les povres chapeleins tormentent,
> Justise vendent e dreiture:
> Mult en avront cil chere cure.

Guillaume also threatens priests who extort money from their parishoners by enjoining masses as penance, demanding pay for the masses, and then failing to say them.[18]

Rutebuf denounces the usual sins: of the prelates, simony; of the lower clergy, the unwillingness to give to the poor or to say mass except for pay. Both prelates and civil rulers are companions of *Covoitise* or of Mistress Simony:

> Je n'i voi ne prince ne roi
> Qui de prendre face desroi,
> Ne nul prélat de Sainte Yglise
> Qui ne soit compains Covoitise,
> Ou au mains dame Symonie,
> Qui les donéors ne het mie.[19]

Rutebuf's attacks on the lesser secular clergy center on the canons, who live comfortably on Christ's patrimony, watching the poor

---

[18] *Le besant de Dieu*, 597–700, pp. 17–21. Cf. also *Romans de carité*, p. 46. The *Manuel des pechiez*, attributed to William of Wadington, one of the many instructional treatises deriving from the thirteenth–century religious revival, discusses simony briefly as one of the parts of the sin of *covoitise*. Cf. *Manuel des pechiez*, ll. 4775–4788; in Robert of Brunne, *Handlyng Synne*, ed. F. Furnival (EETS,o.s., 119–123, London, 1901–1903), I, 180. For discussion cf. Arnould pp. 41–59. On the venality of diocesan officials and lesser clergy cf. also the thirteenth–century verses printed by P. Meyer, "Mélanges de poésie Anglo–Normande," *Romania*, IV (1875), 389–390.

[19] *Œuvres complètes*, II, 23. For more on the prelates cf. II, 36–37.

starve or freeze while they wear a furred cape and carry a purse full of pence. The canon pays no heed to God, for he is the servant of Avarice. "And if he goes to mass, it is not to please God; rather it is to get *deniers*, for. . . if he does not expect to get any, he will never seek to drag his feet there."[20]

The satire of the *Lamenta* of Matheolus, although written in Latin about 1290, had little influence until its translation into French by Jehan le Fevre (ca. 1370).[21] Hence the work became widely known at about the same time as *Piers Plowman*. It is chiefly a blast against women and marriage, deriving partly from the *Roman de la Rose*, but mostly from the author's bitter personal experience as a married clerk; Matheolus, however, devotes some space to most of the major evils of the day. In his treatment of venality he follows the conventions of the other Latin satirists of the time. An attack on clerical luxury leads him to the sale of *spiritualia* and a protest against simony. Prebends go only to those who give; the evil prelate sells them, "pro donis dona rependens," or gives them to his friends. Simon buys, Giezi sells; Peter is dead, Simon lives:

> Venales hodie prostant instar meretricis
> Prebende; solum nummis dantur vel amicis.
> Symon emit, Gyesi vendit: "caro do facioque
> Ut des vel facias"; sibi collidunt in utroque.
> Petrus obit, Simon vivit; modo nemo petrisat,
> Immo procul dubio totus clerus symonisat.
> Ergo suo viduata Petro, cum sit sine scuto,
> Lugeat ecclesia, Symonis subjecta tributo!
> Ve! ve! Symonibus,   prelatis dico prophanis,
> Ve! ve! muneribus   corruptis quottidianis.

[20] *Œuvres complètes*, II, 18–19. On the canons cf. also P. Meyer, "Mélanges," *Romania*, IV (1875), 390.

[21] Wood, p. 7, believes that the French version "attained almost as great popularity as the poem of Jean de Meung."

Jehan le Fevre translates the passage thus:

> Aux mauvais est [la prouvende] pour pris vendue,
> Fraude y est par tout endendue;
> En livrant la prouvende a fraude
> On la vent comme une ribaude,
> Par pris et a personne indigne;
> Tel contract donne mauvais signe.
> Symon vit et mort est saint Pierre;
> On ne fonde rien sus sa pierre.[22]

These comments on clerical venality are representative of the French satire of the time. They show no major change or development in the theme, but are significant only as instruments of its wide diffusion in vernacular literature. Poetically they are negligible.

Satire on the venality of lawyers and judges, especially in the ecclesiastical courts, was as important in French literature as in the Latin. This is not surprising in view of the growing importance of the lawyer; nor, in view of the lawyer's late appearance in medieval life, is it surprising that earlier writers like Etienne de Fougères and Hélinant fail to mention the subject. But Guiot de Provins describes the new tribe: "Often they come to Bologna to make their living at law. I see them come there jangling more than a starling in a cage. All their guile and all their words are turned toward treachery." From a silver mine we get many handsome things; but, through their evil, from the great laws and decrees we get only treachery and corruption:

> On trait de la mine l'argent,
> don l'on fait maint biau vassal gent
> et mainte œvre et belle et chiere. . . .
> et des hauz livres honoreiz

---

[22] *Lamentations*, pp. 277–278.

c'on appelle lois et decreiz
nos traient engig et barat!²³

Guiot says less of the venality of advocates than of their general deceitfulness and treachery. His figure of the caged starling, however, is vivid and amusing.²⁴

The lawyer was still so new in the thirteenth century that Rutebuf, for example, has only a single short passage (in "De l'estat du monde") dealing with him. The lines show his familiarity with the Latin satire on the subject:

Encore i a clers d'autre guise;
Que quant il ont la loi aprise
Si vuelent estre pledéeur
Et de lor langues vendéeur;
Et penssent baras & cauteles,
Dont il bestornent les quereles,
Et metent ce devant derrière.
Ce qui ert avant va arrière,
Car quant dant Denier vient en place
Droiture faut, droiture efface.
Briefment tuit clerc fors escoler
Vuelent avarisce acoler.²⁵

Here *Dan Denier* makes his appearance, the favorite French personification of *Nummus* or *Munera* or the power of the purse. *Dan*

---

²³ *Bible Guiot*, 2435–2453; in *Œuvres*, pp. 85–86.

²⁴ Cf. also the *Manuel des pechiez*, 4695–4708, in *Handlyng Synne*, I, 176–177, which in its condemnation of venal judges and advocates develops didactically the traditional three ways of perverting judgment.

²⁵ *Œuvres complètes*, II, 19–20. Rutebuf liked the idea of the last lines, that all clerks except scholars are avaricious. He repeats it elsewhere (*Œuvres complètes*, II, 26):

Fors escoliers, autre clergie
Sont tuit d'avarisce vergie.

Denier, whose cult we shall discuss below, is the Almighty Dollar of medieval France. Rutebuf's *Denier* couplet is full of the spirit and flavor of much of the earlier Latin verse on the subject. "When money talks," the "Manus ferens munera" of the *Carmina burana* had said, "he confounds the laws." But the same sentiment was so frequent in the Latin verse that it would be difficult to guess where Rutebuf found it.

Evil lawyers and jurymen—"advocatz, countours, legistres e pledours e les gence qu sont en dozeyns"—were a favorite subject of Nicole Bozon, the best of the Anglo-Norman *exempla* writers, who wrote his brief sermon-fillers about 1320.[26] He uses the mineral lodestone as a symbol of truth, for its name in Latin, "Magnes," signified "greyndur," and Truth surpasses all things. "And this stone draws heavy iron to itself, for there was never a case so grievous that it could not be tried, if Truth could show its power." But there is a stronger and very precious stone, the diamond, which makes its appearance secretly: "This is a purse with money, which makes the case start up again and causes truth to fail completely."[27]

Nicole also uses the figure of the cursed hounds with which the devil hunts men's souls. There are four pairs of them with the colorful and bilingual names of "Ricer e Wilemyn, Havegyf e Baudewyn, Tristewel e Gloffyn, Beauvis e Trebelyn." By the device of these hell-hounds Friar Nicole discusses the cardinal

[26] Nicole Bozon, *Contes moralisés,* ed. L. Toulmin Smith and P. Meyer (SATF, Paris , 1889), p. ii. These are *exempla,* allegories and fables for use in sermons. They are frequently very lively, and obviously of English provenance, being full of English words.

[27] *Contes moralisés,* 2, pp. 9–10. Elsewhere (3, p. 10), he speaks of the four brothers who once ruled the earth well: "Dreiture, Verité, Jugement, Equitee." But they have been defeated by an enemy, "Coveitise, *Mikelyerne,* qar un bourse od blaunche monée plus peut en terre que Verité. . . ."

sins.[28] The hound Baudewyn, named after "baudoir" (self-confidence or boldness), is used to hunt lawyers into hell:

> Another dog, named Baudewyn, is loosed on pleaders and lawyers and advocates, many of whom are hunted into hell by the boldness of their reasoning, which they willfully use, through their wiles, against right.... Now if the false party has a purse full of money and the true party gives nothing, you will see that the purse draws toward itself the laws and the decretals, and makes the laws accord with itself against the truth.[29]

The *Contes moralisés* represent most attractively the sermon materials of the mendicant preacher, where *contes*, beast fables, the lore of the lapidaries and bestiaries, and other curious and exotic learning are mingled to hold the attention of the faithful. Especially noteworthy is Nicole's affection for allegorical technique, exemplified by the story of the devil's hounds. Mendicant preachers probably did as much to popularize moral allegory as did works like the *Roman de la rose;* perhaps allegorical romance achieved its greatest influence in this manner. Surely Langland had heard many sermons like that on the hounds of the devil,[30]

---

[28] The third hound, Havegyf, is the vehicle of Nicole's attack on clerical venality: "... Havegyf, ceo est a dire 'pernés et donez', qel est descouplé sur les abbés, priours e chivalers et damez qe ont esglises en lur donison qe pensent en donant de doner e prendre: de doner un esglise de lur doneison e lur seignurage, e pur lur doun receyver ascun avantage. ... Ceaux qe donent a foux e a mauveys en beauté de fevour od de lur terrien aver dussent doner as prodhomes de bone vie.... Veiez ici Havegyf, un chien bien corant qe meynt alme chace en enfer par le seon donant." *Contes moralisés*, p. 31.

[29] *Contes moralisés*, 22, pp. 29–37. Nicole's sixth dog, Trebelyn, is an interesting example of the growing satire, especially among popular preachers, against the avarice of the bourgeois. Trebelyn is used to catch usurers and merchants: "E pur ceo est appellé Trebelyn ceo chien qe lur chace, qar rien ne vendront ne apresteront ne achateront si ils ne eyent le treble a gayn."

[30] G. Owst, *Literature and Pulpit in Medieval England* (Cambridge, 1933),

and I am inclined to believe that venality-satire was widely circulated in the same manner, especially in the fourteenth century.

Matheolus in his *Lamenta* attacks the venality of judges and advocates with great enthusiasm and some originality. Our modern justice, he says, is sold like wine in a tavern. The judge fears not God Himself, but does everything for bribes or favor. Those who grease the judge's palm most generously are masters of the courtroom. Jehan's French translation follows the Latin closely here, with the addition of an occasional didactic passage. Matheolus treats the advocate with even more ire. The idea that venal lawyers prostituted their talents was commonplace, and the figure of the venal tongue invited comparison with prostitutes. Matheolus develops the further curious variation that lawyers were worse than whores to the extent that the member which they sold was more dignified:

> Quid de causidico possum tibi dicere?   dici
> Debet enim similis vel par vili meretrici,
> Immo vilior est, quia, si meretrix locat anum,
> Hic vendit linguam, quod plus reor esse prophanum,
> Cum sit enim lingua membrum preciosius ano.

> Des advocas comment diray?
> Ja pour paour n'en mentiray.
> Il a en eulx plus de diffame
> Qu'en une pute fol femme.
> Chascuns de ses instrumens joue;
> Femme son cul pour deniers loue,
> Et l'advocat sa langue vent;
> Ambdeux ne vivent pas de vent.
> La langue est plus precieux membre

---

has done immensely valuable work in this field and has by no means exhausted its riches. For preaching on venality similar to that of Nicole, cf. the discussion in the next chapter of the later Dominican, John Bromyard.

Que n'est le cul, bien m'en remembre;
Tant est la vente plus honteuse
Com la langue est plus precieuse.

The lawyer will keep no oath, but will sell his tongue to the man who offers most money. He will even represent a stranger against his own father, "out of ardor for meed," for the size of the fee determines his relationship to a client. When he sees money he will unsheathe his violent tongue like a sword. And he is an excellent jouster until his client's purse is empty; then he loses interest. "Il n'aime rien tant que pecune." He would drain the seas dry if they were money.[31] Jehan's looser French does not achieve the conciseness of the Latin; nor can Jehan refrain from a few words of his own, so that his passage on lawyers is almost twice as long as that of Matheolus. Both Latin and French amble along in a pleasant, undistinguished manner.

These and other French satires on the venality of justice[32] can hardly be said to develop the satirical theme or to introduce significant variations. Behind them all lies the concept of the simoniac sale of the *donum Dei*. The commonplaces of the Latin literature are repeated with few changes. The venal tongue is the central image of most of the passages, the catch-phrase on which the

---

[31] *Les lamentations de Matheolus* (Latin), 4569–4617, pp. 282–285; (French), IV, 501–584, pp. 282–285. Even the striking comparison of the lawyer with the prostitute is not peculiar to Matheolus. Like the following, it may have been drawn from the *sententiae* of a preachers' handbook: "Item, advocatus plus vituperandus est quam meretrix, quae partem sui viliorem et turpiorem vendit; ipse vero meliorem et nobiliorem." This *sententia*, printed by Hauréau, *Notices*, IV, 174, was written in the thirteenth century, probably a few years before the *Lamenta*.

[32] Most of the French works mentioned earlier in the chapter touch on venality in the legal profession. There is also a fragmentary *conte du monde* which devotes most of its attention to satire on lawyers and usurers.

versifiers build. The personification which creeps into some of the French satire was already present in the Latin. The tendency toward allegory, however, was growing.

TWO

SATIRICAL GENERALIZATIONS ON THE POWER OF MONEY:
Dan Denier

Satirical generalizations on the power of money like those of Hildebert, Godfrey of Cambrai, and many unknown Latin satirists, are somewhat rarer in French than in Latin. The Latin generalizations were largely clerical *jeux d'esprit*, but most French satirical literature was basically didactic, a part of the great movement of *vulgarization* which began in the thirteenth century, in which clerical authors attempted to make available to lay audiences the religious, scientific and technical knowledge of their time. Fabliaux excepted, vernacular satire (as it has survived) usually justified itself by the moral lessons it taught to a "lewed" audience. Those surviving French satirical generalizations on money which approach most nearly the mockery of the Latin *genre* are exceptions to this didactic tendency, and usually bear the mark of the *jongleur*. Such displays of mocking or cynical wit were valuable tools in his profession. But this literature had slim chances for survival; a good many money-satires probably died with minstrels themselves or were dispersed with their notebooks.

What has survived of the *jongleurs'* venality-satire is almost all connected with the cult of *Dan Denier*, the French personification corresponding to *Nummus*, *Regina Pecunia*, and similar Latin figures.[33] *Dan Denier* seems to have been invented, or at least

[33] I have dealt with *Dan Denier* and other aspects of French venality-satire

popularized, by the minstrels. We know, for example, that there were songs about him in the minstrel repertoires. "Ge sai le flabel de Denier," says a jongleur in the fabliau of the *Deux bordeors ribaus* when he is retailing his repertory to the others.[34] We do not know whether the tale to which he referred is extant, but it is clear that the writer of the fabliau expected it to be familiar to his characters and his audience. The familiarity of that personification in popular literature is also attested by a number of scattered proverbs.[35]

There is a curious French *debat*, probably of the thirteenth century, between Master *Denier* and a sheep, each boasting his power and his value to the world. We are not here concerned with the sheep's side of the argument, but *Denier's* boasts develop into the characteristic lines on the power of money in the world which are already so familiar from the Latin satires. "I work my pleasure with everyone and have whatever I want in the world; I often cause heads to be cut off, both of men and dumb beasts." He is beloved of women and powerful over them; men who amass him are always considered sage. He is everywhere in demand:

> Covoitiez sui par tout le mont,
> Neïs des chardinaus de Romme.

The man whom Denier fails is always disgraced. When a sheep is found dead, he is thrown into a ditch to rot; but no one, afoot or on horse, sees Denier lying in the road without stopping to pick him up. "I carry the banner which attaches the whole world to me; not one ally would march if Denier did not assemble them."

---

in "Medieval French Money Satire," *Modern Language Quarterly*, XXI (1960), 73–82. Some of the contents of this chapter are drawn from that paper.

34 A. Jubinal, *Jongleurs et trouvères* (Paris, 1835), p. 94.

35 J. Morawski, *Proverbes français antérieurs au XV⁵ siècle* (CFMA, Paris, 1925), Nos. 484, 485, 528, 958, 1322, 1882, 1902, 1999.

> Denier fet à maint homme embler,
> Denier relie madelins,
> Denier confont les Sarrasins;
> Sanz moi ne puet nus passer mer.
> Je faz boivre, je faz humer,
> Je faz doner, je faz tolir,
> Je faz chevaus corre et saillir,
> Haubers rompre, percier escuz;
> Champions sont par moi vaincuz. etc.

In rebuttal, the sheep continues the list of money's powers, powers for evil rather than for good:

> Tu fez d'un hermite larron,
> Tu tols à droit, dones à tort.
> D'un mauves homme, boçu, tort,
> Fez-tu tant que plus est amez
> C'uns sages hom plains de bontez.

The argument at this point resembles closely the dispute between Meed and Conscience before the king in *Piers Plowman*, where the ambiguous Lady Meed stresses her services to the nobility on battlefield and in court, while Conscience attacks her for the evils she has wrought throughout the world (III, 124-226; cf. p. 8 above). The French debate closes without a decision, but Dan Denier has clearly had the better of the argument.[36]

The theme is that of the twelfth and thirteenth century *nummus* poems and *munera* passages—we have discussed a similar Latin debate between *Amor* and *Nummus*—but the author's attitude differs. The informality and lack of learned or courtly affectation suggest a minstrel author or minstrel adaptation. The Latin *nummus* verses concentrated on the power of money among clergy and kings. This poet addresses neither clergy nor nobility. He

---

[36] A. Jubinal, *Nouveau recueil de contes, dits, fabliaux et autres pièces* (Paris, 1839), I, 264-272.

is familiar with courtly trappings but does not write courtly poetry. He mentions the clergy only once, with a brief glance at the commonplaces on Rome. Nor does he have the religious and didactic aims of the vernacular books of instruction. He is merely interested in the entertainment of a lay audience.

This shift is noticeable in a better-known money poem entitled in the manuscripts *De dan Denier*. It also purveys the usual generalizations on money's power, and also seems to bear traces of *jongleur* origin or rehandling. After a perfunctory moralizing prologue it begins in minstrel manner:

> Oez bon conte
> De dan Denier qui si haut monte:
> Forment l'ont cher et roi et conte;
> Trestou teirriens denier afronte;
> Cil qui l'aime n'en a pas honte,
> que il a droit
> Qui denier aime et denier croit.

This is the poet's song throughout the 161 lines of the poem. Denier is a privy chamberlain who does his will quietly; he has his way in Rome; whoever brings Denier with his request gets whatever he demands. Denier raises an ignoble lineage, fills an empty house, inspires priests to sing three masses a day, swears great oaths, gives pardons, disinherits orphans, makes wars. It is the familiar story of *Nummus* or *Munera*:

> Denier fes mors ensevelir,
> Denier fet citez assaillir,
> et les murs granz.
> Deniers n'est mie recreanz,
> Ainz est hardiz et combatanz.
> Denier justice les poissanz,
> Denier aprent les non-sachanz,
> Denier a les espiels trenchanz,
> espiels, etc.

As in the *nummus* poems, money rules the world, this time in the guise of Master Denier;

> Or dirons del denier la fin;
> A Denier est li mons aclin.[37]

Legrand d'Aussy records an extract of a fabliau very similar to *Dan Denier*, which he entitles in his modern French prose translation *De dom Argent*. The teller remarks how his mouth watered as he passed the stands of the Paris money-changers, and then bursts into a panegyric which rings the usual changes on the power of the *denier*:

> With him you can buy greatcoats and mantles of ermine, Gascon horses and mules, abbeys and benefices, cities and castles, great estates and beautiful women. He causes the orphan to be disinherited, the excommunicated to be absolved, the villain to receive justice, injuries to be pardoned. . . . Money makes a courtier of a peasant, a gay man of a melancholic, a wit of a sot. Do you have to act on the sly? he is a sure friend. Must you cause a disturbance? he will strut proudly, and speak fiercely. If you have business at Rome, don't go without him, or you will fail; but if you have him I will be security for your success. etc.[38]

It will be recalled (cf. p. 206 above) that the penny-hero was known to Rutebuf when he attacked the lawyers. He appears momentarily elsewhere, when a versifier bewails the scarcity of money in the winter,[39] in a verse treatment of the seven deadly

---

[37] Jubinal, *Jongleurs*, pp. 94–100; also in Wright, *Mapes*, pp. 357–359. Though Jubinal (p. 94) has found the verses only in two MSS, this poem may have been the "flabel de Denier" mentioned by the two *bordeors*. If it had been a regular part of *jongleur* repertoire there is no special reason why it should have been written down frequently. One couplet at least was popular enough to get into the proverb collections. Cf. Morawski, *Proverbes français*, No. 1882.

[38] P. Legrand d'Aussy, *Fabliaux et contes* (3ᵐᵉ éd., Paris, 1829), III, 216–217. The editor gives neither the source nor the original text of his modern French translation, and I have been unable to locate it.

[39] Jubinal, *Nouveau recueil*, II, 165.

sins,[40] in at least one other fabliau,[41] in a legend of the Virgin and St. Katherine, and in the *Roman des romans*.[42] It seems clear that he was a familiar figure in medieval French literature, gathering to himself in the vernacular the same generalizations given to *Nummus* or *Munera* in the Latin satire. But the French *Denier* poems are usually for entertainment, not edification; in the figure of Dan Denier, rather more plebeian than *Regina Pecunia* or *Dea Moneta*, the satirical theme was becoming secularized. Rome, that traditional ultimate in venality, and the other venal clergy are still mentioned, but the interests of the poets obviously lie elsewhere.

THREE

THE MEED-THEME IN FRENCH ROMANCE

A significant development in French venality-satire is the appearance of the theme in romance. Though it is more frequent in allegorical romance, it appears, too, as part of the motivation in at least one non-allegorical romance. This is the late *Bauduin de Sebourc*, a long tale probably written near the middle of the fourteenth century, perhaps the work of two authors.[43] It is clearly calculated to appeal to a middle-class audience. Its latest

[40] An unpublished Anglo-Norman *Petite Sume de les set pechez morteus* quoted by Arnould, p. 56.

[41] R. Johnston and D. Owen, eds., *Fabliaux* (Oxford, 1957), p. 50.

[42] A. Långfors, "Notice du manuscrit français 12483 de la Bibliothèque Nationale," *Notices et extraits*, XXIX, ii (1916), 579; *Le Roman des romans*, p.29.

[43] E.-R. Labande, *Etude sur Bauduin de Sebourc* (Paris, 1940), pp. 66, 70–74. The long romance is summarized briefly by Lenient, *Satire en France*, pp. 187–193, and at length by Labande, pp. 23–50.

student sees in the main author only a demagogue,[44] but Lenient considered the romance a regret for the old world of chivalry, full of a "profonde aversion pour ce monde nouveau, politique, financier, administratif, judicière, qui vient le remplacer avec son cortège de procureurs, de maltôtiers et de sergents."[45]

For us, *Bauduin de Sebourc's* interest lies in Gaufrois, a fiscal villain, the instrument of whose crimes is usually money: "Le gentilhomme," says Lenient, "devenu traitant, usurier, faux-monnoier, marchant, la lance d'une main et la bourse de l'autre, à la conquête du monde." He conceives a passion for the wife of his lord, the King of Frisia, sends him on a crusade to the Holy Land, and there sells him to the Saracens. He returns home wealthy with the price of treason, falsely announces the king's death, and proceeds to make himself popular at court by what Langland would certainly have called "mede": gifts of jewels, rings, gold cups, purses, chests of gold, even castles and towers.[46] Thus he fills the court with friends, "for the man who is rich and successful finds friends who make themselves of his lineage; and the poor man finds neither kinsman nor cousin" (I, 922-924). The queen dares not resist his offer of marriage. Gaufrois plans to kill her son, Bauduin, but the child miraculously escapes his hands. The author meanwhile provides a satirical etymology for the word *argent*:

> E! Diex, qu'est-che d'argent? chieus le sot bien nommer
> Qui argent l'apella: les gens fait embraser.
> .i. deablez d'enfer le fist argent nommer:
> Car une grange fist de monnoie pupler,
> Et puis l'ala tantost a moult de gent conter;

---

[44] Labande, p. 63.

[45] Lenient, p. 191.

[46] *Li romans de Bauduin de Sebourc*, ed. L.-N. Boca (Valenciennes, 1841), I, 879-898.

Chil alèrent tantost le grange deffremer,
S'alèrent le monnoie querquier et entasser;
Et li déablez ala celle grange allumer,
Se fist le gens gens dedans ardoir et embraser.
Pour chou ot nom argens; li noms n'en voelt muer,
Car il art tout le monde, si lons qu'on set aler:
Il n'est si petit enfes, c'est légier à prouver,
S'on li donna .i. denier, qui n'en laist le plourer.

(II, 24-37)

The author of Bauduin, too, had read the venality-satires.

When Gaufrois has married and become king he begins to oppress the commons with taxes to support his spending. He soon becomes a hated tyrant who taxes everything: moving about the country, getting married, enjoying one's wife, slaughtering cattle or sheep. And the tax collectors are to be found everywhere. But Gaufrois now wishes to become king of France. While the young hero, Bauduin, is gaining the kingdom of Jerusalem by arms, Gaufrois is using his familiar technique to become the idol of the French court. He poisons the king and is about to become ruler of France when Bauduin arrives, accuses him, and challenges him to mortal combat. Gaufrois shamelessly tries to buy himself off, expressing perfectly the philosophy of the corrupt grafter of all ages:

Frère, chertainement
Vous avés trop béut à che desjunement;
Venés à moi parler, vous arés de l'argent.
Li autre en ont éut, s'avés le coer dolent
Que vostre part n'avés, s'en arés largement![47]

---

[47] XXIV, 132-136. Another passage, on corrupt judges (XII, 15-26), indicates the author's familiarity with the conventional satire on the venality of the legal profession. One cannot avoid noticing, incidentally, the similarity in conduct between Gaufrois and that avaricious, extortionist connoisseur of the next century, the Duc de Berry.

Bauduin angrily refuses and the ensuing battle terminates in Gaufrois' surrender and hanging.

Bauduin de Sebourc is especially interesting in its use of the venality theme to express its author's economic and social conservatism. The theme becomes, as Lenient has pointed out, a vehicle of protest against a new world of nationalism, money, taxes, and collectors, in favor of a world long past and idealized, of feudal obligations and privileges, of settled class-distinctions, of personal mutual devotion between lord and vassal (such was the idealization) as the basis of social order. This conservatism is combined with an obvious sympathy with, and an appeal to, the lower classes of society, and a fervid conviction that they would benefit from a return to the "normal" feudal society. Now it is exactly this conservatism combined with a strong sympathy for the poor which we find in *Piers Plowman*, written only a few years later. These ideas were in the air, as *Bauduin* makes abundantly clear.

The appearance of venality-satire in allegorical romance suggests significant relations with *Piers Plowman*. Surprisingly enough, the moral-satirical-didactic omnibus which constitutes Jean de Meun's portion of the *Roman de la rose* deals little with venality. Guillaume de Lorris's love-allegory, as we might expect, has even less to offer. But the reader of Guillaume's portrait of *Richece* can hardly fail to recall the similar though less elaborate portrait of Meed in *Piers Plowman*. The liars, traitors, flatterers and envious who surround *Richece* suggest the train of Meed's followers. But her clothing—the rich purple robe with all its gems—is most like Meed's.[48] Robertson and Huppé have pointed out the rela-

---

[48] *Le roman de la rose*, ed. E. Langlois (SATF, Paris, 1914–1924), ll. 1053–1076, II, 54–55.

tionship between Meed and the Whore of Babylon in the Apocalypse of St. John.[49] Possibly all three are literary kin.

Jean de Meun's section of the romance contains a number of passages on the theme. Jean mentions, for example, the venality of lawyers and doctors (ll. 5091-5094) and attacks the avaricious clergy, who devote all their attention to temporal goods and thus lose their own souls while they preach to others (ll. 5101-5110). God has only lent money to greedy men, but they have imprisoned her. Wealth, however, unwilling to be diverted from her natural end, takes vengeance on the miser (ll. 5121-5204). Jean, too, personifies money as a queen:

> Ainsinc Pecune se revenche,
> Com dame e reïne franche,
> Des sers qui la tienent enclose;
> En pais se tient e se repose,
> E fait les mescheanz veilJier
> E soussier e traveillier.
>
> (ll. 5205-5210)

When Jean speaks of judges his language is even closer to the commonplaces of the theme: "Now they sell their judgments and overturn orderly procedure, and tally and count and squeeze, and the poor people always pay" (ll. 5579-5582.)

Jean's other remarks on bribery and venality are more in the spirit of Ovid than of *Piers Plowman*. The doorkeepers must be bribed if the lover is to free *Bel Acueil*, but it is unwise to give too much: small bribes and large promises are better (ll. 7431-7454). The "fol large doneeur" cause trouble for all by their great gifts (ll. 7609-7632). Yet gifts are most important in winning a woman, for poverty is an ugly thing (ll. 8189-8196).

[49] D. Robertson and B. Huppé, *Piers Plowman and Scriptural Tradition* (Princeton, 1951). pp. 49-56.

More important for the history of the satirical theme is an allegorical romance of the fourteenth century, *Le roman de Fauvel*, attributed to Gervais du Bus. It was written in two books, both probably by the same author, the first book dated in the manuscripts 1310, the second book 1314. It appears to have been popular, for it is preserved in a dozen more or less complete manuscripts.[50] The aim of the poem is wholly satirical, its author apparently protesting the submersion of religion and the Church during the close and friendly relations between Philip the Fair and Clement V.[51] The 3274-line romance is an allegorical blast at corruption of all forms among all classes, but especially among the nobility and higher clergy, in particular at the royal court. It is of interest to us not only for its treatment of corruption, but also for its allegorical hero, his successes at court, and his marriage at the close of the romance.

The hero is a horse named Fauvel, a common name for a fawn-colored horse in the Middle Ages.[52] The author explains its allegorical meaning and etymology at length: it is a beast designed to signify worldly vanity and falsehood, compounded of the sins of flattery, avarice, baseness, fickleness, envy and cowardice:

> Fauvel est beste appropriee
> Per similitude ordinee

[50] Gervais du Bus, *Le roman de Fauvel*, ed. A. Långfors (SATF, Paris, 1914–1919), pp. xi–civ.

[51] Cf. Wood, p. 107. For another complaint on Church and State in Philip's time cf. "Dou Pape, dou roy et des monnoies," mentioned above, p. 199.

[52] A. Långfors, in *Le roman de Fauvel*, pp. lxxiv–lxxv. The name appears in medieval texts, but before the time of this romance only as a name for a tawny horse. But the word *fauve* (fawn–colored), from its similarity to *faus*, had acquired an unfavorable sense as early as the twelfth century, so that worldly malice was frequently personified as a fawn–colored ass or mare. Meanwhile the word for falsehood and hypocrisy was the feminine *fauvain*.

A signifier chose vaine
Barat et fauseté mondaine.
Ausi par ethimologie
Pues savoir ce qu'il senefie:
Fauvel est de faus et de vel
Compost, quer il a son revel
Assis sus fauseté velée
Et sus tricherie meslee.
Flaterie si s'en derive,
Qui de nul bien n'a fons ne rive.
De Fauvel descente Flaterie,
Qui de monde a la seignorie,
Et puis en descent Avarice,
Qui de torchier Fauvel n'est nice,
Vilanie et Varieté,
Et puis Envie et Lascheté.
Ces siex dames que j'ai nommees
Sont par FAUVEL signifees:
Se ton entendement veus mestre,
Pren un mot de cescune letre.[53]

Fortune has made Fauvel lord of her house. Everyone wants to curry ("torchier") him, high and low alike: kings, temporal lords great and small, sheriffs, provosts, bailiffs, merchants and peasants. The clergy, too, stroke Fauvel, led by the pope, the cardinals and their retainers, followed by prelates, Dominicans, Franciscans, Augustinians, nuns, clerks with benefices. The poor unbeneficed clerks would like to, but cannot get near enough. The similarity of this miscellaneous rout to the one which surrounds Meed is significant.

The author draws a long contrast between St. Peter and the reigning pope, and between the apostles and the contemporary cardinals. Saint Peter, with a small net, caught little more than

---

[53] *Fauvel*, 235-256.

enough to sustain himself and his friends, "but our present pope fishes in much better places; he has a great and strong net, which brings him so many gold florins that St. Peter and his ship would tremble from them. He fishes up florins without number. . ." (ll. 553-559.) With this wealth the pope carries florins to Fauvel and the cardinals do the same. The apostles were poor and full of charity and humility, but now the pastors pasture only themselves. The wolves have become shepherds and take the wool so close to the skin that the sheep bleed (ll. 610-616). Ignorant youths become bishops through simony and "grant lignage" (624-627, 707-713), and the canons do nothing but take money (743-746). Briefly, in the eyes of Gervais, the spiritual power has surrendered to the temporal when it should be the leader. And the laity are equally curriers of Fauvel, especially the great lords who burden the commons with taxes, forgetting that they no more rode forth from the womb on horseback than their serfs.

Book II is especially interesting as a forerunner of Langland's Meed episode, for it is the story of the marriage of Fauvel. Fauvel is seated in his palace surrounded by his court, a familiar group: personifications of the cardinal sins, Presumption, Spite, Indignation, Vanity, Boasting, Arrogance, Inconstancy, Duplicity, Barratry, Cheating, and many others. Fearing the inconstancy of Fortune, Fauvel wishes to marry her, in order to make his reign permanent and to create a dynasty (1245-1748). His court approves the marriage and glorifies his worldly success. He rules the whole world, having driven his competitors, Good Conduct and Good Parts, to the Western Isles (1797-1808).

Hence Fauvel undertakes a journey to Macrocosme, where Fortune lives with Vainglory seated at her feet, distracting those at the top of Fortune's wheel so that they do not see their approaching fall. Fauvel protests his love and suggests that it would

be to Fortune's advantage to have offspring to continue her rule
(1837-2112). But the answer is a contemptuous rebuff: "How
did it get into your head. . . that I am Lady Pantalon, who would
take Fauvel for a lord?" (2135-2138). Fortune identifies herself
as a daughter of the Eternal King who rules all things, but leaves
the governance of mutable being to her, under the names of
Providence, Destiny, Fate, Accident, or Fortune. She speaks at
great length, quoting Scripture, telling *exempla*, paraphrasing
Boethius, and describing her own symbolism in a thousand-line
moral-scientific sermon. Fauvel, she says, is permitted to reign
only because God has said that war and sin will reign near the
end of the world. Fauvel is the son and messenger of Antichrist
himself.

But before sending him away, Fortune offers Fauvel a fitting
wife: Vain Glory, "la decevante damoiselle" (3157-3162). Fauvel
marries her on the spot in a common-law wedding, "sans bans
et sans clerc et sans prestre." Their offspring have since invaded
every country of the world, "for Fauvel engenders every day,
in every country, new Fauvels, who are much worse than wolf-
cubs" (3220-3226).

There is much in the romance to suggest the Meed episode.[54]
Meed first appears, it will be recalled, in the company of False
and Favel:

> "Loke vppon thi left half   and lo where he standeth,
> Bothe Fals and Fauel   and here feres manye !"
>   I loked on my left half   as the lady me taughte,
> And was war of a womman   wortheli yclothed. . . .
>   (II, 5-8)

---

[54] This striking parallel was first pointed out by Roberta D. Cornelius,
"*Piers Plowman* and the *Roman de Fauvel*," PMLA, XLVII (1932), 363-367.
Miss Cornelius is convinced that Langland had some knowledge of the allegory
in Book II of *Fauvel*, though she acknowledges that it remains beyond proof.

It is Favel, too, who arranges for Meed's marriage (II, 41-42). In the C-Text, indeed, Favel is Meed's father (C Text, III, 25-26). Favel reads the charter for the marriage of Meed and False (II, 78), bribes the crowd of lawyers and notaries to agree to her marriage (II, 143), fetches mounts for the ride to Westminster (II, 162), and helps lead Meed to the courts (II, 183), before he disappears from the action of the poem.

Now "favel," meaning cunning, duplicity and flattery, was not a common English word at the time of *Piers Plowman*. It has been pointed out that Langland was the first known English writer to use the word with that meaning, just as the author of the *Roman de Fauvel* was the first to fuse the common French descriptive name for a tawny horse with the meaning of the word "fauvain."[55] The indirect influence of *Le Roman de Fauvel*, seems probable. Fauvel is precisely the sort of figure which might have gotten into the colorful preaching of the mendicant orders: one recalls, for example, Nicole Bozon's hell-hounds. And the central action of Book II of *Fauvel*, like the Meed episode, is the attempted marriage of an evil hero to a figure (Fortune) who is dual in nature, both good and evil. Both *Fauvel* and the Meed episode express the same social complaint: that men of all estates have sacrificed, or at least lost sight of, their true end in the feverish struggle of "getting ahead." Here, however, the similarity between the poems ends. Gervais is less strongly influenced by religious motives than Langland, and more strongly by political ones. He is more interested in courtly society and less in the poor. Nevertheless, *Fauvel* approaches the plot and imagery of the Meed episode more closely than any other predecessor. It may have suggested, directly or through the vehicle of the popular sermon, the whole

---

[55] Cornelius, p. 365. Cf. "Favel," NED, and "Fauvel," Godefroy, *Dictionnaire de l'ancienne langue française*.

story of Lady Meed.[56] Though *Piers Plowman* was popular in appeal and homiletic in spirit, it could hardly have been written without the allegorical romances and debates which preceded it.

French satire on venality and the power of money tended to move, then, from simple personification toward allegory. *Fauvel* is the most highly developed of the allegories which treat the theme at length, and though its hero is more complex and more general than Lady Meed, the romance is clearly inspired by something of the same feeling which inspired Langland's Meed episode. Such sermon devices as Nicole Bozon's hounds of hell or the legend of the devil's daughters are probably partly responsible for the strength of that tendency. Allegory had long been popular in medieval preaching, but the mendicants especially seem to have bent the allegorical romance to their use, as St. Francis himself had bent the love lyric to his use. After the work of Owst it seems probable that sermons can account for much in *Piers Plowman*, written by a man obviously remote from courtly interests or influences.

---

[56] G. Owst, *Literature and Pulpit*, pp. 92–97, believes that the legend of the devil's daughters, popular in both French and English sermons from the twelfth through the fourteenth centuries, is the most likely source of the Meed episode. In French sermons the legend became almost a traditional type. The sermon would first describe the marriage of the devil to some personification of evil, then describe at length the daughters (usually nine) born of the marriage, personifications of the cardinal sins or other vices. Finally the sermon would describe the marriage of these vices, each to a profession most closely associated with the vice. P. Meyer, "Notice du MS Rawlinson Poetry 241," *Romania*, XXIX (1900), 1–84, has conveniently gathered together six sermons of the type. The device, a simple framework on which to hang commonplaces about the popular sins of the time, seems less likely than *Fauvel* to have inspired the Meed episode.

FOUR

THE EARLIEST ENGLISH VENALITY-SATIRE

We know the popularity of venality-satire in England from the numerous Latin verse satires in English manuscripts and from the comments of men like Walter Map, John of Salisbury and Giraldus Cambrensis; yet the limited nature of the theme and of the audience to which it would appeal kept it almost unknown in the English vernacular before 1350. Henry II's chaplain, Etienne de Fougères, when he dealt with the theme in the vernacular naturally treated it in French. When it does appear in English it is confined to occasional laments for the times and perfunctory treatments in the handbooks of sin and penance. Around 1308, for example, an anonymous poet arraigns corruption in the government in verses which center about a beast fable. "Coveitise," he says, "hath the law an honde," and is ruining the poor. The king's ministers will not enforce the law, for they are all corrupted by meed:

> Hab hi the silver, and the mede,
>   And the catel under-fo,
> Of feloni hi ne taketh hede,
>   Al thilk trepas is a-go.

The poet tells of the wolf and the fox, justly accused of their crimes before the royal lion, and of the simple ass, also accused, who was innocent. Before the trial the fox sent the lion geese and hens, and the wolf sent lamb and mutton. But the simple ass, trusting in his innocence, sent nothing. Hence the fox and the wolf were acquitted and the ass sentenced to death.

> Also hit farith nou in lond,
>   Whoso wol tak therto hede:

> Of thai that habbith an hond,
> Of thevis hi takith mede.

The innocent man is thrown into prison until he pays a fine, but the bribing thief goes free. The poem closes with a general lament over the reign of pride, covetousness and contention, a threat of punishment beyond the grave, and an admonition to honor God and Holy Church and to give to the poor.[57]

The longest and most amusing of these early fourteenth-century satires on the depravity of the times is a sort of vernacular "Apocalypse of Golias." The disgruntled author, of the reign of Edward II, systematically anatomizes the estates, clerical and lay, in *cursor mundi* fashion, beginning with the pope and excepting only the poorest, who bear the weight of the sins of the others. The emphasis is largely on avarice and venality, especially when the poet treats the clergy. Truth lives not at Rome, for fear of violence:

> Among none of the cardinaus dar he noht be sein
>   for feerd,
> If Symonie may mete wid him he wole shaken his berd.

This poem more than other English satires of the time has the familiar ring of the earlier Latin venality-satire. At Rome only money gets a hearing:

> Voiz of clerk is sielde i-herd at the court of Rome;
> Ne were he nevere swich a clerk, silverles if he come,
> Thouh he were the wiseste that evere was i-born,
> But if he swete ar he go, al his weye is lorn
>   i-souht,
> Or he shal singe *si dedero*, or al geineth him noht.[58]

---

[57] Wright, *Political Songs*, pp. 195–205. Cf. also the complaint in the "Song of the Husbandman" (pp. 149–153) of the same period against the king's meed–taking beadles.

[58] This line shows the popularity of some of the older satirical songs. Cf. the Latin verses, *Si dedero*, p. 175 above. The phrase must have been in common

For if there be in countre an horeling, a shrewe,
Lat him come to the court hise nedes for to shewe,
And bringe wid him silver and non other wed,
Be he nevere so muchel a wrecche, hise nedes sholen be sped
         ful stille,
For Coveytise and Symonie han the world to wille.

The Church in England, says the poet, has declined steadily since the death of St. Thomas. Prelates dare not reprimand their clergy, for they lead equally vicious lives. Like Langland and Chaucer, the poet makes archdeacons special followers of Meed:

He wole take mede of that on and that other,
And late the parsoun have a wyf, and the prest another,
        at wille;
Coveytise shal stoppen here mouth, and maken hem al stille.

Whenever a benfice becomes vacant, Simony and Covetousness will be present at the considerations:

Coveytise upon his hors he wole be sone there,
And bringe the bishop silver, and rounen in his ere,
That alle the pore that ther comen, on ydel sholen theih worche,
For he that allermost may ʒive, he shal have the churche.

When one of these simoniac clerks gets a benefice he devotes God's patrimony not to the poor, but to his own pleasures, hunting and whoring:

For thouh the bishop hit wite, that hit bename kouth,
He may wid a litel silver stoppen his mouth;
He medeth wid the clerkes, and halt forth the wenche,
And lat the parish for-worthe. . . .

Such a priest will turn out a good and learned vicar for a fool who will take the duties for less pay.

---

use in England. Cf., e.g., John Lydgate, *Minor Poems* (ed. H. MacCracken, EETS, e.s., 107, o.s., 192, London, 1911–34), II, 577.

The poet then attacks the regulars, the monks for luxury and lack of charity, the friars for venality. The stanzas on the friars recall both Chaucer's *Summoner's Tale* and Lady Meed's friar-confessor (III, 40-50):

> If a pore man come to a frere for to aske shrifte,
> And ther come a ricchere and bringe him a ʒifte;
> He shal into the freitur and ben i-mad ful glad;
> And that other stant theroute, as a man that were mad
>   in sorwe;
> ʒit shall his ernde ben undon til that other morwe.

Officials and deans are rebuked for venality:

> Mak a present to the den ther thu thenkest to dwelle,
> And have leve longe i-nouh to serve the fend of helle
>   to queme;
> For have he silver, of sinne taketh he nevere ʒeme.

Silver will buy a divorce or let a man live in adultery. And silver is the god, too, of false physicians, who look at a man's urine in a glass and invent stories to get money. They ask for half a pound to buy spices, and eight shillings for wine or ale; but the drink they concoct will probably make the patient sicker.

The poet finally turns on the "justises, shirreves, meires, baillifs," all followers of Meed. When these officials gather soldiers for the king's armies they let the strongest stay home for a bribe of ten or twelve shillings, and send some weak and helpless poor man in his place. When they collect taxes they get as much from the poor as the king gets, and the king never learns how the poor are robbed. But his officers grow wealthy: "Theih pleien wid the kinges silver, and breden wod for wele." Lawyers, too, charge outrageous fees and encourage people to begin useless lawsuits for the sake of money. The jurymen follow the example of their superiors, and

Damneth men for silver, and that nis no wonder.
For whan the riche justice wol do wrong for mede,
Thanne thinketh hem theih muwen the bet, for theih
        han more nede

                                to winne.

There the poem breaks off because of a defective manuscript.[59]
It will be noticed that the poet's venal world is almost identical
with that with which Langland surrounds Lady Meed, less than
half a century later. Though he continues to pay great attention
to clerical venality, he depicts many more secular figures than
earlier satirists. Like Langland's exemplars of venality, they are
a grotesque and unpleasant mingling of all estates. The prelates
and archdeacons, the monks and friars, the beadles, bailiffs and
sheriffs, the judges, lawyers, jurymen and false merchants are
all present, as well as the very atmosphere of *Piers Plowman*. For
the episode of Lady Meed, Langland had simply to place such a
group in an allegorical setting like that of the *Roman de Fauvel*.
The personifications of Coveytise and Symonie further suggest
the Meed episode.

It would be unprofitable to summarize here the treatment of
money and venality in the handbooks of religious instruction
which were popular during this period, such as Robert of Brunne's
Handlyng Synne, the *Cursor mundi*, and Dan Michel's *Ayenbite of
Inwit*.[60] Such works are almost wholly derivative, their authors
reproducing with little change the advice of religious or devo-

[59] Wright, *Political Songs*, pp. 323–345. A variant version, somewhat shorter
than that summarized above, has been edited by H. C. Hardwick, *A Poem on
the Times of Edward II* (Percy Soc., XXVIII, London, 1850). Parts of it vary
considerably in form from Wright's version.

[60] Cf. *Handlyng Synne*, 5325–6514, 11079–11154, for sins of covetousness;
also *Cursor mundi*, ed. R. Morris (EETS, London, 1874–1894), Cottonian Version, 27822–27867, and *Ayenbite of Inwit*, ed. R. Morris (EETS, o.s. 23, London,
1866), pp. 34–46.

tional treatises a century older. Their attention to venality, essentially a sin of the clergy and the great, is largely perfunctory.[61]

FIVE

Meed and Secular Economic Developments

In the foregoing pages we have described the relationship between the rebirth of medieval venality-satire and the program of taxation undertaken by the Papacy to support its expanded functions. We have noted that this program was for centuries largely one of enforced gifts—called "gratuities," but actually taxes. Papal finances developed, of course, much earlier and much more fully than those of the slowly emerging national governments. But as the money-theme became at least partly secularized in the fourteenth century, and poets began to complain more frequently about the venality of secular officials, it became clear that taxation by enforced gifts was no longer confined to the Papacy or other ecclesiastical circles. It seems rather to have been one of the characteristic types of medieval tax. The phenomenon was common in England, where financial organization was more advanced than in other European secular courts. The original name for the Fine Rolls was *Oblata* Rolls, derived from the offerings made by applicants for privileges. The name suggests a kind of organized system of bribes or extortions. There were two types of offerings, *oblata in rem* and *oblata in spem*, the first payments for favors received, the second offers to the king of

[61] Cf., e.g., *Ayenbite of Inwit*, p. 46: "þise byeþ þe boȝes of aurice ynoȝ þer byeþ oþre. Ac hy byeþ more to clerekes: þanne to þe leawede. And þis boc is more ymad uor þe leawede: þanne uor þe clerkes þet conneþ þe writinges."

part of the expected proceeds in order to get litigation expedited.[62] If we were to describe these two "offerings" in the terms applied by the satirists to ecclesiastical taxes we would call the first type the Giezi-tax and the second the Simon-tax. It is amusing to hear Henry II's treasurer try to distinguish between the acceptance of offerings *in spem* and mere bribery:

> But offerings are said to be made *in spem*, or for future advantages' when a man offers a sum to the King to obtain justice about some farm or rent; not, of course, to ensure justice being done—so you must not lose your temper with us and say the King sells justice—but to have it done without delay. Note also that the King does not accept all such offers, even though you may think him to overstep his limit. To some he does full justice for nothing, in consideration of their past services or out of mere goodness of heart; but to others (and it is only human nature) he will not give way either for love nor money. . . .[63]

The distinction has an ugly sound to the callow reader. Richard the Treasurer, remarks Winfield, "is probably splitting hairs in the passage, in order to gloss over the evil practice of the Anglo-Norman kings in extorting money for the administration or retardation of justice."[64] But the student of venality-satire is likely to recall the similar practices of the Roman Curia and Pope Adrian's defense of them to John of Salisbury, and to reflect that the development of taxes both secular and ecclesiastical was accompanied by severe growing-pains. However evil the practices, they were certainly common. We have examined the problems of the Papacy. But also in a secular society, originally organized largely

---

[62] P. Winfield, *The Chief Sources of English Legal History* (Cambridge, Mass. 1925), p. 138.

[63] Richard, Son of Nigel, *Dialogus de scaccario*, ed. and tr. C. Johnson (London 1951), p. 120.

[64] Winfield, p. 138.

on personal privileges and obligations, on the direct relation of lord to vassal, the line between tax and bribe was very fine. Richard's discussion treats cases which fell very close to that line.

The king had a more important source of these informal taxes in the fines called *amercements*. Amercements, says Winfield, are "pecuniary mulcts imposed on a delinquent for a crime or a trespass. *Misericordia* is the liability for the mulct, amercement is its assessment in money terms."[65] The frequency and whimsicality with which small freemen and villeins were amerced make it difficult for the modern student to distinguish these mulcts from extortion. Poole notes the frequency of these exactions: "A man for some reason or other, quite of en innocently, gets himself into trouble with the authorities. He is adjudged *in misericordiam*; he is in the king's mercy; he is amerced. Maitland thought that most men must have expected to be amerced at least once a year, and he is hardly exaggerating. The very inevitability of amercement is sufficient justification for regarding it among social obligations."[66] These amercements were not fines for crimes committed (except for very minor misdemeanors), but were assessed on "men who in one way or another failed in their public duties, or. . . made mistakes in their pleading or in the course of procedure."[67] The man on jury duty was especially in danger of amercement. "You were almost bound to come out of court poorer than you went in," says Poole, "whether you were there as plaintiff or defendant, pledge or juryman."[68]

Amercements burdened the small man, but the knight also had his burdens, equally inevitable and usually equally arbitrary.

[65] Winfield, p. 139.

[66] A.L. Poole, *Obligations of Society in the XII and XIII Centuries* (Oxford 1946), p. 77.

[67] Poole, p. 84.

[68] Poole, p. 89.

Most of these obligations arose from the commutation of payment in kind to payment in cash, already well advanced in England by the end of the twelfth century. Knightly service was commuted by scutage, and there were other associated charges. "When in the thirteenth century," says Poole, "the king tried to compel men possessed of a certain amount of landed property to become knights . . . . he doubtless had in mind the pressing need of increasing the number of men available for serving on grand assize juries and performing other administrative functions which were restricted to the knightly class. But the chief object was financial; to gain more money from those fruitful sources of royal revenues, scutages, reliefs, wardships, and marriages, incidental to military tenures. So early does a money economy intrude itself upon the feudal organization of society."[69]   The king and some lesser lords found a source of income in the regular and systematic debasement of the currency, from the eleventh century onward, a policy occasionally attacked by moralists and satirists. It caused less economic disturbance, however, than we might expect, because the steadily decreasing supply of silver in the face of increasing trade produced a consistent rise in silver value.[70]

The rise of trade, of a money economy, and of the resulting governmental financial problems, both ecclesiastical and secular, produced the rise of credit—the usury of the moralists—and the rise of bankers, the hated tribes of the "Lumbardes and Iewes," useful to prelates and kings as sources of ready money and, when convenient, as whipping boys for fumbling fiscal policies.[71] Systematic usury and banking grew first where the money economy

[69] Poole, pp. 3–4. On both money penalties and "voluntary offerings" cf. *Dialogus de scaccario*, pp. 119–125.

[70] Lenient, pp. 181–183; A. Feavearyear, *The Pound Sterling: a History of English Money* (Oxford, 1931), pp. 20–50.

[71] Lenient, p. 182.

was earliest established, in northern Italy, and its development was greatly aided by the complex financial and tax structure of the increasingly-centralized Church. Early in the twelfth century we hear from the satirists of the usurers in Rome who made their living by financing the large *servitia* and other Curial taxes on newly consecrated prelates. As the financial structures of the various royal courts gradually increased in complexity—that is, as the money economy gradually established itself in the rising nations of Europe—the same phenomena took place, and similar objections were heard. The reign of money was inexorably replacing the reign of mutual personal obligation.

This gradual development was thoroughly chaotic. The change from an agrarian, feudal economy to a money economy was certainly not managed according to plan by rulers temporal or spiritual. Every innovation was makeshift, dictated by necessity, and usually by pressing financial necessity. Though the causes were only dimly understood, it was abundantly clear that these rulers had a pressing need for money. They obtained it by whatever means came to hand, and the resulting fumbling led to appalling inequity and misery. It is not surprising that conservative moralists reacted with bitter satirical generalizations on the power of money *in saeculo*. The greatest spiritual pitfall which the world seemed to offer, especially to the souls of its leaders, was symbolized by Money.

Hence it seems clear that much medieval venality-satire is part of a conservative reaction to the surprising economic developments of the times. To a mind cast in the feudal mould all Church taxation must seem to be simony, and almost all secular taxation a form of extortion. Nor were the secular and ecclesiastical lords always able to deny this view. The suspicion of money payments forced both secular and ecclesiastical authorities to devise their taxes haphazardly, often as "gifts," which might escape the obloquy attached to regular cash payments. Only in rare instances, as we have pointed out, can we connect this satire with specific fiscal policies of individual princes. In most cases the feeling is too generalized and too complex to be interpreted in terms of its occasion. "Omnia namque cum pretio hodie," John of Salisbury had observed, and his phrase sums up concisely the bitter complaints of the satirists, as its conclusion sums up their general forebodings: "sed nec cras aliquid sine pretio obtinebis !"[72]

[72] *Policraticus*, VI, xxiv. In Webb, II, 68.

VI

"WHO IS A MAISTER NOW BUT MEEDE:"

THE VENALITY-THEME IN ENGLISH

AND OTHER VERNACULARS

ONE
THE SERMON AS A VEHICLE OF THE MEED-THEME

The moral-religious substratum of late fourteenth-century satire appears most vividly and characteristically in the sermons. Some of these, like the first part of *Jacob's Well*, have been published in scholarly editions. The massive *Summa praedicantium* of the Dominican preacher, John Bromyard, was printed several times in the fifteenth and sixteenth centuries with only minor changes. But much more remains in manuscript, though the invaluable work of G.R. Owst has brought this material forcefully to the attention of scholars. It is useless to look for novelty in these sermons. The age placed little value on originality, and sermons have never been the place for it. The preacher's obligation to produce regularly and to repeat the essential elements of the Church's teaching tends to make the sermon, ancient or modern, a collection of moral and religious commonplaces, more or less expertly phrased. These circumstances have their special value, for they provide us with emotional and ideological norms, with the ideas, phrases and attitudes which produced the moral-religious tone of everyday life—what men expected to hear—and therefore with a record of the steady, if unexhilarating, moral currents of the age. The fourteenth century produced preachers, indeed, of great verve and brilliance, but they exercised their originality, if at all, in their method of expression rather than in their ideas. In the mass of sermon-literature, as in the great body of early commentary and exegesis, we hear not so much the individual thinker as the almost impersonal and unvarying voice of Holy Church.

This material when it deals with money and venality does not depart in essentials from the channels of earlier moralizing on the subject. It is an instrument of diffusion rather than innovation. Hence we observe the same time-worn themes; the same groups are attacked, the same commonplaces and catch-phrases appear. The sermons catch up worn ideas from the satirists, *exempla* from earlier writers and material from older commentators, and recirculate them, frequently in simpler or more earthy form, to be taken up again by a new generation of satirists, perhaps with new techniques, but with essentially the same moral attitudes as their predecessors. The words of such sermons must have been almost daily in the ears of Langland himself. *Piers Plowman* was written by a man experienced in the common methods of discussing private and public morality in his day. The sermon material makes this clear.[1]

As in the vernacular verse treatises designed essentially for popular instruction, the fiscal vices of the pope and Curia receive less attention than they did from earlier Latin satirists. The subject

---

[1] Owst's chapter, "The Preaching of Complaint," in *Literature and Pulpit*, pp. 210–470, is especially useful. I have used little Wyclifite material, since some of its fundamental assumptions are not typical of the period. It does not differ from the orthodox sermon in its attacks on venality.

was not immediately important to the hearers of most sermons, and certainly not likely to edify a lay audience. Nevertheless, it receives sufficient attention to prove its continued popularity as a satirical theme. Bromyard, for example, makes scattered references to it, and discusses it at length under the heading "Honor," where he suggests that the bad example set by the highest prelates has produced a host of evils, and encouraged venality throughout the diocesan structure. "If those presiding in the highest court of the Church . . . would show such eagerness, and make such stern penalties, for the salvation of souls as they do now about florins and the collecting of money, there would not be among clergy and people so many adulterers, fornicators, perjurors, whoremongers, and similar destroyers of the mandates of God and honor." To Bromyard the multiplicity of regulations about the collection of money, of excommunications for money matters and of assessments of pecuniary penalties indicates how deeply the whole Church is absorbed in the search for meed. When prelates are blamed for exactions from their priests and people, they lay the blame on their costs at Rome, and especially visitation taxes and *servitia*, to the great scandal of the Church in the eyes of all the world. Bromyard does not himself make the charge of simony, but describes the papal taxes as the" abusum, uel consuetudinem" of the time, which causes Christians to question whether any of the higher clergy are free of the taint of simony. Such expenses lead to heavy exactions from the clergy or to recourse to usurers. [2] Bromyard thus describes papal taxation not as simony, but the cause of simony, usury, and other crimes. Elsewhere he notes the usual comparison of the papal doorkeepers to voracious watchdogs, and warns that there is no end to such extortion: "For among such people a bribe suppresses

[2] *Summa praedic.*, "Honor," 14–19.

hidden anger (Prov. XXI) [only] as long as the bribes are continued; for when payments once begun are withdrawn or dis-
continued their wrath is greater than if they had never been
given anything. . . ."[3]

Venality among bishops and lesser clergy receives considerably
more attention in the sermons. The charges are the usual ones:
the purchase of bishoprics and the sale of benefices by the bishops,
extortion by the administrators of ecclesiastical law, and the sale
of sacraments by small parsons and vicars. The author of *Jacob's
Well* conveniently summarizes these fiscal crimes of the clergy:

> þis fote brede of symonye is vi. inche thycke. The firste inche
> is whanne þou leryd man ȝeuyst ȝiftes for to ben orderyd. An-oþer
> inche is whan þou ȝeuyst mede, or byest a benefyse, cherche, or
> prouendre, fre chapell, or chauntrye, for temperall lucre, or ȝeuyst
> to him þat þou owyst dette to, or for frenschip, but ryȝt nouȝt for
> charyte. þe thridde inche is chaungyng of benefyce, as to chaungyn
> a more & a lesse, & he þat hath þe lesse schal haue bote. þe ferthe
> inche is in eleccyoun of prelacye or dygnite. for whan a college
> or a couent schal chesyn here prelate, thrugh prayere or pro-
> curyng of a lord, þei schal chese one þat is onworthy. þe fyfte
> inche is comyng in-to relygioun be procuryng or be prayere, for
> profyȝt or for hope of here kyn to þe couent, & noȝt princypally
> arn receyvid for charyte. þe vi. inche is in schewyng of goddys
> woord or in mynystryng of sacrament. for he þat wyl noȝt preche
> goddys woord, but he be payid for his trauayle, or þe preest þat
> wyll noȝt synge masse, or heryn confessioun, or ȝyuen þe housyll
> or oþere sacramentys, wyth-oute mede; all þis is symonye . . . .[4]

This six-point summary of the types of simony makes an interesting comparison with Peter Cantor's more general twelfth-century
list of the six types of meed (cf. p. 134 above).

The old exegetical tradition of the three types of meed is popular with the preachers. John Myrc, for example, recurs to it

---

[3] *Summa praedic.*, "Munus," 8.

[4] *Jacob's Well*, Part I, ed. A. Brandies (EETS, o.s., 115, London, 1900), p. 127.

in his unpublished *Manuale sacerdotium,* where he laments that simony seems to have become incorporated into the fabric of the Church: "For scarely anyone at all is promoted without bribe of hand or tongue or sycophancy. For, either he gives bribes with his hand or flattering words with his tongue, or else fawns by performing some toilsome office."[5] Archbishop Fitzralph of Armaugh preaches the same charge. "Scarcely is there a single one amongst those promoted," he says, "who is innocent of the crime of Simony. . . . For I hear from many quarters that there are a number of prelates who rarely confer a benefice on anyone, unless they have received payment at their hand, or else have made sure of their reward when the deed is done—which is too disgraceful in the Church of God!"[6]

Bromyard speaks of the bishops who have gained their sees "either by prayer or by price,"[7] and mentions the constitutions of Boniface VIII enjoining bishops to prevent buying and selling in church. "But the contrary is true," he says, "among modern prelates: for in parliaments where prelates gather together the Church is full of selling, contrary to the word of God."[8] Elsewhere he treats simony systematically under the figure of the four entrances to the Church: the doors of Simon, of Caesar, of the Devil, and of God. The three types of *munera* appear in the discussion. Those who "obtain ecclesiastical ordination or a benefice through a bribe of the tongue or of service enter through the door of Simon." Through that door robbers and thieves achieve entry into the place of God. The sellers of these offices

---

[5] *Manuale sacerdotium,* I, xiii; translation in Owst, *Literature and Pulpit,* pp. 276–277.

[6] *Literature and Pulpit,* pp. 244–245. Owst here cites a number of other examples from unpublished MSS.

[7] *Summa praedic.,* "Mundus," 12.

[8] *Summa praedic.,* "Praelatio," 15. Cf. also 2.

are worse than Judas, for Judas returned the money which bought Christ, but they keep it and spend it on themselves. The buyers, having laid out money for their benefices, now look to them only for returns from their investments. They sing the services merely to avoid losing their income. A priest of that sort "celebrates mass more frequently for love of money than for love of God." Let each priest search his heart: "What brought him into Orders or his benefice, love of God, or of money? the lucre of purses, or of souls?" Is he a corrector of sin or a collector of silver? And let him look, too, to the way he expends the goods of the Church. Bromyard describes the state of the Church in the common image of the woman, very beautiful from the front, but from the rear utterly foul. The front represents Christianity in its early beginnings, but the rear shows it as it is at present, "turpissima, & quasi destructa." Like so many of his predecessors he uses a punning grammatical analogy to explain how priests scale the heights of the Church. Some climb in the nominative case, chosen for real merits; others in the dative, "for meed given or promised"; others in the vocative, by invoking the help of wealthy friends; and others in the ablative, taking positions away from the worthy.[9]

The officials of the ecclesiastical courts receive as much attention as the prelates. "Purs is the ercedekenes helle," said Chaucer's summoner, expressing one of the chief complaints of the sermons of the day. The pecuniary penalty became one of the satirists' symbols for the grass-roots venality of the whole ecclesiastical system. An anonymous sermon-writer expresses their attitude with characteristic force and sardonic bitterness:

[9] *Summa praedic.*, "Ordo clericalis," 9, 11, 13, 14, 20, 70, 71. The image of the beautiful–foul woman has interesting literary and doctrinal affinities with the figure in Dante's dream of the Siren (*Purg.*, XIX) and esp. with the *Frau Welt* of medieval German poetry and sculpture. On the latter cf. W. Stammler, *Frau Welt* (Freiburg, 1959).

For every vice and for every sin they prescribe only a single
medicine—that which is called by the popular name of "pecuniary
penalty." This certainly appears to be well called "a penalty,"
because it is very "penal" to many; nevertheless, whether it ought
to be called a "medicine" I do not know. Yet, in truth I think
that if it is a medicine, it deserves rather to be called "a laxative
medicine for purses," rather than "a medicine for souls!"[10]

Bromyard, too, attacks this regular application of the pecuniary
penalty to all sinners. The body and the soul, he says, sin together
but the purse is punished. He likewise takes up the medicinal
image, which had its origin in the language of the courts themselves:
"Behold a blind leach, a bad doctor, who does not direct his
medicine against the disease. . . ." True punishment should accord with the nature of the sin and of God's law. Yet the court
officials are like watchdogs who can be quieted by a piece of meat;
a little money will stop their threats. Officials who for *munera*
ease the penalties due to sin are vile. Since many of them undertake their duties with the sole aim of enriching themselves it is
not surprising that they fail to perform them adequately. Not
only do they dismiss men for meed, but they sometimes in-
tensify punishments when none is offered.[11]

The idea that consistory courts function more for love of money
than for hatred of sin is a commonplace of the fourteenth century.
The court officials are the ecclesiastical counterparts of extortionist
sheriffs and bailiffs. Thus they are attacked in *Jacob's Well*:

Offycyallys & denys þat oftyn settyn chapetlys, to gaderyn þat
þei may getyn, þow3 þei do wrong, þei recche neuere, for þei

[10] Translated in *Literature and Pulpit*, p. 280. Cf. the verse on Rome's "physica
bursis constipatis," in the "Utar contra vitia," *Carmina burana*, I, i, 77.

[11] *Summa praedic.*, "Correctio," 38–42. Cf. also "Judices," esp. 22. The concept of legal punishment as *medicina* rather than *ultio* was becoming common
in the fourteenth century. It was supported, for example, by Lucas de Penna.
Cf. W. Ullmann, *The Mediaeval Idea of Law* (London, 1946), pp. 146–147.

haue more affeccyoun to gadere syluer þan to don correccyoun. and ȝit þei do noȝt so scharpely reddour to ryche men as to pore, for ryche þey forbere for mede, & pore men þei greue wrong-fully, wyth cursynges & puttyng out of cherch to penaunce, to paye vnryȝtfully. þis may be clepyd raueyn & extorcyoun.[12]

The complaint seems stereotyped. At least one other anonymous preacher of the period lifted this passage bodily fom *Jacob's Well* for his own sermon—if indeed he is not himself a source for *Jacob's Well*.[13]

Even more violently attacked are the subofficials of these courts who, like Chaucer's Summoner, use the threat of the court's power to extort money from innocent and guilty alike. Dr. John Waldeby, an Austin Friar contemporary with Bromyard, says, for example, that they heap their punishments upon the poor but permit any fornicator for a bribe to keep his woman as long as he wishes.[14] An anonymous writer of sermons comments on "sompnoures and bedelles, that beth mynistres to this lawe, that procureth to do men be accused, and in other wyses greveth men by colour of her offices, to have of her good, and so robbeth the peple. . . . ,"[15] and *Jacob's Well* echoes the accusation.[16] Chaucer's summoner was well established in the train of Lady Meed.

From these officials of the ecclesiastical courts it was a short step for the preachers to the judges and lawyers, secular or clerical, favorite objects of fourteenth-century satirical sermons.

---

[12] *Jacob's Well*, p. 129.

[13] Quoted in *Literature and Pulpit*, p. 282.

[14] *Literature and Pulpit*, p. 266.

[15] *Literature and Pulpit*, p. 282.

[16] *Jacob's Well*, p. 129. Because of the summoner's appearance in the *Canterbury Tales*, the type of the venal summoner has been thoroughly canvassed by modern scholars. Hence we have dealt briefly with him here. Cf. esp. I. A. Hazelmeyer, "The Apparitor and Chaucer's Summoner," *Speculum*, XII (1937), 43–57.

"For bothe Cristen courte and seculere courte . . ." says one, "goon for golde and ȝeftes, and trewthe is forsakon."[17]   The careful hearer of the sermons of the time might have concluded that venality was the rule in law courts. "We have law, it is true," says Bromyard, "good indeed in itself, but they use it as reapers use a sickle to gather sheaves. Wherefor the law in their hands is as they wish strict or lenient. To the man who gives nothing it will be strict. . . . and whoever gives freely (*large*) will find the laws easy (*largas*). . . . Such men are like the rooster on the steeple; as it turns itself toward every wind, they turn themselves toward every piece of silver."[18]   Elsewhere Bromyard records the traditional four banes of the judge: "munera, amor, fauor, odium."[19] He recurs to the common conceit comparing the judge to a balance weighing right and wrong, just and unjust, and his tongue to the tongue of the balance which indicates truthfully the difference between right and wrong. But if the devil, through "amor, munus, consanguinitas, affinitas, vel falsitas," moves the tongue which God placed in the center, the balance will cease to read properly; the guilty will be freed and honored, the innocent with no meed will be condemned. A rich man able to distribute *munera* can always get his business done at court while a poor man waits.

Bromyard cites examples from the classics, the Fathers, saints' lives, and from St. Bernard's *De consideratione*. He wonders at Christian judges who, "a short time after they have been given

---

[17] Quoted in *Literature and Pulpit*, p. 341.

[18] *Summa praedic.*, "Acquisitio," 23.

[19] *Summa praedic.*, "Aequitas," 4. Cf. also Bishop Brinton of Rochester, a contemporary of Bromyard and Langland, as quoted in *Literature and Pulpit*, p. 343: "Quando, producti et pro utraque parte in judicio constituti, jurant dicere solidam veritatem, illam celant pretextu odii vel favoris, muneris vel timoris, amicitie vel dominationis, pro quorum perjuria unus terra hereditatis vel jure patronatus privatur, et alius injuste lucratur."

power as judges or in various other offices, buy lands and build houses out of their bribes and usury and iniquity, and treasure up much money, and many curses. . . ." He recurs to the figure of the balance: "For with them justice is not as perceptible and palpable as money. Money is heavier, and therefore the balance inclines in that direction. And justice, which cannot be seen or felt, is held to be worthless, and the poor man is excluded from their courts. . . ." Bromyard turns to Hélinant (whose *Vers de la mort* we have discussed above, p. 191) for satirical sauce, in a passage which exemplifies admirably the manner in which four-teenth-century preachers gathered up the strands of the old sa-tirical tradition to weave them into their own sermons:

> In the houses of prelates and princes, everything today is venal. You trust in vain to the testimony of your conscience or the honesty of your conduct, unless a price intervenes. For according to Ovid, "the court is closed to the poor—money brings office; from money the grave justice, the austere knight"—grave and austere, indeed, toward those who give nothing,
>
> sed audito nummo   surgunt, quasi principi summo,
> dissiliunt ualue   nihil auditur nisi salue.[20]

Unjust judges are like musical instruments, which produce no concord unless they are well stroked. Likewise false judges and jurymen will not come to concord with law or litigant, or even among themselves, unless they are well stroked by bribes. And

[20] This passage is an interesting tissue of satirical reminiscences. It appears first in the *Policraticus* of John of Salisbury, V, x (cf. p. 163 above), where the quotation is from Ovid's *Ars Amatoria*. It was picked up by Hélinant in his tract *De bono regimine principis* (PL, CCXII, 741), not, as Bromyard says, the *Chronicon*. Either Bromyard or an earlier copyist changed the Ovid quotation to *Amores*, III, viii, 55–56. The leonine distich which concludes the passage was probably added by Bromyard. It appears in at least two earlier Latin satires (cf. p. 96 above).

they must be stroked equally, for otherwise the man who receives least will be in discord with the others; like the jurymen who were asked if they were in agreement, whereupon one of them answered that they were not; for some of his companions had received 40 shillings, while he had received only twenty. Thus, concludes Bromyard, where money reigns and poverty cannot win a lawsuit, justice is nothing more than public merchandise.[21] The man who approaches the courts of the false singing the right tune will find the doors open and will be greeted, not by "benedictus qui venit in nomine domini," in the manner of the ancients, but in the new mode, "benedictus qui venit in nomine nummi." Meanwhile the poor man stands outside and hears them sing, "Come, let us oppress the just, for he is contrary to our works."[22]

Bromyard has collected many exempla on the subject, including the common tale of the old woman who took literally the bystander's advice to grease the palm of the judge (cf. pp. 196-197 above, and note).[23] Similar exempla on judicial venality are scattered throughout his work.[24] Both Bromyard and *Jacob's Well* tell the story of the false judge who was bribed by one of the litigants in a certain case with the gift of an ox. But the opponent bribed the judge's wife with a cow, so that she begged him repeatedly to favor the man who gave the cow. In the trial, when the judge

[21] *Summa praedic.*, "Iudices," 4–18.

[22] *Summa praedic.*, "Iustitia," 2–13. The last sentence is an echo of Wisdom, II, 12.

[23] *Summa praedic.*, "Iudices," 20.

[24] For other material on judges cf. *Summa praedic.*, "Iustitia," "Acquisitio mala," "Dominatio," "Falsitas." Cf. also *Jacob's Well*, p. 131: "þe xi. inche is, whanne a fals iuge doth more wrong þan evynhed in iugement, for auantage fauouryng a wrong, or ȝif he take mede on boþe sydes, & fauouryth him þat ȝeuyth him most, & ȝeuyth doom wyth hym þat hath no ryȝt, or taryith a ryȝt be his assent."

inclined toward the party of the cow, the party of the ox spoke up: "þou oxe, speke for me as þou hy3test me!" But the uneasy judge replied, "þe oxe may nou3t speke, for þe cowe wyl no3t sufferyn hym."[25] Bromyard adds that a judge who may be ashamed to receive bribes himself may nevertheless yet receive them through his wife, his friends, or family.[26]

The sermons attacked venal lawyers even more fiercely than venal judges. "How mony cursed falsnes and how mony vyces," says one writer, "buthe menteynyd in this world by the lawe. . . . For gold or sylver or som other 3efte wol turne the lawe a-non, and make the wronge as hit were very ry3t, and of the ry3t, the wronge."[27] Bromyard is severe. False advocates, he says, like the wandering stars, have a double motion, *pro* and *contra*: "*Pro* when something is given them. *Contra*, if more is given by the adversary." A lawyer's fees, he insists, should accord with the wealth of the client and the amount of work done, and no lawyer should defend evil for money, "since he who denies truth for money sells Christ Himself, who is Truth." The false lawyer's sharp tongue, like the thief's knife, cuts the purses of many men. Bromyard quotes a proverb: "A lawyer's tongue is damning unless it is bound by ropes of silver."[28] Venal lawyers are merchants of the devil, his companions in lucre, and deserving

---

[25] *Jacob's Well*, p. 213.

[26] *Summa praedic.*, "Iustitia," 25. Bromyard's remarks recall the vivid picture in Theodulf's *Paraenesis ad judices* of the judge besieged by the pleas of his bribed wife, children, and servants. Cf. p. 44 above.

[27] Quoted in *Literature and Pulpit*, p. 343. Cf. also *Jacob's Well*, p. 131.

[28] *Summa praedic.*, "Aduocatus," 21. The same proverb was used by John of Salisbury in his discussion of courtiers two centuries earlier. Cf. *Policraticus*, V, x, p. 162 above. Bromyard's language in this place is almost identical with that of selections from an earlier preacher's handbook (probably from the second half of the thirteenth century) printed by Hauréau, *Notices*, IV, 194.

to be his companions in eternal punishment. They use every possible method to protract cases for their own profit. The man who has no money will never get a decision in his case, and the man who has much will wait long. They should not begin their processes with the usual formula, "in dei nomine, amen," but rather with the new formula, "in nummi nomine, amen." "For there, everything obeys money, and in their courts *Nummus* rather than *Deus* is heard and sped."[29]

But the worst lawyers are those who argue against their Father, God—that is, against the truth—and against their mother the Church; those who for meed curse their Father, calling the good bad and the true false. Bromyard tells of a lawyer who was tortured after his death by fiery horses, cattle and other beasts placed in his mouth, which had become immense. In a vision he explained to his friend that he had gained these animals evilly through his speech and was now fittingly tortured by them. The exemplum ends with a distich:

O uos iuridici qui linguam venditis illi,
Vos uocat infernus, uos respuit ordo supernus.[30]

[29] *Summa praedic.*, "Aduocatus," 4–32. Cf. also Wyclif's very similar complaint in the English Works, ed. F.O. Matthew (EETS, o.s., 74, London, 1880), p. 182. The harshness of justice to the poor man is suggested by the story of the false accuser in Gregory's *Chronicle*, ed. J. Gairdner, *Historical Collections of a Citizen of London* (Camden Soc., n.s., 17, London, 1876), p. 199: "And thoo men that he appelyd were take and put yn stronge preson and sufferde many grete paynys, and was that they sholde confesse and a–corde unto hys false pelyng; and sum were hongyd that hadde noo frende shyppe and goode, and thoo that hadde goode gate hyr charters of pardon."

[30] *Summa praedic.*, "Aduocatus," 44–47. Cf. also "Gloria," "Mors," "Munus," "Dominatio," and *Literature and Pulpit*, p. 343. The concluding distich was not original with Bromyard. The following earlier version is printed by L. DeLisle, "Notice sur les manuscrits du Fonds Libri conservés à la Laurentienne," *"Notices et extraits*, XXXII, i (1886), 68:

Venal jurymen, too, were frequently the objects of the preachers' scorn. "This false queste-mongeres," says one, "...for a litill money, or els for a good dyner will save a theffe, and dampne a trewe man. And ʒitt, and he be wrouthe with is neyʒbore and com to asyse, he will for a peyre of gloves of vi pens put hym from is londe."[31] Sheriffs, bailiffs, and other court officers fare no better. A sermon by Robert Wimbledon, preached at Paul's Cross in 1388, suggests the attitude of the preachers toward these officials:

> o lord· god, what abvisioun is þer among officerys of boþe lauys now on dayes! if a grete man plete with a pore to haue ouʒt þat he holdyþ, euery offycyr schal be redy to hiʒe al þat he may þat þe ryche man myʒt haue soche a eende as he desyriþ. but if a pore man plete with a riche man, þanne þer schal be so many delayes þat, þow þe pore manys ryʒt be open to al þe contre, for pure de faute of spendyng he schal be glad for to cejce. schyreuis and baylyes wollyn retorne pore menys wryttys with tarde venit but if þei fele mede in her hondys. and ʒut j here seie of men þat han seen boþe lauys þat þat court þat is clepyd cristyn is more cursyd.[32]

Wimbledon tells how "sacrates, þe philosopher" laughed as he watched the law courts. When asked why, he replied: "for i see grete þeuys lede a litil þef to hangyng."[33]

O vos, causidici, qui linguas venditis *ici*
Vos manet infernus, vos respuit ordo supernus.
It also appears in Bibl. Nat. MS Latin 1249, f. 42.

[31] Quoted in *Literature and Pulpit*, p. 343. Cf. also Wyclif, *English Works*, p. 183: "iurroris in questis wolen forsweren hem wittyngly for here dyner & a noble, & þat so custumablice þat þouʒ a man haue neuere so opyn riʒt to a lordi-schipe anemptis mannys lawe & also goddis, þat many questis wolen wittyngly swere þat it is not his for a litel money." Cf. also *Summa praedic.*, "Dominatio," esp. 9.

[32] R. Wimbledon, *A Famous Middle English Sermon*, ed. K. Sunden (Göteborg, 1925), p. 12.

[33] Wimbledon, p. 13.

Bromyard's *Summa* contains an interesting description of the activities of men selected to go to London when a case was appealed, to attest to the truth of testimony already given in the original suit. This custom produced a sort of traveling jury, whose members apparently often tried to get as much financial profit as possible out of their appointments; twelve apostles of falsehood and Antichrist, Bromyard calls them. On the first day they try to get an offer from one party, swearing that they will support him; and so they get what they can. On the next day they make their offer to the other party. Whichever offers more receives their support. Meanwhile each juryman takes great pains to assure himself that he has received as large a bribe as his fellows.[34] Meed's trip to London immediately comes to mind. "Have we not actually here," says Owst, ". . . the fundamental idea which inspired Langland's incident . . . when the supporters of the Lady *Mede* 'wenden . . . to Westmynster', to witness to her disputed deed of marriage?"[35]

In the fourteenth century the venality of royal courts and their creatures, as well as other representatives of the king, was coming increasingly under attack in the sermon literature. The extortionist jailer, for example, attracts Bromyard's attention. He describes a man who exacted huge payments from the friends and relatives of noble prisoners of war for the privilege of visiting the prisoners. When reproved for it he answered that his lord had given him the position for his advancement, and he felt no qualms about his conduct, since this was his only opportunity for profit.[36] Another

[34] *Summa praedic.*, "Munus," 12. A useful brief summary of the problems and complexities of fourteenth century legal practice appears in the introduction to *Mum and the Sothsegger*, ed. M. Day & R. Steele (EETS, o.s., 109, London, 1936), pp. xxvi–xxix.

[35] *Literature and Pulpit*, p. 347.

[36] *Summa praedic.*, "Dominatio," 8.

jailer would, for meed, change the identities and clothes of criminals with those of innocent men so that the guilty were set free and the innocent hanged.[37] Much of this corruption among petty officials of great lords comes, says Bromyard, from the illiberality of the lords themselves, who place in office

> poor relations, or even those who have served them long, whom they should pay from their own wealth. . . or what is worst, sometimes they sell them some foreign or domestic office, or one in their household or domain, where there is not any income on which the official can live, but everything is from graft (*turpilucrum*). Or if there is some income attached it is too small to sustain the official. Hence these officials, having succeeded with difficulty to the reward of past service, collect—with an addition—the equivalent in money given by people whom they do not serve or to whom they gave no money, without conscience . . . .[38]

We have seen in a previous chapter how similar policies helped to produce the grasping minor officials who gave scandal at the Roman Curia. But Bromyard is not especially interested in clerical venality. He attacks corruption among all officials, "tam ecclesiasticis, quam mundialibus," and the corrupt system which makes underlings derive their support from those who do not employ them. Lords, he says, appoint ministers not for the public good but for their own; and thus they appoint those who will bring in most money, not those who will be most just. Hence the underlings try harder to collect money than to correct faults, more eager to please their grasping master than to please God.[39]

One is tempted to believe that the multitude of mendicant preachers like Bromyard, who preached frequently to large groups of laymen, was the chief instrument in secularizing a theme which

---

[37] *Summa praedic.*, "Falsitas," 32.

[38] *Summa praedic.*, "Dominatio," 8.

[39] *Summa Praedic.*, "Ministratio," 15.

had once been confined to clerical abuses and clerical audiences. In this respect as in others the author of *Piers Plowman* seems to have been following the lead of the friars. The more learned of these preachers were especially adept in catching up the characteristic attitudes, phrases and structure of the older satire and reworking it for a broader audience. The personifications and tags of the learned satires reappear in the sermon, along with material which must have been popular and proverbial. "Now nys no god but gold alone," says one preacher in the midst of a Latin sermon. Later he adds another English phrase: "God schal be god, wan gold nys none." These scraps suggest that there may have long been popular parallels to the learned Latin satire on the power of the purse. Certainly the people were vividly aware of the growth of the money economy: "Lo! what great miracles gold works in days such as these."[40] Thus the familiar song of three centuries of venality-satire.

Bromyard's work is full of the flotsam of the satirical tradition. Alas, he sighs, quoting Ecclesiastes (X, 19), "pecunia obediunt omnia."[41] He expands the idea repeatedly throughout his *Summa*. "The hearts and deeds of all evil men," he says, "obey money. Hence a certain man used to say that if he wished a god other than the God of Heaven, he would choose Money for his god; for just as the man who has God is said to have everything, so the man who has money can have everything; for all things on earth, and in hell, and in the heavens, and even redemption from sin, are bought with money. . . ."[42] Bromyard preserves another fa-

---

[40] Quoted in *Literature and Pulpit*, p. 316. Cf. also pp. 317–319.

[41] *Summa praedic.*, "Dedicatio," 13.

[42] *Summa praedic.*, "Avaritia," 40. In "Avaritia," 58, he illustrates the power of money by the exemplum of Hannibal's escape from an ambush. He filled a casket with lead and had it deposited openly in the temple, as if it were a great treasure. The conspirators, thinking he would not suddenly leave a city where

vorite figure of the money-satirists, the "Cross of Silver."[43] This god Denarius with his cross, he says, cures moral lepers, for the cross gives respectability to known sinners. It evangelizes the poor, for it places the unworthy in office. In this manner Simon Magus can perform false miracles, as Peter performed true ones. Indeed there are ways in which the cross of Silver is more efficacious than the cross of Christ, for the cross of Christ can protect us from fiends, but not from evil men. Yet a man with a purse "copiously marked with silver crosses" can go anywhere and, holding the cross before him, succeed in everything. "Thus," says Bromyard, pushing on in the style of the ironic parodist, "this Cross of Silver leads us forward and back. This cross conquers, rules, and erases all guilt; against this sign no danger prevails. It kills and it raises from the dead, it leads into hell—but not out; it makes men poor and enriches them, it humbles and it exalts. . . ."[44] The preacher caps one of his attacks with a pas-

---

he had such great wealth, were in no haste to capture him and he slipped away secretly.

[43] Cf., e.g., "De cruce denarii," pp. 177–178 above, and *Piers Plowman*, XV, 500–509.

[44] *Summa praedic.*, "Crux," 37. The passage is so throughly saturated with the language and spirit of the earlier satire that it deserves to be quoted at length:
Iste Deus cum Cruce sua in carius, & officiis, & ubi falsi dominantur, omnes leprosos mundat, & sic leprosi mundantur, non per aurum comestum, sed per aurum datum, quia peccatores iusti, & mundi reputantur, & mortui resurgunt: quia morte digni abire permittuntur. Et pauperes euangelizantur: quia indigni in moribus, & scientia pro muneribus prae-mouetur. Et sic, sicut miracula, que Petrus uere fecit, Simon Magus fecit ficte. Ita omnia miracula, quae Christus uel Crux eius fecit, haec crux cum Deo suo denario facit false. Et non solum talia facit miracula, sed etiam a multis periculis custodit, a qua Crux Christi non custodit. Signatus enim Cruce vera in corde, & corpore potest se a daemonibus custodire . . . sed non custodit a malis hominibus, immo simplicioribus, qui in Cruce

sage from the *De planctu naturae* of Alain de Lille, ending with the common parody refrain, "Nummus vincit, nummus regnat, nummus imperat universis."[45]   In the manner of other preachers and satirists he compares the meed-hunter to various beasts, the hydra, the dog, the wolf, the beaver, and the lynx, typing in characteristic bestiary fashion the curiosities of classical and medieval natural history.[46]   Bromyard's treatment of the theme shows everywhere his broad familiarity with the satirical tradition and his obvious belief in the fundamental social importance of the venality he attacks.

The evidence from sermons, then, suggests that the preachers, especially the mendicants, provided a major vehicle for popularizing the older satire on the power of the purse. What Bourgain has said of the twelfth-century French sermon is equally applicable to that of fourteenth-century England: "Elle admet tous les genres, toutes les formes, tous les tons. Elle aime l'allégorie, la satire, l'élégie, joyeuse, théâtrale, puérile, touchante. L'esprit simple des

---

Christi plus confidunt, plus quandoque nocent. Sed qui habent bursam de Cruce argentea copiose signatam, & sciat de Cruce illa benedictionem largam iugiter infundere, intret curiam quamcunque, & secure uadat, ubicunque voluerit, quia uix debebit hominem timere, vbi Crux illa ante eum portatur, nec est, qui in diocesi sua, & ad domum suam eam portari prohibeat. Crux ergo haec argentea ducit, & reducit. Crux haec uincit, Crux regnat, & expellit omne crimen, hoc contra signum nullum stat periculum. Mortificat, & uiuificat, deducit ad inferos, sed non reducit, pauperem facit, & ditat, humiliat, & subleuat . . . .

[45] *Summa praedic.*, "Munera," 11. The passage from Alain is in Prose **IV**: "Si in aure vel Aduocati susurret pecunia, etc." Cf. p. 173 above.

[46] *Summa praedic.*, "Munera," 1–5. The long discussion under this heading is a most useful summary of the commonplaces of venality-satire in the fourteenth century. The importance of the subject to Bromyard may be measured by the fact that over thirty of his subject-headings contain material which bears on our satirical theme.

auditeurs le demandait ainsi. Il réclamait tout ce qui parle aux sens; il cherchait même avec bonne foi des leçons de morale sous les crudités. La cause de tout de variétés libres, dramatiques, familières, n'est pas ailleurs."[47] In these sermons, then, the earlier venality-satire reappears, secularized, and usually without the witty neo-classicism of the earlier writers. The central ideas and much of the imagery remain, but we begin to feel a hint of the vivid, realistic, homely scenes which burst and dissolve like star-shells throughout *Piers Plowman*. It would seem as if the preacher more than all others established the tone of fourteenth-century English satire.

TWO

THE FOURTEENTH-CENTURY ENGLISH SATIRISTS

The venality-theme appears almost everywhere in the English satire of the second half of the fourteenth century. The tone is generally similar to that of the sermons, more secular and often somewhat more vigorously realistic than much of the material from earlier centuries. Any discussion of English satire of this period might best begin with Chaucer.

Yet, considering Chaucer's ironic bent and the venality-theme's popularity in the fourteenth century, he wrote surprisingly little on it. The plan of his *Canterbury Tales* was not essentially satirical and in any case would hardly have permitted him to satirize venality in the highest clergy or nobility. His extortionist summoner is of all his characters most clearly and conventionally a part of the satirical tradition. The summoner's venality had long been a common theme and was, as we have seen, a frequent target of

[47] Bourgain, *Chaire française*, pp. 231–232.

the sermons of Chaucer's own time. Chaucer's unpleasant character follows the type:

> He wolde suffre for a quart of wyn
> A good felawe to have his concubyn
> A twelf month, and excuse hym atte fulle.[48]

The summoner's own view of the archdeacon and of the punishments of the ecclesiastical courts is equally in the tradition:

> And if he foond owher a good felawe,
> He wolde techen him to have noon awe
> In swich caas of the ercedekenes curs,
> But if a mannes soule were in his purs;
> For in his purs he sholde ypunysshed be.
> "Purs is the ercedekenes helle," seyde he.
>
> (I, 653-658)

The summoner of the *Friar's Tale* is cast in the same mold. His
extortions have made him into a thief comparable to Judas (III,
1346-1368). He is always "feynynge a cause, for he wolde brybe."
He is interested in his office only for the wrongful profits he can
draw from it. And the archdeacon by whom he is employed
follows faithfully the satirical tradition in his application of the
"pecunial peyne" (III, 1301-1320). But the friar who tells the
tale is himself venal, like Lady Meed's confessor:

> Ful swetely herde he confessioun,
> And pleasaunt was his absolucioun;
> He was an esy man to yeve penaunce,
> Ther as he wiste to have a good pitaunce.
>
> (I, 221-224)

---

[48] *The Works of Geoffrey Chaucer*, ed. F.N. Robinson, 2nd ed. (Boston, 1958),
Fragment I, ll. 649-651. Reference should be made again to Hazelmeyer,
"The Apparitor and Chaucer's Summoner," *Speculum*, XII (1937), 43-57. Cf.
also M. Bowden, *A Commentary on the General Prologue to the Canterbury Tales*
(New York, 1948), pp. 262-273, for a convenient brief summary of scholarship
on the summoner.

He knew that men too strong to weep for their sins might instead validate their contrition by giving "silver to the povre freres." (Cf. *Piers Plowman*, III, 35-50.) And the friar of the *Summoner's Tale* was drawn to match.

The pardoner, Chaucer's most telling picture of the venal ecclesiastic in action, was a relatively new figure on the social scene in Chaucer's time, as the regular sale of indulgences had not become a source of papal income until the fourteenth century.[49] In Chaucer's character there is a touch of the traditional venal clerk who preaches and administers the sacraments only for money. His pardoner is certainly supremely and ferociously venal, but this venality is so boastful and so thoroughly entangled in neurosis, so much a part of the pardoner's psychic armor and self-esteem, that we miss the characteristic flavor of venality-satire—the suave hints, the money furtively offered or demanded and slyly received, the greased-palm smile, the nod and the wink. He steals, to use the words of Chaucer's Reeve, not "curteisly," but "outrageously." His vices, though typical of those which fourteenth-century satirists attributed to the quaestors,[50] have been subordinated to the larger study of his character.

Other appearances of the theme in the *Canterbury Tales* may be mentioned briefly. In the *Tale of Melibee* Dame Prudence, that

[49] Lunt, *Papal Revenues*, I, 93-136.

[50] For a discussion of fourteenth-century views of the pardoner cf. J.J. Jusserand, *Chaucer's Pardoner and the Pope's Pardoners* (Chaucer Soc. Essays on Chaucer, London, 1884). J.M. Manly, *Some New Light on Chaucer* (New York, 1926), pp. 122-130, is brief but enlightening. Heiserman observes acutely (*Skelton and Satire*, pp. 230-231) that Chaucer more frequently than not uses conventional satirical material to construct comic actions, and that attempts to analyze these actions as satire are misleading. This sound principle must be kept in mind in considering the Chaucerian characters discussed above. Chaucer's aim is rather rarely satiric.

indefatigable medieval Poor Richard, unburdens herself of a number of the satirical commonplaces on the power of money: it brings for example, a husband, friends, and social respectability (VII, 1555-1559). But the *Parson's Tale* deals more directly with the theme. This sermon has long been recognized as indirectly derivative from two of the many books of instruction designed for parish priests, all ultimately springing from the canons of the Fourth Lateran Council. *Jacob's Well*, *Handlyng Synne*, the English *Cursor mundi*, and the *Ayenbite of Inwit* are all of the same lineage, though in different ways.[51] Hence the parson's material differs little from that of these and similar manuals. He repeats the scriptural commonplaces on avarice, attacks simony, and condemns false witnessing for gain: "Ware yow, questmongeres and notaries !" One of his most significant passages, since it exhibits clearly the secularization of the venality theme, is the attack on civil amercements, which the parson castigates as extortion:

> Of Coveitise comen thise harde lordshipes, thurgh whiche men been distreyned by taylages, custumes, and cariages, moore than hire duetee or resoun is. And eek taken they of hire bonde-men amercimentz, whiche myghten moore resonably ben cleped extorcions than amercimentz.[52]

Whether this is Chaucer's own contribution we cannot tell, but it seems unlikely.

Chaucer's treatment, then, of the summoner and the friar especially, suggests his familiarity with the traditions of satire against

---

[51] For details cf. the summary of scholarship in the Robinson *Chaucer*, pp. 765–766, and the discussion by Mrs. Dempster in W. Bryan and G. Dempster, *The Sources and Analogues of Chaucer's Canterbury Tales* (Chicago, 1941), pp. 723–760. For the manuals of instruction and penance which grew out of the canons of the Fourth Lateran Council cf. Arnould, *Le manuel des péchés*, pp. pp. 1–59.

[52] X, 751. On civil amercements cf. p. 234 above.

venality. But though his characterization is brilliant, his attitude is essentially conventional and his treatment largely unsatiric.[53] He does not favor the theme, partly, no doubt, because of his position at court, but even more because of the plan of his work. Only among the lower clergy does he show venality in action. Chaucer was no crusader, and he probably found the venality-theme somewhat inharmonious with his own relatively benign irony. What Chaucer the courtier probably dismissed with an ironic shrug seemed far more important to social moralists like Langland and Gower.

It is hardly surprising to find the venality-theme well represented in the works of Gower: virtually every characteristic medieval theme or device appears somewhere in his ample pages. He is conservative and derivative, and his satire resembles closely the work of earlier centuries. The theme appears frequently in his major works, English, French, but especially Latin. The subjects of his satire are those which were already popular at the close of the eleventh century. In his Latin satire on the Court of Rome, for example, we meet again the formulas and imagery which had accumulated over three centuries. There is no freshness of concept or imagination:

> Roma manus rodit non dantes, spernit et odit,
> Donum pro dono sic capit omnis homo.
>
> . . . .
>
> Qui precium ponit diues preciata reportat
> Munera, nam tali curia tota fauet:
> Assumens oleum secum non intrat ibidem,
> Aurea ni valeat vngere gutta manum:
> Copia nil morum confert vbi deficit aurum,
> Nam virtus inopum nulla meretur opem.
> Auro si pulses, intrabis, et illud habebis

---

[53] On the satirical background of his treatment of friars cf. A. Williams, "Chaucer and the Friars," *Speculum*, XXVII (1953), 499–514.

Quod petis, et donum fert tibi dona tuum:
Si tibi vis detur large, da munera larga,
Nam si pauca seras, premia pauca metes.[54]

This passage is nothing if not derivative, almost every line echoing
the language and imagery of the earlier satirists; and Gower's
other attacks on venality are similar. He contrasts the venal present,
for example, with the golden past,

For thilke tyme I understounde
The Lumbard made non eschange
The bisschopriches forto change,
Ne yet a lettre for to sende
For dignite ne for Provende,
Or cured or withoute cure.

.   .   .   .

Bot now men sein is otherwise,
Simon the cause hath undertake. . . .[55]

Archdeacons and deans place sin on sale for their own profit:

Car pour les lucres temporals
En tous paiis u l'en devient
Achater poet quiconque vient
Les vices qui sont corporals.
     Le dean, qui son proufit avente,
Par tout met les pecchés au vente
A chascun homme quelqu'il soit,
Maisqu'il en poet paier le rente: etc.[56]

---

[54] J. Gower, *Vox clamantis*, III, 1197–1212; in *Works*, ed. G.C. Macauley (Oxford, 1899–1902), IV, 139. Gower says much the same thing in the French *Mirour de l'omme*, 18449–18588, 18781–18792, 18853–18925, 18984–19033; in *Works*, I, 214–221.

[55] *Confessio amantis*, Prol., 206–241; in *Works*, II, 10–11. Cf. *Vox clamantis*, III, 1357–1402; in *Works*, IV, 143–144. Elsewhere he describes Simony as one of the five daughters of avarice; she is at home in Rome, among the clergy, and at the courts of kings. Cf. *Mirour de l'omme*, 7345–7488; in *Works*, I, 85–87.

[56] *Mirour de l'omme*, 20096–20104; in *Works*, I, 226. The indictment continues through l. 20208.

The attacks on clerical venality in his Latin poetry are equally derivative. The old puns, for example, appear once again:

> Sic non pastor oues pascit, set pastus ab ipsis
> Lac vorat et vellus, alter vt ipse lupus:
> Sic libras siciens libros non appetit, immo
> Marcam pro Marco construit ipse libro:
> Summas non summa memoratur, et optima vina
> Plusquam diuina computat esse sacra.[57]

The other estates are not ignored. Gower attacks the extortions which covetous kings practice on Church and people,[58] the rapacity of knights,[59] and the venality of judges.[60] Lawyers also appear in their common venal role:

> . . . . .tant sont esbauldiz
> De lucre, comme l'en puet oïr,
> Q'ainçois la loy font pervertir,
> Dont font le povre droit perir:
>
> .   .   .   .
>
> Car povere droit, qui donne nient,
> Pour null clamour escoulte pas,
> Mais riche tort, qui parle bass,
> Vers luy se tret isnele pass,
> Escoulte, et de sa part devient: etc.[61]

The attack on the venality of the law includes long, conventional passages on venal sheriffs, bailiffs and jurymen.[62]

---

[57] *Vox clamantis*, III, 995–1000; in *Works*, IV, 133–134. On the lesser clergy cf. also *Mirour de l'omme*, 20270–20352, 20497–20509, 20553–20556; in *Works*, I, 228–232.

[58] *Mirour de l'omme*, 22297–22360; in Works, I 250.

[59] *Mirour de l'omme*, 23820–23832; in *Works*, I, 263.

[60] *Mirour de l'omme*, 24673–24684; in *Works*, I, 272–273.

[61] *Mirour de l'omme*, 24193–24225; in *Works*, I, 267. The attack on the venality of lawyers continues through l. 24624.

[62] *Mirour de l'omme*, 24865–24889, 24949–24984, 25045–25104. Gower then turns to an attack on the avarice of merchants, physicians, and grocers.

Gower moralizes like Ovid on the Golden Age, when money was unknown and hence there was no war or misery,

> So mai men knowe, hou the florin
> Was moder ferst of malengin
> And bringere inne of alle werre . . .[63]

He finds a place for the characteristic, conventional litany on the power of money, whose praise he places in the mouth of Midas:

> "The gold," he seith, "may lede an host
> To make werre ayein a King;
> The gold put under alle thing,
> And set it whan him list above;
> The gold can make of hate love
> And werre of pes and ryht of wrong,
> And long to schort and schort to long;
> Withoute gold mai be no feste,
> Gold is the lord of man and beste,
> And mai hem bothe beie and selle;
> So that a man mai sothly telle
> That al the world to gold obeieth."[64]

Rarely does the commonplace money-litany of the Latin satires appear so baldy in English.

Gower's restatements of the venality-theme contribute nothing to its development and have little intrinsic value; yet his imitative mediocrity makes his handling of the theme more typical than

---

[63] *Confessio amantis*, V, 341–347; in *Works*, II, 411.

[64] *Confessio amantis*, V, 243–245; in *Works*, II, 408–409. The passage is followed by the common comparison of avarice to dropsy (ll. 249–262). Other passages treating the venality-theme may be found in *Mirour de l'omme*, 6469–6480; *Vox clamantis*, III, 35–62, 194–226, 753–772, 841–858, VI, 40–76, 171–182, 254–275, 427–456, VII, 41–56, 93–112, 793–816. The two brief Latin poems, *Carmen super multiplici viciorum pestilencia*, ll. 225–311, and *De lucis scrutinio*, ll. 1–12, 55–62, contain excellent examples of the conventional Latin treatment. Cf. also *Cultor in ecclesia*.

Langland's. Like the sermon-writers, he provides an excellent saturation-gauge of the theme's diffusion, and a useful dictionary or guide to the old clichés; his correct and soporific lines repeat in three languages almost all the ancient commonplaces on the subject, indicating clearly the theme's importance at the close of the century in the mind of a secular moralist. Moreover, Gower was with Chaucer the master of the fifteenth century, and transmitted to later writers a ponderous legacy of venality-satire.

The appearance of the venality-theme in the guild drama, like its appearance in Gower and the sermons, again suggests its popularization and secularization. Sermon and drama were the only literary forms of learned authorship directed to a truly popular audience, the only forms beside folk literature and the minstrel-romances in which circulation was not largely limited to the literate. In the drama the theme appears most frequently in the plays which center around the Passion and the Last Judgment. The violent Pilate of the Towneley Plays, for example, is a legist and a typical corrupt judge. Even Caiaphas worries, lest Pilate release Jesus for meed:

> ffor I am euer in drede wandreth, and wo,
> lest pylate for mede let ihesus go;
> Bot had I slayn hym indede with thise handys two,
>> At onys,
> All had bene qwytt than;
> Bot gyftys marres many man.[65]

Pilate himself in his ranting boasts of his own venality:

---

[65] *The Towneley Plays*, ed. G. England and A. W. Pollard (EETS, e.s., 71, London, 1907), XXI, 434–439. Pilate's satirical function in the Towneley Plays is thoroughly discussed by A. Williams, *The Characterization of Pilate in the Towneley Plays* (East Lansing, 1950), pp. 37–51, with illustrative material on the corruption of lawyers and judges.

ffor like as on both sydys the Iren the hamer makith playn,
   So do I, that the law has here in my kepyng;
The right side to socoure, certys, I am full fayn,
   If I may get therby a vantege or wynyng;
Then to the fals parte I turne me agayn,
   ffor I se more Vayll will to me be risyng.
                          (XXII, 14-19)

He gives aid and comfort, too, to other venal figures of the law-
courts:

      All fals endytars,
      Quest-gangars, and Iurars,
      And thise out-rydars
        Ar welcom to me.
                          (XXII, 23-26)

In all the cycles, Judas is the epitome of venality as the seller of
Christ, but the corrupt Judas of the York and Towneley plays
betrays Jesus partly for revenge. He objects to the woman's
anointing Jesus, and says that the ointment could have been sold
for 300 pence and the proceeds given to the poor. As keeper of
the common purse he had been accustomed to keep a tenth for
himself; he will regain his lost profit by selling Christ:

      And this, to discouer, was my skill,
      For of his penys purser was I,
      And what þat me taught was vntill,
      The tente parte þat stale I ay still;
      But nowe for me wantis of my will,
      þat bargayne with bale schall he by.

    . . . .

      And þerfore faste forþe will I flitte
      The princes of prestis vntill,
      And selle hym full sone or þat I sitte,
      For therty pens in a knotte knytte.[66]

---

[66] *York Plays*, ed. L.T. Smith (Oxford, 1885), XXVI, 135-152. Cf. also
Towneley Plays, XX, 270-281. This interpretation was common. Cf., e.g.,

The guard set over Christ's tomb must, as Scripture stated (Matt. XXVIII, 12-15), be bribed to keep the truth of the Resurrection from spreading. They are instructed to say that a large number of armed men came to remove the body by force, or else they are to keep silence entirely. This bribing of the guard occurs in all the English Resurrection plays, the price, where stated, running as high as 10,000 pounds![67] In the *Ludus Coventriae* Annas, who suggests the bribe, generalizes on the power of meed in the familiar manner of the earlier satirists:

> Ffor mede doth most in every qwest
> and mede is mayster bothe est and west
> now trewly serys I hold þis best
> With mede men may bynde berys.[68]

The York *Resurrection*, too, closes with a characteristic cynical comment by Pilate on the sale of truth, after he has assured himself that meed has sealed the lips of the guard:

> Thus schall þe sothe be bought and solde,
> And treasoune schall for trewthe be tolde . . . .[69]

---

the material printed by P. Lehmann, *Erforschung des Mittelalters* (Stuttgart, 1941–60) II, 235–6, 265–6. The Gospels (Matth. XXVI, 8–9; Luke XIV 4–5) do not specify Judas as the objector.

[67] Cf. *Towneley Plays*, XXVI, 532–561; *York Plays*, XXXVII, 407–454; *Ludus Coventriae*, ed. K.S. Block (EETS, e.s., 120, London, 1922), pp. 326–327; *Chester Plays*, Part II, ed. Matthews (EETS, e.s., 115, London, 1916), XVIII, 300–308 (nothing is said about money in the passage from the Chester Play, but cf. the stage direction: "Tunc tradet eis pecuniam et discedunt . . . .").

[68] *Ludus Coventriae*, p. 326.

[69] *York Plays*, XXXVIII, 449–450. In the Chester *Last Judgement* the satirical theme appears in the laments of the damned. The damned pope is a simonist:

> Also Siluer and Simonye
> made me Pope vnworthy;
> that burnes me now full bitterly,

There is no better testimony of the venality-theme's popularity with both satirists and the common man than its appearances in these dramas.

The theme is scattered throughout the anonymous moral and satirical literature of fourteenth-century England. There are perhaps many little fragments on money buried in sermon manuscripts, like the verse in John of Grimston's sermon book, written around 1376:

> maket wrong rith.
> Pecunia maket day nith.
> maket frend fo.
> maket wele wo.[70]

The unknown author of the alliterative *Wynnere and Wastoure* (ca. 1353), that curious debate between avarice and prodigality, places the usual subjects of venality-satire in the camp of Wynnere, the representative of avarice. The pope and the other clergy are there, especially the friars; the lawyers are there, and the merchants, who are naturally avaricious.[71] Wynnere's followers include the whole rout with which Langland surrounds Lady Meed, though their social reach goes higher. When the king parts the two opponents and sends each to live "in a lond þer he es loued moste," Wynnere is sent to Rome:

> þe cardynalls ken þe wele, will kepe þe ful faire,
> & make þi sydes in silken schetys to lygge,
> & fede þe & foster þe & forthir thyn hert,
> As leefe to worthen wode as þe to wrethe ones.[72]

---

for of Blis I am full bare.
The damned emperor, king, and judge, all accuse themselves of similar crimes of covetousness and venality (XXIV, 181–308).

[70] Quoted in *Literature and Pulpit*, p. 317.

[71] *Wynnere and Wastoure*, ed. I. Gollancz (Oxford, 1930), 143–196.

[72] *Wynnere and Wastoure*, 462–465.

This promised reception suggests the welcome given Meed by the lawyers and others when she makes herself at home in the king's court.

Examples appear in other poems on the times. A poet writing on the earthquake of 1382 sees the catastrophe as a warning against the venality of a world which would betray father and mother for money.[73] Another poet recurs in macaronic verse to the worn but pertinent theme of simony.[74] A "Song of Merci" describes the woes of the contemporary world at least partly in terms of venality:

> And symonye   haþ chirches solde
> And lawe is waxen   couetise
>
> .   .   .   .
>
> Who is a Maister   now but meede.[75]

The burden of many of the Lollard sermons, tracts, and satires is directed against venality and the power of money among the clergy. The Lollard attitude here does not differ discernibly from that of the orthodox. The late fourteenth-century *Plowman's Tale* which survives (probably much modified) only in sixteenth-century and later prints, is a sufficient example. The greater part of the allegorical pelican's complaint is devoted to clerical luxury and love of money.[76] The clergy from prelate to parson are depicted as simonists who "sellen churches and prioryes:"

---

[73] *Political Poems and Songs*, ed. T. Wright (Rolls Ser., London, 1859–61), I, 252. This volume also contains a number of fourteenth-century Latin satires of English provenance which deal with the theme.

[74] *Political Poems and Songs*, I, 277.

[75] F. Furnivall, *Early English Poems and Lives of Saints* (Berlin, 1862), pp. 122–123.

[76] *The Plowman's Tale*, esp. 261–987; in Chaucer, *Works*, ed. W.W. Skeat (Oxford, 1894–97), VII, 147–190.

> With purse they purchase personage,
> With purse they paynen hem to plede. . . .

They will bless nothing "but for hyre," they make parsons for pennies, and they sell absolution in their courts, even when no crime has been committed. The pope and the cardinals are (again) fishers of gold rather than of souls:

> They layeth out hir large nettes
> For to take silver and gold,
> Fillen coffers, and sackes fettes
> Ther-as they soules cacche shold.[77]

The ecclesiastical courts sell fornication by the year; priests demand "shryft-silver," and determine that

> None of the sacraments, save askes,
> Without mede shall no man touche.

This part of the Lollard tale is quite as traditional as the orthodox satire of its age.

The theme is applied to secular life in scattered passages of the late *Mum and the Sothsegger*. Like the *Plowman's Tale* and many other late works it is heavily influenced by *Piers Plowman*. It repeatedly attacks venality in the law and rapacity among the king's retainers. The author urges that instead of flooding the country with badges of the king's authority, carried by criminals, badges be given to upright judges. The judge who remains firm, so

> þat no manere mede   shulde make him wrye,
> For to trien a trouthe   be-twynne two sidis,

deserves some honor and recompense for his conduct.[78] For, says the author, the common practice today is to do nothing without

---

[77] N.b. the striking parallel in *Le roman de Fauvel*, 553-559, p. 223 above. There are also other parallels. Cf., e.g., p. 278 below.

[78] *Mum and the Sothsegger*, ed. M. Day and R. Steele (EETS, o.s., 199, London,

meed, to "prien affter presentis" (III, 306-307). All the king's legal officers, from the chancellor downward, favor the rich and ignore or oppress the poor (M Frag., 1-28). Against the rich man, the poor man "wircheth al in waste and wynneth but a lite."

The king's extortionate taxes, too, receive attention (IV, 19-38), and the venality of the clergy comes under the usual attack. The friars are followers of Mum:

> Thay mellen with no monaye more noþer lasse,
> But stiren hit with a sticke and staren on hit ofte.
>
> (M Frag., 429-430)

The secular clergy

> . . . bisien more for benefices þenne bibles to reede,
> And been as worldly wise and wynners eeke
> As man vppon molde, and asmuche louen
> Mvm and þe monaye, by Marie of heuene,
> For mayntenance and mede been þaire two mates.
>
> (M Frag., 669-673)

Nor are there any greater followers of Mum than the church courts, who condone sin for money:

> . . . penys . . . þay fongen
> For lemmans and lotebies in þees late dayes . . .
>
> (M Frag., 1350-1351)

One unusually interesting late satire from the first decade of the fifteenth century is a disputation between two men, one poorly clad, praising "moche thank," the other, dressed finely, praising meed. The wealthy man has obtained riches, not by facing danger for his lord, but by pleasing him at home with servile flattery in small matters. He now makes himself "mery

---

1936), II, 81-90. The poem seems to have been written between 1403 and 1406. Cf. pp. xix-xxiv.

with mede." The poor man who wielded spear and lance for his lord gets only thanks; the flatterer gets meed. The flatterer is like a weathercock, swinging toward money; he is a war profiteer:

> Thou woldest euere more were werre,
>   (ffor profyt and pilage thou myght glene,)
> . . . .
> Thou noldest not come ther but for mede.[79]

In fine, the wealthy man, too soft for war but well able to serve himself at meals, does nothing gratuitously, but "seruest al for mede."

The theme lived on healthily in fifteenth-century England but by then there were few poets with social interests who had not fallen under the influence of *Piers Plowman*. Langland's own ideas on venality and the power of the purse are those of the age and the tradition rather than the individual. The vivid character of Lady Meed helped popularize the theme but she did not alter its central ideas, and even she was not wholly original. The theme would have continued to be significant for moralists, preachers, and satirists, even if she had not appeared to give venal worldliness its most complex and perhaps most profound medieval expression.

---

[79] *Twenty-Six Political and Other Poems*, Part I, ed. J. Kail (EETS, o.s., 124, London, 1904), II, 67–72, p. 8. All these poems were apparently written by the same author, and many of them deal with meed and its dangers. Cf., e.g., II, 156–158, IV, 137–138, VIII, 17–20, 33–36. The poet busies himself almost wholly with commonplaces.

THREE

THE MEED-THEME IN OTHER VERNACULARS

We have pursued the venality-theme in detail through a rich array of evidence from the Latin, French and English satirical literatures. Though we have confined our investigations to these literatures, the theme itself was certainly not confined to them. It is an almost unexceptionable rule, indeed, that whatever appears with frequency in the Latin and French literatures of the Middle Ages will somewhat later make its appearance in other major vernaculars. Though this is eminently true of venality-satire, a systematic investigation of the theme in other literatures would add greatly to the bulk of our work without contributing appreciably to our understanding of the theme's significance or development. The flavor, tone, and idiom of venality-satire vary little, as we have seen, from country to country. The evidence here offered is by way of appendix, to confirm this impression of uniformity and to demonstrate the theme's wide diffusion.

Though venality-satire was not especially popular in Italian literature, its familiarity to Italian writers is sufficiently attested by Dante's frequent and savage assaults in the *Commedia* against papal simony and the barratry of the Italian city-states. This material is too well-known to require repetition. One example from the many scattered throughout the *Commedia* may serve as representative. The poet, from the Heaven of Justice, calls on God to take notice of the venality of the Avignon Papacy:

> Wherefore I pray the mind wherein thy
> motion and thy power hath beginning, to look
> upon the place whence issueth the smoke that vitiates thy ray;
> so that once more the wrath be kindled

against the buying and selling in the temple
which made its walls of miracles and martyrdoms.
    (*Par.*, XVIII, 118-123; tr. Carlyle-Wicksteed)

Dante was too bold a genius to fall long into the clichés and con-
ventionalities of the tradition, but even he recurs in this canto
to a variation of the familiar image of the *crux denarii*: the face
of Saint John on the florin, imitated at Avignon by Pope John
XXII. Thus he addresses the pope, alluding with characteristic
dense indirection to the saint and to the pope's love of the coin:

Though thou indeed mayst urge: "I have so
fixed my longing on him who lived a solitary,
and by tripping steps was drawn to martyrdom,
that I know not the fisherman nor Paul."
    (*Par.*, XVIII, 133-136)

The venality-theme was immensely popular in German satirical
and didactic literature. Much of the earliest Latin satire on the
subject seems to have originated in Germany. There is at least
one example of a mixture of the languages, where German macaronic verses expressing the usual ideas about the power of money
are appended to a Latin *Nummus*-grammar:

Qui caret nummis,
dem hilfft nit, das er frumm ist,
sed qui dat summis,
der macht schlecht, das krumm ist.[80]

The theme appears repeatedly in German verse from the twelfth
century onward. Heinrich von Melk, the earliest significant satirist in the German tongue, expresses it in both *Priesterleben* and
Von des tôdes gehugde, where he directs it especially against the
lesser clergy for the sale of the sacraments[81] and for the difference
between the treatment of the poor and of the rich:

[80] Lehmann, *Parodistische Texte*, p. 16.
[81] Heinrich von Melk, *Von des tôdes gehugde*, ll. 9-32. Both this work and

> Swer in ze gebene hât
> Der mac tuon swaz er wil . . . .

He who has given can do what he will, so that in any way he pleases he can do many bad things, for his pennies will do his penance. They [the clergy] strain at gnats, they swallow camels: they reprove only the poor, when they should pity them. Whatever the rich man does, that they think sweet and good.

(Tôdes gehugde, 116–126)

Heinrich makes elaborate use of the traditional comparison of the venal, sacrament-selling priest with Judas, punctuating his attack in the *Priesterleben* (ll. 303–378) with the words of Christ (Luke, XXII, 21) at the Last Supper:

> Sîn hant diu mich verraetet,
> Diu ist mit mir ob mînem tische.

In the first quarter of the thirteenth century the bitterness of the struggle between pope and emperor encouraged a large amount of German venality-satire against the papacy. Some of this verse shows a strong vein of secularism and lay contempt for the clergy, well before it is found elsewhere in Europe. The theme of Roman venality is well represented in poems written almost concurrently by two laymen of strikingly different temperaments, between 1215 and 1230. These are the *Bescheidenheit*, that strange, moralistic miscellany by the wandering poet who called himself Freidank, and the political *Sprüche* of Walther von der Vogelweide. Walther is thoroughly courtly in attitude, completely within the tradition of *Hohe Minne*; Freidank not at all courtly, but full of earthy, sardonic practicality, bourgeois in flavor. Both men are united, however, in their distaste for the taxation imposed on Germans by the papacy—exactions which were becoming especially large

---

the *Priesterleben* are printed in *Deutsche National-Literatur* (Stuttgart and Berlin, n.d.), IX, 69–120.

because of the demands of the Crusade. Walther was the most famous—and one of the most bitter—of writers of anti-papal satire in his time. He pictures Pope Innocent III laughing with his Romans as he profits by fostering civil strife in the Empire:

> Oh, how Christian-like the pope now laughs, when he tells his Romans: "I've done it thus!" (What he tells then he should never have thought of.) He says: "I have brought two Germans under one crown, so that they may confuse the Empire and destroy it. Meanwhile we will fill our coffers. I have driven them to my cage; everything they have is mine. Their German silver wanders into my Roman chest. You priests, eat chicken and drink wine, and let the German laymen grow thin, and fast."[82]

The German clergy, says Walther, are being misled into simony by the example and encouragement of the papacy, though all Christians have renounced the buying and selling of the gifts of God at their baptism. The cardinals have covered their altar with a beautiful roof, while German altars lie shabbily under the eaves. The pope is the "junge Jûdas," who acts in the same manner as his original (33,20). Walther addresses the papal crusade offering-box angrily, as a traitor sent to rob and plunder the Germans for the enrichment of Rome, for little of its silver reaches the Holy Land:

> ich waen des silbers wênic kumet ze helfe in gotes lant:
> grôzen hort zerteilet selten pfaffen hant.
>
> (34, 20-21)

Elsewhere (e.g., 10, 25-32) he attacks the clergy generally for living luxuriously on the patrimony of the poor, and in the spirit of Dante laments the Donation of Constantine as destructive of true holiness in the Church.

---

[82] *Die Gedichte Walters von der Vogelweide*, ed. K. von Kraus (Berlin, 1959), 34, 4-13, pp. 45-46.

Freidank devotes over a hundred lines of his long poem to an attack on Rome and papal venality which includes most of the commonplaces of such satire. The section opens with a conventional picture of Rome as the bottomless pit into which all of the wealth of the world is poured:

> All the streams of treasure go to Rome, and there
> they stay, and yet she can never become full; it
> is a cursed hole. Likewise all sin goes there.
> There everything is taken from the people: what
> they can keep is a matter of luck.[83]

The poet contrasts the poverty of Saint Peter and his rejection of wealth with the luxury and avarice of the contemporary papacy. He has recourse to the common figure of the new net of Saint Peter, which catches wealth instead of fish:

> Daz netze kam ze Rôme nie,
> Dâ mite sant Pêter vische vie . . . .

The net never came to Rome with which Saint Peter used to fish; that net is now despised. The Roman net catches silver, gold, castles and land; that was unknown to Saint Peter. Saint Peter was a proper vassal, whom God commanded to care for his sheep: He did not command him to shear his sheep. Now they cannot do without shearing them.

(p. 337)

Such ideas lead Freidank, as they led so many other versifiers, to observations on the universal power of money:

> Now men honor riches more than God Himself, soul and honor.
> Man's heart is always wherever his treasure is hidden. He who
> loves riches properly commits no evil: but now men honor the
> penny as the only worthwhile thing.

(p. 334)

---

[83] Freidank, *Bescheidenheit*, p. 334. Selections in *Deutsche National-Literatur*, IX, 251-353.

These generalizations were as popular in German as in Latin, and soon led to the typical personifications of money. By 1250 Reinmar von Zweter, a minnesinger of strong political interests and satirical tendencies, much influenced by Walther, was commemorating *Herr Pfennig*:

> Her Pfennink, daʒ ir waeret liep . . . .
> Sir Penny, if only you were good, and not entirely the thief of honor, that is what I would wish for rich and poor.[84]

By the fourteenth century *Herr Pfennink*, or *Junker Pfenning*, [85] or *Meinherr Pfenning*, was thoroughly established, the naturalized version of the French *Dan Denier*:

> Was doch der pfenning wunders tuet!
> mein her pfenning, ir seit ze fruet.
> mir ist laid, das man ewer gert
> so geitecleich . . . . .

How many wonders penny performs! *Meinherr Pfenning*, you are so fruitful! It makes me sad that you are desired so eagerly. You are so valuable that you are in the counsel of high princes. The wise must make room for you. You buy churches and chaplains; you have hurt the honor of many women, I hear say. You make many a great one tremble; you take the thief from the gallows and from prison, yet you are not as big as a span. He who would win city and castle must always have many pennies. The penny tells false tales; the penny perverts true justice; the penny buys all advice; he buys God, who made us. etc.[86]

[84] F. H. von der Hagen, *Minnesinger. Deutsche Liederdichter des zwölften, dreizehnten und vierzehnten jahrhunderts* (Leipzig, 1838–61), II, 188.

[85] A poem entitled "junker Pfenning" appears in a Munich manuscript. Cf. H. Schletter, "Die poetischen Werke Hans Rosenplüts," *Serapeum*, II (1841), 353–358. It is probably of the fifteenth century.

[86] Hans Vintler, *Blume der Tugend*, p. 195. Selections in *Deutsche National-Literatur*, XII, i, 195–206. This work was a translation by Vintler of the *Fior di vertu* of Tomaso Leoni (ca. 1320), but the penny poem is Vintler's own addition. Cf. also the interesting poem "Von dem Phenning" of Suchenwirt (ca.

But already a generation before this effort of Hans Vintler, Hugo von Trimberg, probably under the influence of Freidank, from whom he borrowed freely, had placed a similar *Spruch* on the penny in his massive *Renner*. It is a familiar tale:

> Pfenninc lêrt predigen manigen man
> Der wênic der heiligen schrift kan . . . .

Penny teaches many a man to preach who knows little of Holy Scripture. Also he makes many a woman unstable who rarely would sin without a gift. Penny perverts religious minds, Penny teaches much faithlessness, Penny can argue, make peace, make war, Penny can swear, lie, deceive, Penny can sing, jump, strive, Penny can drive out righteousness and honor. Penny is a relic of high renown in Rome. etc.[87]

Hugo's *Renner*, incidentally, is rich in the venality-theme,[88] which is well exemplified in his discussion of the faults of priests. Here he develops a long litany on alms—"almuosen"—in which he treats the ambivalent nature of these offerings in the manner in which Langland treats Lady Meed, or earlier satirists had treated *Nummus*, or *Munera*:

> Almuosen nert manigen frumen pfaffen:
> Almuosen nert ouch tôrn und affen;

1385), which is relatively original. The poet describes himself as riding alone through the countryside and meeting an old man, who turns out to be Pfenning himself. The body of the poem retails at length the conversation between the two. Printed in *Deutsche National-Literatur*, XII, i, 316–324. Personifications of *Pfenning* seem to be very numerous in fourteenth and fifteenth-century German literature. In the same volume cf. the *Reimspruch*, p. 361: "Die minne uberwindet alle ding. / 'Du liugest' sprach der pfening." This is curiously echoed in the Latin title of a fifteenth-century English money-poem by Lydgate: "Amor vincit omnia mentiris quod Pecunia." Printed in J. Lydgate, *Minor Poems*, II, 744–749.

[87] Hugo von Trimberg, *Der Renner*, ed. G. Ehrismann (Bibliothek des Litterarischen Vereins in Stuttgart, 247, 248, 252, 256, Tübingen, 1908–11), IV, 84.

[88] Cf., e.g., *Der Renner*, I, 95–100, 174, IV, 8, 84–86, 127, 240–243.

Almuosen prediget, bíhtet, singet . . . .
Alms nourishes many a pious priest: Alms also nourishes fools
and apes; Alms preaches, prays, sings: Alms dances, carols, leaps . . .
Alms saves many a soul: Alms brings about much evil; Alms has
pride, avarice, envy, anger, lust, gluttony, and sloth . . . .Alms
can do evil and also good, according to the disposition of its
receiver; etc.[89]

Clearly "almuosen" is intended to signify the ambivalent "munera"
of the German cleric. The passage shows a characteristically
growing awareness of the impersonality and ambiguity of a money-
economy.

Pfenning's characteristics, then, are those of *Denier*. By the
fourteenth century the tone, contents, and poetic development
of these penny poems had become thoroughly conventional in
all the major vernacular literatures of Europe. One of the most
interesting examples of this outgrowth of the venality-theme is
a chapter from the remarkable *Libro de buen amor*, written by Juan
Ruiz, Archpriest of Hita, perhaps a dozen years before the birth
of Chaucer. The Archpriest or his scribes entitled the digression
"Enxienplo de la propriedat que'l dinero há." It is relatively
long—over 150 lines in four-line stanzas—and does no more
than set forth the doctrine which we have now pursued through
many pages. Its tone is virtually identical with that of the penny
poems in other languages, as a scattering of its stanzas will suffice
to suggest:

Mucho faz' el dinero, mucho es de amar:
Al torpe faze bueno é ome de prestar,
Pfaze correr al coxo é al mudo fablar,
El que non tiene manos, dyneros quier' tomar . . . .
The penny has much power, and gains much love. He makes
a good and a useful man of a worthless one. He makes the lame

[89] *Der Renner*, I, 97–98.

run and the dumb speak. Even the man without hands wishes to grasp after *dineros*.

. . . .

If you have pennies you will have consolation, pleasure and joy, and a prebend from the pope. You will be able to buy Paradise, you will gain salvation: where there are many *dineros* there is much blessing.

In Rome, where sanctity resides, I have seen all men show great humility to Penny: they show him great honor, with great solemnity. Everyone humbles himself to him, as to a great majesty.

He makes many priors, bishops and abbots, archbishops, doctors, patriarchs, powers: he has given prelacies to many ignorant clerks. He turns truth into lies and lies into truth.

. . . .

He makes the poor man lose his house and his vinyard, and disorders all his goods and his lands, for he spreads his scab and his itch over the whole world. Where Penny judges, there the eye winks.

He makes knights of worthless peasants, counts and great men from villeins; with Penny all men grow healthy. . . .

But we are already well versed in all these powers of the penny, and may conclude this survey abruptly with the Archpriest's hardly novel observation that money makes the world go 'round:

> En suma te lo digo, tómalo tú mejor;
> El dinero, del mundo es grand rrebolvedor. . . . [90]

These scattered examples of vernacular venality-satire, then, will indicate that the theme which we have traced from its earliest eleventh-century revival had become in the course of the centuries a universal literary and homiletic phenomenon throughout Christendom. It is hardly too extreme to describe venality as the single most popular subject for satirists in the Middle Ages, if we except

[90] Juan Ruiz, Arcipreste de Hita, *Libro de buen amor*, ed. J. Cejador Y Franca (Classicos Castellanos, 6th ed., Madrid, 1951), I, 182–194.

such broad general areas as the cardinal sins. At a number of points in our study we have commented on the causes of the theme and its significance for the economic, social and intellectual history of Europe. It may be of use, by way of recapitulation, to return to Langland's *Piers Plowman*, with which we began our analysis. Though Langland is not one of Europe's greatest poets, he thought and felt profoundly, and his Lady Meed episode remains in many ways the recapitulation *par excellence* of the medieval venality-theme. If a reconsideration of this part of *Piers Plowman* does nothing else, it may help us pay tribute, in the light of the satirical tradition, to Langland's balance and sanity.

VII

THE LINEAGE OF LADY MEED:

THE CULMINATION AND SIGNIFICANCE

OF THE THEME

ONE

Piers Plowman ONCE MORE

In the context of a centuries-long tradition of venality-satire Lady Meed, then, had her origin. Yet her episode forms only the center-piece of Langland's venality-satire in *Piers Plowman*. It serves, indeed, to establish for Langland the fundamental importance of uncontrolled *munera* as a social evil, the chief of all the evils which afflict the Field Full of Folk as organized society. The lady in white, Holy Church, is the guide of the Folk to their supernatural end as men; but Lady Meed is her eternal opponent, the gracious and attractive epiphany of venal worldliness, who distracts society from that end. Having established his view of meed's importance as the fundamental social evil, Langland applies it broadly throughout his poem in attacks on traditionally venal groups. He deals harshly with visiting cardinal-legates (XIX, 411-413) and with venal prelates (XV, 239-243). He lashes pardoners (Prol., 80-83) as well as chantry priests who hasten to London "And syngen there for· symonye for siluer is swete" (Prol., 83-86). Meed's friar-confessor is an image of venality,

THE ANIMAL FACES OF AVARICE

From the Hortus Deliciarum *by Herrade de Landsberg, a 12th-century manuscript. Bibliothèque de la Ville, Strasbourg.*

Avarice rides in her car, which is pulled in opposite directions by the fox which personifies fraud and trickery, and the lion which represents gnawing ambition.

From the top, the dirty pig points to the head of Avarice. The vulture standing for the morbid desire to acquire the goods of others, is followed by the blustering bear. The wolf at the bottom stands for rapaciousness, the ox for the hunger to accumulate more and more, while the barking dog signifies the tenacity of the avaricious person.

and the poet indicates that the friars are almost all more interested in silver than in souls (XI, 71-74). Venal lawyers are the true *bêtes noires* of the poem, attracting attention almost from beginning to end. Everywhere they are devotees of Meed, and plead only

> . . . for penyes   and poundes the lawe,
> And nou3t for loue of owre lorde   vnlese here lippes onis.
> Thow my3test better mete the myste   on Maluerne hulles,
> Than gete a momme of here mouthe   but money were shewed.
> (Prol., 210-215)

The seriousness of the crime committed by these merchants of the divine gift of knowledge is suggested by the treatment of lawyers in the pardon of Piers Plowman: "Men of lawe lest pardoun hadde that pleteden for mede. . ." (VII, 39). Piers himself warns his followers against the venal lawyer's ally, the venal juryman, who is always ". . . frithed in with floreines and other fees many" (V, 590). The corruption of justice is the most notable activity of the personified Simony as he attempts to defeat Conscience. Directed by Covetousness, he

> . . . boldeliche bar adown   with many a bri3te noble
> Moche of the witte and wisdome   of Westmynster halle.
> He Iugged til a Iustice   and Iusted in his ere,
> And ouertilte al his treuthe   with 'take-this-vp-amendment.'
> . . . .
> For a mantel of menyuere   he made lele matrimonye
> Departen ar deth cam   and deuors shupte.
> (XX, 130-138)

The bold, ironic image of Simony jousting in the justice's ear characterizes vividly Langland's attitude toward the legal profession of his time. Significantly, Langland hastens to label the arguing of cases for money as simony. He agrees with the canonists about the sale of knowledge, but usually ignores their concession that the laborer is worth his hire.

Like older venality-satirists, Langland gives less attention outside the Meed episode to other estates. He warns kings and knights not to leave truth for love of silver (I, 98-101) and burghers not to buy knighthood for silver (C Text, VI, 65-79). He advises the knight to make ". . . Mekenesse thi mayster maugre Medes chekes" (VI, 41), and like Chaucer alludes to the love of physicians for the cordial gold (XX, 170). To all estates he issues warning in a figure already hoary with age, that the world's woes stem from lust for money:

> And tho was plente and pees   amonges pore and riche;
> And now is routhe to rede   how the red noble
> Is reuerenced or the rode   receyued for the worthier
> Than Crystes crosse, that ouer-cam   deth and dedly synne!
> And now is werre and wo   and who so 'why' axeth,
> For coueityse after crosse   the croune stant in golde.
> Bothe riche and religious   that rode thei honoure,
> That in grotes is ygraue   and in golde nobles.
> For coueityse of that crosse   men of holykirke
> Shul tourne as Templeres did   the tyme approcheth faste.
>
> (XV, 500-509)

This fourteenth-century Cross of Gold speech, touched with nostalgia for a past, gold-free Utopia that is reminiscent of Ovid or Virgil on the Golden Age, summarizes the poet's preoccupation with the corruption which springs from avarice. Never was the *crux denarii* image used with greater earnestness. The indictment which centers in the episode of Lady Meed actually extends from the opening scene of the "faire felde ful of folke" to the closing picture of the battle for Holychurch. Professor Kane insists that in *Piers Plowman* cupidity is the vice "which in the first and last instance comes nearest to undoing both church and state. . . Cupidity corrupts the clergy until they sell absolution for silver: this wounds Contrition, and once he is out of the fight Holychurch falls."[1]

Another scene in *Piers Plowman* summarizes even more impressively the central position which the poet gives to the problem of human venality. In a remarkable, Lucretian passage in Passus XI, the dreamer views the wonders of Nature, to learn, like the Psalmist, wisdom from them. Reason rules all created being except man. In the center of the magnificent panorama is man, turning to evil and corrupting himself with meed:

> I seigh the sonne and the see   and the sonde after,
> And where that bryddes and bestes   by here makes thei ʒeden
> Wylde wormes in wodes   and wonderful foules,
> With flekked fetheres   and of fele coloures.
> Man and his make   I myʒte bothe byholde;
> Pouerte and plente   bothe pees and werre,
> Blisse and bale   both I seigh at ones,
> And how men token mede   and mercy refused.
>   (XI, 318-325)

It will be profitable here to return to the heart of Langland's assault on venality, and reconsider the Meed episode itself. In the light of the satirical tradition its major personifications fall easily into place. Lady Meed's lineage goes back to the very beginnings of medieval satire, not to mention the satire of Augustan Rome: Queen Money, Mother or Mistress or Goddess Purse, the saints Albinus and Rufinus, or the god Albus and his pope Rubicundus, Saint Nummulus, Dan Denier, Munera, or simply the personified Nummus. In allegory, too, she had a predecessor. The French Fauvel, however ungracefully bestial in his courtly surroundings, had many of Meed's attributes. He represented, however, a broader aspect of the preachers' "World" than Meed, *vanitas* rather than venality; but venality was one of his most

---

[1] G. Kane, *Middle English Literature* (London, 1954), p. 246.

important attributes. His success at court was like Meed's and his marriage suggests strongly the proposed marriage of Meed. Meed herself, as Langland describes her on her first appearance, is a curious fusion of the Whore of Babylon and *Richesse* of the *Roman de la rose*, Saint John's oriental vision of evil reclothed in courtly medieval splendor.

Meed is first introduced by Holy Church as the enemy of Loyalty, and especially of loyalty to Holy Church herself:

> "That ys Mede the mayde," quod she   "hath noyed me ful oft,
> And ylakked my lemman   that Lewte is hoten,
> And bilowen hire to lordes   that lawes han to kepe. . . ."
>
> (II, 20-22)

Meed, the rewards of this world (considered apart from just wages or honest merchandising) continually disrupts the life of the spirit, and that disruption begins at the top, *Caput Mundi*. Meed is "in the popis paleys. . . pryue as" Holy Church herself (II, 23). Variously identified as the bastard daughter of Wrong (A Text), False (B Text), and Favel (C Text), she is also the true descendant of the august Queen Pecunia, who had found papal Rome to her liking as early as the eleventh century:

> Hic erit mea requies; hic stabit mea facies;
> Hic figam sedem stabilem inter plebem amabilem.[2]

Like earlier satirists Langland was moved to bitterness by the paradox that both Holy Church and Venality had established their homes at the same court.

Meed's identity with the *Munera* of the older moralists and satirists is obvious from the scriptural passages which are associated with her in *Piers Plowman*.[3] Like *Munera* she is ambivalent, as her mixed parentage signifies: bribery or corrupt worldliness

---

[2] Du Méril, *Poésies populaires latines*, p. 234. Cf. p. 81 above.
[3] Cf., e.g., III, 96, 241, 247, 333.

on the one hand, honorable rewards on the other. The question of her marriage—the central problem of the Meed episode—is a further extended anatomy of this dual nature of meed or *munera*. Shall Meed be placed in the lordship of evil or can she somehow be placed in the service of good? Left to herself she will gladly marry False Fickle-Tongue; but the king wishes her to marry Conscience, and Meed, who is common to all, good and bad, is willing to do so. One of Meed's remarkable characteristics throughout this episode is her agreeableness to all parties, her general warm affability. She spreads her favors indiscriminately wherever she comes. Through the king's proposal of her marriage to Conscience Langland develops on a human level the contrast between actual and ideal which underlies the whole episode. Meed, considered only as the rewards of this world, should belong to those who are guided by conscience, but with the connivance of corrupt and venal officialdom she is about to become the possession of the false and faithless of the world. The king, whose vision is at first that of the unaided human reason, sees this as the essential problem. In the hands of evil men Meed is barratry, simony, bribery, human venality; dispensed with conscience she becomes just rewards, though they go beyond the limits of earned wages. The king would have justice, honor, integrity rewarded with the goods of the world, and would have falsehood, flattery, venality stripped of the meed which they too frequently and too easily acquire on earth. This is his purely human and ethical and worldly analysis of the opposition of ideal and actual, and this the solution he proposes. *Prima facie* it seems admirable.

But Conscience, the probing, speculative, visionary moral center of the human soul, has "cam late fro biȝunde." With the eyes of Grace he sees deeper than the king and, significantly, rejects the proposed marriage, which the king's prudence had seen as a reasonable method of controlling earthly rewards, of forestalling the deadly alliance between *munera* and venal officialdom. Conscience, mindful of the ideal of apostolic poverty and of the injunction "gratis accepistis, gratis date," perceives the subtle entanglements of the soul which may arise from even the most honorable of gifts in the highest of causes. At the beginning of the episode Lady Meed was introduced as the natural enemy of Christian loyalty; now she is pictured as naturally destructive of the Christian conscience. In even their most innocent form this world's goods can provide a distraction to the conscience, cloud the human vision ever so slightly, cause ever so small a precession in the judgment, just enough perhaps, to give *entrée* to Mammon. The king is falling victim to the subtle snare. In this manner Langland re-examines the problem of the Christian and the World, a crux ever since the Fathers of a growing Church had been forced to acknowledge the limited applicability of the ideal of apostolic poverty. Saint Jerome had recognized both the necessity of gifts and the danger that they might taint the receiver, "lest... we be called, not indeed thieves ourselves, but the companions of thieves" (cf. p. 28 above). The infiltration of feudalism into the Church, and later papal taxation, had brought the problem to the attention of the satirists, who labelled such taxes simony. Consequently too the twelfth-century Petrus Cantor described the acceptance of permissible gifts as "dangerous... because by that we sell our liberty" (cf. p. 134 above). Conscience's clear insight comes close to the ethical center of all medieval satire on money's power.

Hence Conscience, recognizing the subtly corrupting effects of worldly goods, indignantly rejects the marriage with Meed in a long speech which climaxes the Meed episode. Here Langland summarizes more fully and directly than elsewhere the devastation wrought by *munera*, and his summary is constructed largely of the commonplaces of the satirical theme. The passage is the closest approach in *Piers Plowman* to the *munera* or *nummus* litanies of the earlier Latin satirists. Conscience attacks in turn all the traditional objects of venality-satire, and some not regularly a part of the tradition. Rome fittingly comes first:

> [Mede] hath apoysounde popis   and peired holicherche;
> . . . .
> For she is priue with the pope   prouisoures it knoweth,
> For sire symonye and hir-selue   seleth hire bulles.
>   (III, 127, 146-147)

The other clergy follow:

>   She blesseth thise bisshopes   thei3e they be lewed,
> Prouendreth persones   and prestes meynteneth,
> To haue lemmannes and lotebies   alle here lif-dayes
>   (III, 148-150)

In accord with Langland's own feelings, Conscience devotes more attention to the venality of the law than to that of the others:

> Bi Iesu, with here ieweles   3owre iustices she shendeth,
> And lith a3ein the lawe   and letteth hym the gate,
> That feith may nou3te haue his forth   here floreines go so thikke.
> . . . .
> Lawe is so lordeliche   and loth to make ende,
> With-oute presentz or pens   she pleseth wel fewe.
>   (III, 154-161)

The king's officers as well as those of the church courts are Meed's servants:

> Sisoures and sompnoures   suche men hir preiseth;
> Shireues of shires   were shent 3if she nere;
> For she doth men lese here londe   and here lyf bothe.
> She leteth passe prisoneres   and payeth for hem ofte,
> And gyueth the gailers golde   and grotes togideres,
> To vnfettre the fals   fle where hym lyketh;
> And taketh the trewe bi the toppe   and tieth hym faste,
> And hangeth hym for hatred   that harme dede neure.
>   (III, 133-140)

Other familiar conventional ideas appear in the speech. Meed, for example, is an instrument of seduction (III, 124-125), and never fears the curse of the consistory courts (III, 141-142). Langland, like Chaucer, Bromyard, and others of his century hated the application of the "pecuniary penalty."

At this point in the C-Text Langland reminds his readers of the distinction between *meed* and *mercede*. Mercede is clearly wages, or recompense for work done,

> As a leel laborer   that by-leuyth with hus maistre
> In hus paye and in hys pyte   and in hus pure treuthe,
> To paye hym yf he performeth   and haue pyte yf he faylleth,
> And take hym for hus trauaile   al that treuthe wolde.
> (C-Text, IV, 350-353)

But meed has a boundless, indeterminate quality, is unrelated to accomplishment, to work done. It is the indiscriminate scattering of pelf, the random feeding of the bottomless pit of avarice,

> inliche to coueyte
> To a-corde in alle kyndes   and in alle kynne numbre,
> With-oute cost and care   in alle kynne trauaile,
> With-oute resoun to rewarde   nauȝt recching of the peple.
> (C-Text, IV, 373-376)

Langland's long distinction at this point is clearly a conscious application or affirmation of the distinction of legists and canonists between money paid for knowledge and money paid for the laborer's hire. The term *mercede* itself echoes the *merces* of the canonists and of St. Luke.

This, then, is the ideological framework within which Meed and her entourage act out their tableaux of venality, dumb-shows which adumbrate the vital satirical content of the episode. Langland uses the larger framework, which involves the question of Meed's dual nature and that of the choice of a lord for Meed, to present the problem in casuistry which surrounded all venality:

how can the necessity for material returns, for the things of this world, be reconciled to the spiritual posture which Reason and Conscience demand of the Christian? How, in other words, can the Christian in public life escape the taint of the World, and thus achieve salvation for himself and happiness for his society? More fundamentally, how can the Christian adjudicate between the demands of body and soul? This is the problem with which the Fathers and the later moralists had wrestled, and which did most to produce the dominant tone of the medieval money-satirists; but none of the earlier satire had succeeded in presenting its subtleties and complexities as well as Langland's allegory of the King, Meed, False, and Conscience. The remainder of *Piers Plowman* is almost wholly devoted to the solution of this basic problem of Christian civilization.

The framework of the Meed episode, then, is the fundamental problem of the relationship of the City of God to the City of Man, an image or echo of the foundation-problem of *Piers Plowman* as a whole. The detail within the framework is largely the commonplace material of the conventional satire on venality. Meed's chief retainers are Simony and Civil. Simony—who had been personified as early as the eleventh century—is official venality in general rather than ecclesiastical corruption in particular, in agreement with the general suspicion that all venality in high station was a sort of simony. His companion, Civil, represents the characteristically scheming and venal lawyer. These and other abstractions are mingled promiscuously with flesh-and-blood individuals from traditionally venal groups.

Meed herself is masterfully drawn in her ambiguity. At first sight (except during her climactic argument with Conscience) she seems a passive, complacent, almost dependent figure. When we first meet her she is entirely in the control of her companions and retainers, Favel, Guile, Liar, Simony and Civil. Later she makes no attempt to escape the king's officers, but waits to be seized, trembling in her apparent helplessness. This is an excellent touch. She is obsequious to the king, quite ready to glaze her confessor's window, perfectly willing to marry Conscience at the king's behest. She refuses no one his desires. But this is the very nature of her whoredom, her *modus operandi*. As Conscience puts it, she is

> As comune as a cartway   to eche a knaue that walketh,
> To monkes, to mynstralles   to meseles in hegges.
> (III, 131-132)

Her indiscriminate pliability whether for good or for evil constitutes her true danger to the soul of man and to society in general. She is anybody's friend. This had been noticed by earlier satirists:

> Nummus mendicus,   nunquam comes, omnis amicus.[4]

> Denier ne garde où il descent;
> Si plus mauvès l'a plus sovent.[5]

Meed—who is one of the rewards of fortune—is as amoral and unstable in her affections as *Fortuna* herself. She reflects perfectly the economic amorality of the money economy which Langland so detested. Her passivity, however, is deceptive. When she falls into the custody of the king that very passivity or compliance becomes her tactical weapon. Meed corrupts, as Conscience well knows. Her charms are sufficient to attract a throng of admirers from the lawyers, judges and clergy, the traditionally venal groups of medieval satire:

> They that wonyeth in Westmynstre   worschiped hir alle;
> Gentelliche with ioye   the iustices somme

---

[4] Yunck, "*The Carmen de nummo* of Godfrey of Cambrai," *Duquesne University Studies Annuale Mediaevale*, II (1961), 78. Cf. p. 171 above.

[5] Wright, *Mapes*, p. 357. Cf. p. 214 above.

> Busked hem to the boure   there the birde dwelled,
> To conforte hire kyndely   by clergise leue. . . .
> (III, 12-15)

The debased part of political and sacerdotal mankind rush to curry Favel, or to woo Meed.

"The prince of darkness," said Shakespeare's Edgar, "is a gentleman." Likewise Meed, his minion, is ever the courtly lady, politely friendly to all who offer their admiration, and willing to help whom she can. Her conduct would have graced any of the courtly romances:

> Mildeliche Mede thanne   mercyed hem alle
> Of theire gret goodnesse   and gaf hem vchone
> Coupes of clene golde   and coppis of siluer,
> Rynges with rubies   and ricchesses manye,
> The leste man of here meyne   a motoun of golde.
> (III, 20-24)

Just so had the corrupt Gaufroi established his position at court in the romance of *Bauduin de Sebourc* (cf. pp. 216-219 above). Meed now assures the clerks who comfort her that their names shall be called in consistory:

> Shal no lewdnesse lette   the leode that I louye,
> That he ne worth first auanced   for I am biknowen
> There konnyng clerkes   shul clokke bihynde.
> (III, 32-34)

The victory of *munera* over *scientia* in the race for ecclesiastical advancement had been lamented from the very beginning of medieval satire. Egbert of Liège's *Pecunia* had easily dispatched *Sophia* (cf. p. 63 above). Amarcius had commented on it:

> Cur rarus nunc est sapiens?   quia blanda videntur
> Ocia proque libris sectatur fenora quisque,
> Tractat non secum: tu tantum collige quod des,
> Munera stultus amat,   sapientem munera mulcent.[6]

---

[6] *Sermones*, III, vii, 896-899. Cf. p. 66 above.

The cry had become a great chorus in the twelfth century, especially when applied to advancement at Rome:

> Si venit ante fores bona vita, scientia, mores,
> Non exauditur; si nummus, mox aperitur.[7]

Few ideas were more popular among the venality-satirists than
this victory of pelf over learning. The dread charge that Money
was the measure of Man joined that of the simoniac sale of the
donum Dei as a central part of the satirical theme.

Thus Meed seduces the lawyers and the clerks, the two learned
groups of the king's court, who at that very time should have
been investigating her misdeeds. Her confession to the venal
friar is a part of that subversion. By offering to help build the
friar's church she extends her influence, and in return for her
gifts she expects the confessor to deal lightly with "lordes that
lechery haunteth." Besides its literal meaning, this lechery is
probably (as it often appears to be in the Old Testament) a figure
of the love of worldly rewards which the courtship of Meed herself represents,[8] for it leads to a digression depicting Meed as
the patroness of small-scale municipal graft. The author describes
the frauds which break loose among unscrupulous tradesmen when
Meed has corrupted the city officials whose duty it is to guard
against such acts:

---

[7] I. Zingerle, "Sterzinger Miscellaneen-Handschrift, "*Wiener Sitzungsberichte*
LIV (1866), 314–315. Cf. p. 95 above. This was, one recalls, a favorite complaint of Walter of Châtillon; and before Walter, Petrus Pictor had sung it in
his "Cur ultra studeam":
> Artes scire bonas nunc pro nichilo reputatur,
> Nummos scire bonos hoc praevalet, hocque probatur;
> Hoc hodie studium deducitur absque labore:
> Quod quicumque tenet, hic sublimatur honore. etc.
Printed by Werner, *Beiträge*, pp. 139–140.

[8] Cf. Robertson and Huppé, p. 59, n.2.

Ac Mede the mayde   the maire hath bisouȝte,
Of alle such sellers   syluer to take,
Or presentz with-oute pens   as peces of siluer,
Ringes or other ricchesse   the regrateres to maynetene.
    'For my loue,' quod that lady   'loue hem vchone,
And soffre hem to selle   somdele aȝeins resoun.'
                                  (III, 87-92)

This attention to municipal graft is a relatively new element in
the satirical theme. It can be found in Gower,[9] for example, but
the older clerical satirists ignore it. Their interests did not extend
to such activity, even if urban society had developed sufficiently
to provide them with material, nor did this type of small-scale
corruption strike them as qualitatively the same as the sale of the
gifts of God. Yet Langland's attention to the scoundrels, swindlers
and shysters of the lesser world, mingling with his allegorical
abstractions, is one of the chief elements in *Piers Plowman's* remarkable flavor of earthy realism.

When Conscience attacks Meed in the presence of the king,
she replies with three sophistical devices: an open appeal to the
king's lower self-interest, a deliberate blurring of the distinction
between meed and wages, and the misquoting of scripture out
of context. All three of these arguments suggest the power of
material gain to obscure honest reasoning, the subtle distortion
which worldly goods introduce into the public man's rational
processes. The human conscience has a difficult battle against
the wordly spirit. Meed's next opportunity to work in her characteristic manner comes during the argument between Peace and
Wrong, which involves the unpleasant spectacle of Meed conquer-
ing the principles of the victim himself (IV, 47-109). Meed not
only enslaves her own special devotees among clergy and officials,
but overcomes the complaints of the loyal and peaceful commons,

---

[9] *Mirour de l'omme*, 25237-26604. In *Works*, I, 279-295.

so that they participate in the destruction of the very principles designed to protect them. Peace, pathetically, is satisfied with his gold:

> For Mede hath made me amendes   I may namore axe.
> (IV, 103)

Wrong fails to escape only because the king has subjected himself wholly to the guidance of Reason and Conscience.

Meed makes a final effort to avoid expulsion from the king's court. Attacked by both Reason and Conscience, shunned by the better people of the court, she turns to the lawyers, who are always her favorites:

> For I seiʒe Mede in the moot-halle   on men of lawe wynke,
> And thei lawghyng lope to hire   and lafte Resoun manye.
> (IV, 152-153)

But in the end Meed retains the devotion only of her most stubborn followers: the venal confessors, the men of law, a juryman, a summoner, and a sheriff's clerk.

These die-hard devotees of Meed are conventional enough, though some of them do not come to the attention of satirists until the fourteenth century. In the earlier satire deans and subdeacons bore alone the opprobrium which they later share with the summoners. The summoner himself was usually concealed under the general title, "officiales episcoporum." The "shireues clerke" who mourns the paucity of meed in his office is the true descendant, on a lower level, of the notaries of the papal and royal courts attacked by earlier satirists. They had received attention in the thirteenth century, seated in court at the feet of the judge:

> Ad pedes sedent clerici,
> Qui velut famelici
>   sunt, donis inhiantes;

> et pro lege dantes,
> Quod hii qui nichil dederint,
> Quamvis cito venerint
> Erunt expectantes.[10]

Meed's flesh-and-blood followers, then, emphasize the conventional elements of the satirical theme

> As sysours and sompnours   shireues and here clerkes,
> Bedelles and bailliues   and brokoures of chaffare,
> Forgoeres and vitaillers   and vokates of the arches. . .
>   (II, 58-60)

Her most slavish followers become mounts for the journey to Westminster: sheriffs, assizors, summoners, provisors, deans and subdeans, archdeacons and diocesan officials (cf. p. 7 above). Thus Meed's human followers bear the burden of the evil personified in her retinue: Fals and Favel, Meed herself, Simony and Civil.

These abstractions present no difficulty. Among the most interesting are "One Waryn Wisdom and Witty his fere" (IV, 26), who go to Westminster at the same time as Reason, of whom they are perversions. They are excellent foils for Reason, for though they are superficially like him they represent something near his opposite. If the end of Reason is Truth, the end of Wisdom and Witty is Success and Acceptance. They are the genius, intelligence and wit of the trained mind applied to worldly gain or advancement without regard for spiritual obligations and they personify a timeless phenomenon, intellect diverted from its end, sophisticated and corrupted by infinite acquisitiveness. Like many of Langland's villains they appear as lawyers of the *grand monde*, so vividly drawn that they seem to be flesh-and-blood. They are worldly, clever, deft, cynical, adept at smoothing their paths with meed in exchequer and chancery. They dwell with Meed, as Conscience explains, and

[10] Wright, *Political Songs*, p. 226.

> There as wratthe and wranglyng is there wynne thei siluer. . . .
>
> (IV, 34)

They take no stand on principle. When Wrong is in trouble they warn him not to be bold, but

> To make his pees with his pens handi-dandi payed.
>
> (IV, 75)

Their wisdom is the sly and unctuous prudence of the World the technique of the greased palm. They question, for example, the king's severe justice with Wrong. If a man makes (pecuniary) amends, bail should have him and the injury be forgotten. Wisdom is unrepentant and remains to the end one of Meed's adherents, expressing his sentiments with the slippery jocoseness of the hardened grafter:

> Waryn Wisdome wynked vppon Mede,
> And seide, 'Madame, I am ȝowre man what so my mouth
> iangleth;
> I falle in floreines,' quod that freke 'an faile speche ofte.'
>
> (IV, 154-156)

This cynical pledge of allegiance recalls characters out of the older satire, like the pope of the *Tractatus Garsiae* or the suave cardinals of Walter of Châtillon's "Propter Sion non tacebo."

The Meed episode, then, unifies the venality-satire of the whole poem. It strengthens the impact of other scattered passages, comments on their meaning, and above all underscores the centrality of the problem of *munera* to Christian public life. As the enemy and opposite of Holy Church, Lady Meed is the social embodiment of Antichrist. But despite the traditional nature of the episode's theme, characters and imagery, Langland has made certain changes in emphasis. His references to papal venality and episcopal simony, for example, are brief, almost perfunctory, as if he were merely paying his respects to the truth of the convention. Langland is not really interested in these groups, but in the efflorescence of venality on the lower levels of officialdom. In every instance he emphasizes the official venality which impinges directly on the average man, the poor but loyal subject. Hence his fierce contempt for venal lawyers, who with the help of corrupt judges and jurymen keep justice forever out of reach of the poor. Pope and Curia receive little abuse, but visiting cardinals, whose luxury must be supported by poor parishes, are attacked. Simoniac bishops are barely noticed, but priests who run to London for an easy chantry are specifically denounced. The notaries of the royal court are untouched, but sheriffs' clerks appear repeatedly in Meed's retinue. The expenses of clerical appeals to Rome go unmentioned, but the activities of archdeacons, deans and summoners, whose courts persecute the poor and turn fornication into graft, receive full attention. Langland also focuses on the relatively new profession of pardoner, the latest swindler in the religious life of the parish.

Nor are these abuses the special problems of the poor priest, though Langland was apparently a clerk. They are the problems of the poor layman, whether peasant or citizen. The theme has been wholly secularized in *Piers Plowman*. What had begun in the eleventh century as clerical property has become in Langland's poem an outcry, instinctively conservative, of the loyal commons against the corruption of venal officialdom, whether secular or ecclesiastical, and against a world dominated by money or meed which causes that corruption. It is the voice of the Common Christian Man crying in the economic wilderness. An important part of that cry is the protest against the venal oppression of the poor. Thus, though Meed herself has had her forerunners, though her unsavory retinue—pardoners, sheriffs and their clerks, beadles, bailiffs, advocates and legists of all sorts, officials of the church courts, friars and other clergy of every rank, assizers, false jailors, provisors and tradesmen, judges and notaries—though this retinue contains the traditionally venal figures of the satirical theme, Langland has radically shifted the emphasis to depict official venality as it showed its face to the impoverished layman.

This shift of emphasis, this broadening and secularization of the theme, is not, as we have seen, wholly original with Langland. It appears in the sermons of the period and in some of the earlier English verse; it was probably in the air in the second half of the fourteenth century. Nevertheless, Langland enriched the development through the subtlety, complexity and palpableness of his allegorical analysis. Langland's ability (like Bunyan's) to naturalize his abstractions to the English countryside is most striking. His is one of the rare allegories which encourages us to visualize the action. Most allegory takes place in the land of faerie, in a green world beyond some stream where no reader expects to stumble on gross humanity. Even *Fauvel*, which perforce deals with gross elements, maintains its unreality and lack of locus: a carelessly visualized court in which brittle figures of nobility and clergy curry a misplaced circus-horse. This, like other allegories, has the characteristics of a charade, a curious groundlessness, a lack of foundation, of firmament. No one tries to believe in the composite horse, in his court, in his grotesque interview with Fortune, in his even more grotesque marriage to Vainglory. Other allegories are even more unreal. No one feels the urge to visualize the tears of Architrenius, the elaborate love-warfare of the *Roman de la rose*, or the journeys of Deguilleville's pilgrim. One merely translates the material into its didactic terms; and it is difficult to believe that the medieval reader, whatever his sense of symbol, did otherwise. But in Langland's bold compound of flesh and allegory the confused scenes virtually force themselves upon our vision, like Breughel paintings or Hogarth prints. His allegorical abstractions are mingled pell-mell with very palpable rascals, and in the mingling take on some of their flesh:

Meed laughing and winking with the Westminster lawyers, Liar going his way from pardoners to physicians to grocers to minstrels to friars, Simony and Civil appealing their case to Rome. The complementary effect also takes place: the abstractions confer some of their evil universality on the concrete villains, so that the poem achieves in its own way that fusion of concreteness and universality which is the essence of all important literature. Nor does this mixture of flesh and abstraction damage the coherence of the episodes. The effect is rather the opposite, and often results in an emotional density rare in allegory. *Piers Plowman* is undoubtedly guilty of much incoherence, but it is not the result of Langland's peculiar mixture of concrete and abstract.

The best sections of *Piers Plowman*, then, are that very rare achievement, perfectly realized allegory. The personifications are consistent with their types and as tangible and earthy as the common English people who surround them; yet they need no translation into abstract terms to secure their generalized satirical effect. Lady Meed is a wealthy, charming and courtly lady, at home in the highest places of Church and State, but able to mingle gracefully with lesser people, essentially evil but nevertheless attractive and capable, if carefully controlled, of good. Yet we never forget that she is the Power of Money. Most moral allegory can be enjoyed only one way or the other; we must translate *Fauvel* into abstract terms for enjoyment, just as we must forget Spenser's allegory to enjoy the *Faerie Queene*. In the best parts of *Piers Plowman* both aspects please simultaneously; so they do in the Meed episode. Paradoxically, even the kaleidescope confusion of the scenes adds to its realism, and produces a powerful effect of breadth and spaciousness.

Piers Plowman contains as many grotesqueries as less effective allegories. Fauvel, for example, compounded of cardinal sins and placed in a royal court for the admiration of the great, is no more grotesque than Langland's reversal of the figure, where sheriffs, assizers, flatterers, summoners, and others are saddled as mounts for Meed, Simony, Civil, and their retinue. Yet the one is strained and artificial, while the other pulses with the blood of English life. Where most earlier venality-satire, both Latin and vernacular, repeatedly fell into static recitation or moralizing, with long, arid stretches of iteration, the Meed episode is filled with a feverish activity and bustle which accurately reflects the busyness of meed-fever—a truly dramatic movement which sweeps the reader along with it. Even the disputation between Meed and Conscience is permeated with the tension of a courtroom situation. It is not surprising that Meed left her mark on the theme, that Skelton rediscovered her and Spenser revived her as Lady Munera.

The problem of Langland's immediate source and inspiration remains unsolved. One is inclined to agree with Owst that the sermons of the day played the largest part in the literary background of Lady Meed. Langland's personification of fiscal corruption, the groups against whom his satire is directed, even some of his imagery, are common in sermon as well as learned satire, and with particular liveliness in mendicant preaching. On the evidence of sermon-books themselves it seems likely that preaching was the most important single factor in popularizing themes long confined to learned satire or to handbooks of moral instruction. The contemporary drama has also been suggested as a source or inspiration for the vigorous realism and the vivid, pictorial quality of much of *Piers Plowman*. This too is presently beyond proof. An explanation for the realism seems hardly necessary, for it is one of the most abiding characteristics of the English literary spirit, gradually emerging in the fourteenth century from continental influences. The "earth" of Langland or the mystery plays is not much different in kind from the earth of Chaucer, or Skelton, or Greene, or Shakespeare, or Sterne, or many other English writers, early and late. *Piers Plowman*, plays, and sermons are of the same atmosphere, and expressions of the same spirit.

Despite unevenness, surface-incoherence, and walking abstractions, *Piers Plowman* forcefully maintains the illusion of reality. In the Meed episode and similar scenes we find, not God's plenty, but the devil's, gatherings of antic rascals mingled with the deadly sins themselves and their offspring. Langland is humorless, except for some displays of the crabbed humor of the stern preacher; but he makes his moral earnestness powerfully persuasive, and n the end evokes a portion of the English spirit as vividly real as any in literature.

TWO

THE CONTINUITY OF THE THEME AFTER *Piers Plowman*

With *Piers Plowman* the medieval tradition of venality-satire may be said to have reached its culmination. There was nothing new to say, and to say the old commonplaces in new ways required literary modes and techniques little practiced in the Middle Ages. Hence—though all *termini* in literary history are arbitrary and often misleading—it seems wise to close our study with the year 1400. The old style of satire on human venality did not, of course, vanish at that date; even Latin compositions on the theme continued to be written. A fifteenth-century German poet, for example, asks his reader to suppose himself the master of all knowledge: the seven arts, theology, medicine, necromancy, alchemy, and law. The portrait he draws is that of a veritable Doctor Faustus. Yet, without money all this would avail nothing:

> in omnibus scientiis
> si sis magister summus

sentencus [sententiosus?]
illud juro certissimus
hoc totum nauci proderit
si tibi de est nummus.[11]

Another poet of the fifteenth century writes verses in hymn-stanzas, in the form of a debate between himself, as a preacher against the sin of avarice, and the avaricious public. He opens with a parody of the Athanasian Creed:

Quincunque vult salvus esse
Ut contempnat est necesse
Crimen avaricie.

But the reply of the avaricious is the common parody appeal to the *crux denarii*:

Nos oportet gloriari
In cruce nummi domini.

To the author's advice to give freely, for the Lord loves a cheerful giver, they can only reply, "Dilige denarium." Their paean in praise of money is thoroughly familiar:

O quam felix, quam amena
Opulenta fit crumena
Et nummorum copia!
Ubi nummi ibi census,
Ubi amor ibi sensus,
Ibi pax et gloria.

In this manner the debate continues for an even dozen stanzas.[12]

Vernacular venality-satire continued to be produced in large volume; the cult of the Almighty Penny remained especially

---

[11] O. Kernstock, "Mittelalterliche Liedercompositionen," *Anzeiger für Kunde der deutschen Vorzeit*, XXIV (1877), 72. The poem may well be as early as the fourteenth century. The bracketed conjecture is Kernstock's.

[12] W. Wattenbach, "Lateinische Reime des Mittelalters, IX," *Anzeiger für Kunde der deutschen Vorzeit*, XVIII (1871), 130–131.

popular. In Germany, for example, verses like this imitation or echo of Vintler's penny-verse were being written:

> Her pfenning, was ir wunder thut! ir seyt ain tayl zw wert. . . .

Sir Penny, what wonders you perform! You are a bit too valuable. I am sorry that the world desires you so greedily. You are preferred to the counsel of the wise; you take the place of high lords. You donate churches, monasteries, and many a chaplain; you have greatly damaged the honor of beautiful women, etc.[13]

Around 1440 Hans Rosenplüt, the popular writer of *Sprüche* and *Fastnachtspiele*, conceived a similar long *Spruch* on the pfennig:

> Nun sweigt so wil ich heben an
> Was der pfennig wunders kan
> Der pfennig kan wurcken vnd schaffen
> Mit leyen vnd auch mit pfaffen. . . .

Quiet now, while I set out to tell what wonders Penny can perform. The penny can produce and work with laymen and also with priests. As long as man has lived, there lives no order on earth who does not always love penny, be he a murderer or a thief. If you wish to corrupt someone, you should have many pennies: though his sorrow be deep, the penny makes all right. The penny makes great feasts, pennies are always good guests, etc.[14]

---

[13] I. Zingerle, "Bericht über die Wiltener Meistersänger-handschrift," *Wiener Sitzungsberichte*, XXXVII (1849), 378–379.

[14] H. Keller, *Fastnachtspiele aus dem fünfzehnten Jahrhundert* (Bibliothek des litterarischen Vereins, XXVII–XXX, Stuttgart, 1853), III, 1183. The reference to *Pfenning* as a wonder-worker, with which so many of the poems begin, seems to have developed into something like a heroic epithet. We have it, for example, in proverb-form:

> Von dem pfenning sagt ein man
> Was er wunders machen kan.

Printed in Keller, *Fastnachtspiele*, III, 1437.

Sir Penny also came into his own in England and Scotland during the fifteenth and early sixteenth centuries, in a number of short poems, some of them carols, no different in tone or content from similar earlier satires in other vernaculars:

> Peny is an hardy knyght;
> Peny is mekyl of myght;
> Peny, of wrong he makyt ryght
> In euery cuntre qwer he goo.[15]

Two of them, carols with refrains ending in "Gramersy myn owyn purs," are interesting parallels to a fifteenth-century Welsh *cywydd* by Sion Cent, whose stanzas end with the identical refrain: "Fy mhwrs, gormersi am hyn."[16] The sixteenth century produced, too, Barnfield's Lady Pecunia and Spenser's Lady Munera, both modeled on Langland's Lady Meed.

It may be mentioned parenthetically that the traditions of venality-satire did not escape the attention of the graphic artists of the Renaissance. A single example will suggest the sort of material in which the theme occurs. In Holbein's famous woodcuts of the Dance of Death, published in Lyons in 1538, the prints of Death overtaking the judge and the advocate catch both these men in the traditional venality of their professions. The judge is accepting a bribe from a wealthy litigant while his poor opponent

---

[15] R. Greene, *Early English Carols* (Oxford, 1935), p. 261. I have dealt with these fifteenth-century English and Scotch penny-poems in "Dan Denarius: the Almighty Penny and the Fifteenth Century Poets," *American Journal of Economics and Sociology*, XX (1961), 207-222. The reader is referred to this paper for further examples and bibliography.

[16] The English carols are printed in Greene, *Early English Carols*, pp. 260–263, and the Welsh *cywydd* in H. Lewis, T. Roberts, and I. Williams, *Cywyddau Iolo Goch ac Eraill* (Wales University Press, 1937), pp. 259–261. I am indebted to my colleague, Professor W.W. Heist, for calling my attention to Sion Cent's poem.

stands forlornly and helplessly aside.   Likewise the advocate is
absorbed in accepting a fee from a wealthy client while a mournful
poor man in the background is unable to attract his attention.
The print of Death and the cardinal may also involve venality,
but is ambiguous. It seems clear that Holbein was more interested
in secular venality.

The seventeenth century saw Rowley's personification of *Mon-
sieur l'Argent* in his *Search for Money*, Jordan's comedy, *Money
is an Ass*, and Meriton's (?) *Pecuniae Obediunt Omnia*, among others.
Sir Penny remained a literary hero in Spain, where Quevedo
(1580-1645) chose as the refrain for one of his satirical *Letrillas*
the apparently proverbial personification, "Poderoso caballero es
don Dinero."[17]   There are undoubtedly a great many similar
satires in the old manner in other vernacular literatures of seventeenth and eighteenth-century Europe. The venal or extortionist
villain, too, grew naturally with the growth of prose fiction.
The theme is eternally popular.

Yet, though the evil of venality is as timeless as the struggle
between man's spiritual ideals and his acquisitive instincts, there
was an unmistakable change in the problem's significance after
the close of the Middle Ages, and a consequent relaxation in
the satire which concerned it. With the growing secularization
of society, the broad expansion of a money economy, the fading
of the personal relationship as the foundation of social organization, the decline of the sacramental view of the world and the
sacerdotal view of learning, the decay of the concept of political
and intellectual eminence as *dona Dei* with responsibilities incom-
mensurate with economic reward—with these changes, venality-

---

[17] F. de Quevedo y Villegas, *Obras*, III, 93-94 (*Biblioteca de Autores Españoles*,
LXIX, Madrid, 1926). I am indebted to my colleague, Professor Donald Yates,
for calling my attention to Quevedo's poem. Quevedo wrote other *Letrillas*
on the subject, e.g., "La pobreza—El dinero," *Obras*, III, 88.

satire lost much of its centrality and tautness, and the satirists themselves much of the profound sense of outrage which had once been kindled by the vision of venal officialdom eternally involved in a repartition of the garments of Christ.

THREE

THE IMPORT AND SIGNIFICANCE OF THE MEED-THEME

The literary lineage of Lady Meed, then, is a long one, and leaves no doubts of that affable maiden's significance to the soul of man in the Middle Ages. Our lengthy examination of her forebears in satire has made it abundantly clear that venality seemed to the medieval moralist a far more radical and desperate evil than twentieth-century "graft" or fiscal corruption has seemed to most of its enemies. Revolutions in economic attitudes are of course a matter of history. Since the death of Langland much of the civilized world has accepted the profit-motive as a not unwholesome spring of human action. We are on speaking terms, at least, with Economic Man. Yet the difference lies deeper than these shifts in attitude would suggest. To the medieval satirist *munera* was not merely a sin among sins. Saint Paul had described avarice as the root of all evil, and *munera* was its classic expression in organized society. Lady Meed was indeed the polar opposite of Holy Church, her eternal enemy; the dramatic structure of *Piers Plowman* at this point is profoundly meditated. Though we have touched repeatedly in our study on the significant reasons for this deeply-felt revulsion from the crime of *munera*, a brief retrospective survey may serve to emphasize the unity of vision which lay behind the vast accumulation of satire.

For the Christian Middle Ages the problem was profoundly rooted—as we suggested at the beginning of our study—in the dual nature of man. It presented itself to the Christendom of the Fathers chiefly in the form of the Old Testament passages on *munera* which served to establish the term's meaning as "bribes" or "corrupting gifts" for all the Middle Ages. *Munera* was no abstract problem to the Fathers, faced with providing the material necessities for an organized Church, one of whose chief teachings was *contemptus mundi*. Baptism was not only a spiritual rebirth, but a very real renunciation of the things of the world under certain aspects. Nevertheless the young Church, composed of men, needed to live. To the Fathers this problem was one manifestation of an essential Christian paradox: man's dual nature, corruptible body and immortal soul. More deeply, this was an image of the sacramental paradox—Body and Blood as Bread and Wine—and even of the most sacred of all paradoxes, God as Man. For the public life of the Church the paradox was stated in those two closely-yoked admonitions of Christ to his apostles: "Gratis accepistis, gratis date," and "Dignus est enim operarius cibo suo" (Luke: "mercede sua"). Throughout the Middle Ages the problem of avoiding the guilt of *munera* was fundamentally the problem of mediating between these two admonitions.

When, in the mid-eleventh century, a reviving culture began once again to produce social satire, the problem of *munera* was making itself felt most strongly in the form of simony. The battle of the papacy against the the simoniac bishops was becoming a large-scale conflict. Most of the simony, one recalls, resulted from the infiltration of the reigning economic system—feudalism—into the Church, so that ecclesiastical sees and benefices had frequently become, as feudal fiefs, the pawns of secular policy. The Church found herself unfree: the Bride of Christ was prostituted to worldliness. This is the tenor of the earliest satire on simoniac bishops, and the rallying cry of the battle carried on by the papacy from Leo IX to Innocent III. The freedom of the Church meant essentially freedom from feudal infiltration. Herein there is also a paradox, for economic feudalism had almost certainly first appeared to the Church as her protector and temporal guarantor, the enfiefment of the Church with feudal lands as the condition which liberated her from secular control. By the eleventh century, however, ecclesiastical feudalism had begun to seem to the popes much like one of the subtler destructive kindnesses of Lady Meed. The images of Simon Magus and Giezi filled the satires, and the saints Albinus and Rufinus were bitterly invoked as the most powerful intercessors for those who wished advancement in the Church.

History, however, is rich in ironies. The price of the Church's freedom from feudalism was centralization, intensely increased papal activity in controlling ecclesiastical affairs, the assumption of responsibility in provincial problems, devices which are sometimes castigated today as "big government." All this was extremely expensive, and the Papacy quickly discovered that its activity had far outgrown its traditional revenues. Papal Rome had burst its own feudal economic confines. The only resource of the popes was to develop their rudimentary and informal system of ecclesiastical taxation well beyond its former scope, and hence to become unwitting leaders of an economic revolution which was to issue in the destruction of feudalism. Well before the time when these taxes were defined and formalized the higher clergy throughout Europe began to feel their painful effects. Imperial publicists were quick to describe these developments as papal simony, and satirists began to take up the ancient cry of Juvenal: "Omnia Romae cum pretio." In a few decades papal simony and venality became the chief subject of the venality-satirists, and such they remained throughout the Middle Ages: Peter was deposed, cried the satirists, and Simon, Giezi, Judas, and Mammon reigned. This long-lived pre-eminence of Rome among the venality-satirists resulted partly from tradition, partly from continued financial pressure which kept the papacy hunting for new revenue until the Reformation, and partly from the sheer exasperation of conservative moralists at policies which outraged their sense of the sacredness of the *donum Dei*.

The centralization of ecclesiastical control and the new fiscality of papal Rome produced similar effects in all parts of the Church. New financial policies in the Curia meant new financial policies in diocese and hence in parish. Clerical efforts to raise money became more intense, and complaints of the sale of prebends by bishops and sacraments by priests began once again to increase in volume. It seems certain that the diocesan courts began to turn increasingly to the application of fines—the "pecunyal peyne," as Chaucer called them—in order to raise more revenue. These financial moves in diocese and parish produced a new sense of outrage and new outbursts of protest from the satirists. The disease—as they liked to explain—had communicated itself from Rome, the head, to the members. By the middle of the twelfth century the satirical chorus attacking clerical venality from Rome at the top down to the least sacrament-selling vicar had reached enormous volume.

But already economic feudalism was in full retreat, though this fact was certainly not apparent to medieval observers. One of the earliest indications of the breakdown was a tendency to commute feudal services or payments in kind to payments in cash; and this was well under way before the close of the twelfth century. Though the structure long remained, these commutations attacked the spiritual heart of feudalism. The forces which had helped cause this change to cash payments were also at work in other ways. Trade had increased rapidly from the beginning of the eleventh century, and with this increase had come the rapid growth of cities—often built around cathedral towns—and the increased circulation of money. Royal courts—frequently allied with the new burghers—increased in complexity, and their rulers did not ignore the lessons to be learned from ecclesiastical taxation:

> Dant populis reges nova iura, novas quoque leges,
> Census ut ipsorum crescat novitate malorum.[18]

For example, kings soon learned that the knighting of a man of wealth made some of that wealth available to them in commutation of the knightly obligations to society. We need not attempt to trace this complex development. It is sufficient to suggest that with these events the satirists began to find themselves in the wilderness of economic impersonality which a money economy introduces into social organization. Honor was becoming dependent on the power of money, and the ordering of life a function or adjunct of cash payments:

> Cesar, reges, marchiones,
> Duces, comites et barones,
> Omnes principes terrarum
> Possident de fide parum.
> Inter omnes vix est unus,
> Qui non respicit ad munus,
> Et iusticiam transponunt
> Pro eis qui munera donunt.[19]

Hence the repeated satirical cry that wealth was the transmuter of all values and the gauge of all success, that money was the measure of man. One of the favorite—and most easily managed—devices for expressing this complaint was the extended litany

---

[18] C. Fierville, "Notices et extraits des manuscrits de la Bibliothèque de Saint-Omer," *Notices et extraits des manuscrits*, XXX, i (1884), 149. This verse was written ca. 1316.

[19] W. Wattenbach, *Monumenta Lubensia*, p. 28. A variant version is printed by Du Méril, *Poésies populaires latines du moyen âge*, p. 141.

on the powers of *nummus* or *munera* or *aurum* or *pecunia* or some similar symbol or personification of wealth. The complaints of the satirists were frequently tinged, too, with the self-pity of the poor but learned clerk who looked on in his poverty at the preferment of those (in his own opinion) less qualified but wealthier:

> Artes scire bonas nunc pro nichilo reputatur,
> Nummos scire bonos, hoc prevalet, hocque probatur. . . .
> Est gravius studium bene scribere, versificari,
> Quam nummo nummis, libras libris cumulare
> Aut ex usuris usuras multiplicare.[20]

Or again:

> Soli nummati digni reputantur honore:
> Ingenium, virtus animi absque decore.[21]

Simon Magus was obviously the enemy of learning in distress.

After the twelfth century the history of the venality-theme in satire was that of its gradual broadening to include ever more secular targets, though the clergy themselves did not cease to be heavily satirized. As national governments grew and their taxes increased, they and their officials became increasingly more frequent targets of the satirists. This broadening of the theme was especially rapid in the fourteenth century. Lady Meed's train of attendants and admirers is a characteristic and revealing example.

In a passage quoted at the beginning of this study (p. 2) Lenient described medieval satire as a solvent of older values and a sort of harbinger of modern free thought. If he was referring

---

[20] C. Fierville, "Notices et extraits des manuscrits de la Bibliothèque de Saint–Omer," *Notices et extraits des manuscrits*, XXX, i (1884), 130. This 80–line attack on the venal clergy includes an interesting pun on *arithmetica: aerismetica*, the art of making money and enjoying it, which was replacing the old corner-stone of the quadrivium among the clergy. The verses are an expansion of Petrus Pictor's "Cur ultra studiam."

[21] Werner, *Beiträge*, p. 149.

merely to the destructive effects of the critical spirit his remarks
may be just; but if he was identifying the medieval satirists with
the *avant-garde*, the spirit of innovation and of change for the
sake of novelty, we must conclude that his comments do not
describe the medieval venality-satirists. In the satirists there is
mockery and irony aplenty, occasionally some thoroughgoing
cynicism; but the spirit of innovation was on the side of their
enemies, the clerks and administrators whose fiscal experimentation
was helping to change the economic face of Europe. It must
be confessed, too, that these men were usually unwilling inno-
vators, acting without plan under the pressures of unforseen necessities. The satirists themselves were from the beginning whole-
heartedly reactionary, like the Roman poets who were frequently
their models. Juvenal especially had despised the commercialized
Rome of his day, in which money ruled, class lines were obscured
and the vigorous, newly freed, sycophantic entrepreneur was
carrying the day. Against all of this he preached the Rome of
the Republic and the earlier Kingdom, evoking an image considerably more severe than history would support.

The Roman poets had in their own fashions looked to the
ideal past. Virgil, Horace and Ovid had celebrated the Golden
Age and an early Roman past loosely identified with it, an era
of lean heroism, of stern, vigorous and ascetic idealism, of sparse,
acorn-and-goats'-milk diet, of homespun piety and grave mores.
Likewise the venality-satirist of the Middle Ages was tireless in
contrasting the modern Roman ecclesiastical marketplace with
the Rome of the Fisherman or of Silvester, the reigning pope's
wealth and luxury with Peter's poverty and spirituality, the modest
fish net of Peter with the massive fiscal net of the current papacy.
The fishers of men had become fishers of florins.

Like so much good satire, then, these medieval attacks on venality were marked by a retrospective idealism, a reactionary

utopianism. The utopia implicit in the satires is usually—where its outlines can be determined at all—an idealized feudalism in which class lines do not change, in which popes, bishops and secular rulers live within their customary feudal incomes, in which men's relations to their world are not modified by their wealth or poverty. These writers belabored most vigorously wealth in the form of money, for money's objectivity and impersonality signified the destruction of the system of personal relationships which their ideal assumed. Meed by its nature could not care where it descended; hence meed killed loyalty. The venality-theme was haunted from its Roman beginnings by the ancient vision of a "state of nature"; and in the medieval satirists this state was usually identified with an idealized, static and cashless feudalism. Significantly, William Langland offers as his best solution of social problems on a worldly level the return to a strict observance of feudal class and feudal obligation, to the idealized personal relations which seemed to be disappearing in the universal solvent of meed.

The significance of the venality theme and its centrality as an expression of certain medieval ideals are, then, inescapable. The theme is complex, distilled from a mixture of religious and secular principles not as perfectly compatible as the satirists seemed to think; a mixture of feudalism and the sacramental view of life, of religious idealism and social conservatism. In almost all instances its fundamental assumption is that any kind of venality is a variety of simony, the accursed sale of the gifts of the Holy Ghost. Applied, as it was in its first medieval appearances, to the feudal traffic in episcopacies, prebends and sacraments, this was simple enough. But, ironically, it was then applied to the taxes of a Papacy which sought to extricate the Church from its feudal entanglements, and Rome became celebrated as the headquarters of simony. Further, all learning and talent were *dona Dei*, and their possessors to that extent a sort of priesthood of learning. The lawyer or teacher or doctor who accepted needless fees was betraying the gift, and hence a simonist. Associated with this attitude was the view of the Church as the sacred custodian of the patrimony of the poor, the special guardian of the widow and orphan. This view had been actively expressed in the social theory of the early Church and drew its strength from the Old Testament's repeated assertions of society's special obligations to these unfortunates. The learned man who ignored these special wards of the Church because of their poverty was doubly betraying his sacerdotal function.

If learning, then, like Holy Orders and the other sacraments, was essentially sacramental, meed or lucre, considered as payment for these gifts, was the great anti-sacrament, the destroyer of spirituality, the outward and visible sign of an inward rejection of grace, devilish in a very special and significant sense, far more damning than simple theft or robbery. It was fundamentally an attempt to deny the divine freedom itself, to bind the channels of grace to vulgar commercial transactions. Hence the peculiarly savage anger of the venality-satirist. Meed attacked the divine foundations of all social order, flew in the face of the natural law:

> Hic est nummus   Iudex summus,
> Decretista   et legista
>   abs omni pudore
>
> Justos punit   reos munit
> Dignos sternit   et prosternit
>   et indignos prehonorat.[22]

Though the satirists nowhere said so specifically, they clearly viewed the functions of secular officials as analogically sacramental,

[22] W. Wattenbach, "Aus dem Briefbuche des Meister Simon von Homburg," *Anzeiger für Kunde der deutschen Vorzeit*, XX (1873), 72.

when the venality of these men came under attack. The corrupt bailiff or sheriff was greeted with the same indignation as the simoniac cleric, and implicitly for the same reason.

The idea of the *donum Dei* gave rise to another important cause of venality-satire. Unlike *merces*, *munera* represented payment not for work done or services rendered, but literally for nothing that could be sold. At its most innocent this sort of payment was simple graft, something for nothing. Viewed more severely it was, as we have seen, a fiendish trafficking in the gifts of God. But the very concept of material value unconnected with land or labor was essentially repugnant to most medieval minds. The consistent medieval attitude toward usury is sufficient illustration of this profoundly felt belief, most suggestively illuminated by the *Divine Comedy*. Dante, it will be recalled, placed the usurers along with the sodomites in the third part of the seventh circle of hell, the barren ground containing those who had attempted violence against God by violating Nature. Their sins were complementary. As the sodomites had perverted sexuality—the reproductive force—into something barren, fruitless and meaningless, the usurers had perverted a barren instrument—money—into a reproducing organism. Many medieval thinkers regarded *munera* as a similar perversion. The giver or taker of bribes was equating the unsaleable spiritual gifts of God with values produced by land or work. But to act on the belief that a gift of God—the sacraments, prebends, *scientia*—was in any way commensurate with monetary value was to act as unnaturally as Dante's usurers and sodomites.

Ironically, these attitudes, so closely associated in their origins with the Church's early battle against ecclesiastical feudalism, ultimately became confused with, or associated with feudal social concepts in the minds of many satirists, especially those who did battle against ecclesiastical taxation and against the venality of jurists and lawyers. The ideal tacitly implied in their satire was a Church (or jurists) supported by the land, feudally enfiefed, and thus free to distribute the gifts of God without temptation or excuse to sell them. For most moralists and satirists this assumption was probably unconscious, but it seems to have taken shape in their minds as the specifically and uniquely Christian way of social organization. In any major economic or social innovation, whatever its ethical complexion, they tended to detect the destruction of Christian principles. This identification of economic and social conservatism with a religious ideal is not, as we know, a rare phenomenon. It seems to have been especially characteristic of the venality-satirists.

Lest we be thought to attribute an intellectual or philosophical awareness to numerous versifiers whose only thought was to fill out a page, to take advantage of a popular theme or to decorate ephemeral verse with satirical grace-notes, we hasten to admit the thorough conventionality of the theme in the hands of many writers, whether morally earnest or merely cynical, amused and playful. The *munera*-satire reached the proportions of a fad among the *litterati*, and one feels in reading some of its products that their authors fell into excoriations of venality almost by a literary reflex. When any literary form, subject, or theme achieves such popularity it will attract those who take it up merely because it is currently sensational or attractive, and because the road has been already cleared for them. There are no difficulties to face. They can broach the subject without thought.

But the mere specious triteness or conventionality of many of the contributors to the venality-theme should not be confused with the deep sense of literary and ethical tradition reflected by the best examples. The inherent and self-conscious traditionalism of medieval art and the corporate sense of the medieval artist are nowhere more apparent than in the reworking of this theme by successive generations of moralists and satirists. Everywhere and in all centuries they reach back to Holy Writ and its commentary for artistic as well as theological support. They reiterate the most striking phrases from the Roman poets for mere decoration, for ironic intensity, as *auctoritates*. They catch up old images, phrases, refrains, and borrow and rework old personifications. They make extensive use of parody—a powerful device for setting tradition before the minds of its readers. They collect, anthologise, quote one another, until their satires have the effect of so many haphazardly scattered mirrors, reflecting one another's light at random. This corporate sense contributes much to the strength and effectiveness of the satire. In the end it conquers the literary, intellectual, and ethical trivialities of its individual authors.

We must grant, then, a large measure of traditionalism, of conventionality, even of triviality to the writers whose work contributed to the venality theme. We must admit further that many of its products, quoted or described in our study, are sub-literary or at best only marginally literary. We may also guess that the venality-satires veil a good deal of petty self-seeking, of wounded vanity, of posturing cynicism, of the vengeful backbiting of disgruntled benefice-seekers. There clings to many of these pieces the faint, acid residue of sour grapes. We may also observe that the idealized feudal solution to economic and social problems which the satirists offer or imply is based on an order and stability which never existed in fact. Nor is this feudalism especially compatible with the deeply spiritual view of the world implied by their concept of simony and the *Donum Dei*. Like the writers of the old romances, they look wistfully backward to an imaginary and idealized past against which they can measure the spotted present. This is not necessarily a defect. In Western culture this retrospective utopianism has been an abiding vehicle for the expression of man's highest ideals.

These things granted, the study of Lady Meed and her forebears provides us nevertheless with valuable insights into the reactions of thoughtful men of the Middle Ages to the chaotic economic developments of that period and to the frequently disreputable maneuvering which accompanied them. It shows us the angry expressions of men caught as it were by surprise, by social changes which they could not understand or tolerate. It provides admirable examples of the interdependence of literature, law, Scripture and its commentary, social and religious ideals, and homiletics, and it shows us clearly the origins, circumstances and development of a significant literary tradition. Most important, perhaps, it provides us, through the haze of scurrility and self-interest, with a view into certain of the most profound and noble ideals of medieval Christendom. The best of the satires are mere surface manifestations, the corona-discharge of a world-view charged with the highest spirituality. The satirists faced the proposition that man is venal, and that all things obey money, with fierce, embattled indignation. Their answer, implicit or explicit in the very cast of their satire, was that man's end was eternal and could not be betrayed for crass temporalities, that man's nature was spiritual and would not be corrupted by coin, that man's highest earthly function was to be the temple of the Holy Ghost, who could not be bartered and who would in due time destroy both buyers and sellers.

LIST OF WORKS CITED

TEXTS:

Adam, Abbot of Perseigne. *Epistolae.* In J.-P Migne, *Patrologiae cursus completus, Series latina* (PL), CCXI, 579-694.
Alain of Lille. *Anticlaudianus.* In T. Wright, *Anglo-Latin Satirical Poets,* II, 268-426.
—— *De planctu naturae.* In Wright, *Satirical Poets,* II, 429-522.
—— *Summa de arte praedicatoria.* In PL, CCX, 109-198.
Amarcius. *Sexti Amarcii Galli Piosistrati sermonum libri IV,* ed. M. Manitius. Leipzig, 1888.
Augustine, St. *De civitate Dei.* In PL, XLI, 13-804. *The City of God,* tr. J. Healey and R. Tasker, 2 vols. (Everyman's Library). London, 1945.
—— *Enarrationes in Psalmas.* In PL, XXXVI, 67-1028.
Baehrens, A., ed. *Poetae latini minores,* 4 vols. Leipzig, 1910.
Barnfield, R. *Poems,* ed. M. Summers. London, 1936.
Bedae Venerabilis, in psalmorum librum exegesis. In PL, XCIII, 483-1098.
Bernard of Clairvaux, St. *De consideratione libri quinque ad Eugenium Tertium.* In PL, CLXXXII, 727-808.
Bernard of Morval. *De contemptu mundi,* ed. H. Hoskier. London, 1929.
Bernoldus. *De emtione ecclesiarum.* In *Monumenta Germaniae historica* (MGH), *Libelli de lite,* II, 106-108.
Biblia sacra juxta vulgatam Clementinam. Tournai, 1938. *The Holy Bible* (Rheims-Douai Translation). London, n.d.
Boethius. *Philosophiae consolatio,* ed. and tr. H. Stewart (Loeb Classical Library). London, 1918.
Bonizo. *Liber ad amicum.* In PL, CL, 803-856.
Bozon, Nicole. *Contes moralisés,* ed. L. Toulmin Smith and P. Meyer (SATF). Paris, 1889.
Bromyard, J. *Summa praedicantium.* Venice, 1586.
Bruno of Segui. *Libellus de symoniacis.* In MGH, *Lib. de lite,* II, 546-565.

Burton, R. *The Anatomy of Melancholy*. London, 1891.

Caesarius of Heisterbach. *The Dialogue of Miracles*, 2 vols., tr. H. Scott and E. Bland. London, 1929.

Carmen de bello Saxonico, ed. O. Holder-Egger. Hanover, 1889.

"Carmen historicum occulti auctoris saec. XIII," ed. C. Höfler, *K. Akademie der Wissenschaften zu Wien. Philos.-hist. Klasse. Sitzungsberichte*, XXXVII (1861), 183-262.

Carmina in simoniam et Romanorum avaritiam, ed. H. Boehmer. In MGH, *Lib. de lite*, III, 697-699.

Chaucer, G. *The Works of Geoffrey Chaucer*, ed. F. Robinson, 2d ed. Boston, 1958.

Chester Plays, Part II, ed. F. Matthews (EETS, e.s., 115). London, 1916.

La "Comédie" latine en France au XIIe *siècle*, 2 vols., ed G. Cohen. Paris, 1931.

Cursor mundi, 7 vols., ed. R. Morris (EETS, o.s., 57, 59, 62, 66, 68, 99, 101). London, 1874-1893.

Dante Alighieri. *Opera di Dante Alighieri*, ed. E. Moore. Oxford, 1894. *The Divine Comedy*, tr. Carlyle-Wicksteed (Modern Library), New York, v.d.

DeLisle, L. "Notice sur les manuscrits du fonds Libri conservés à la Laurentienne," *Notices et extraits des manuscrits*, XXXII, i (1883), 1-120.

Deusdedit. *Libellus contra invasores et symoniacos*. In MGH, *Lib. de lite*, II, 300-365.

Dobiache-Rojdesvensky, O., ed. *Les poésies des goliards*. Paris, 1931.

"Dou Pape, dou roy et des monnoies," *Société de l'histoire de la France. Bulletin*, II, ii (1835), 221-224.

Dreves, G., and others, eds. *Analecta hymnica*, 55 vols. Leipzig, 1886-1922.

Du Méril, E., ed. *Poésies inédites du moyen âge*. Paris, 1854.

—— *Poésies populaires latines antérieures au douzième siècle*. Paris, 1843.

—— *Poésies populaires latines du moyen âge*. Paris, 1847.

Egbert of Liège. *Fecunda ratis*, ed. E. Voigt. Halle, 1889.

Ekkehart I. *Waltharius*, ed. K. Strecker. Berlin, 1924.

Esposito, M., ed. "A Thirteenth-Century Rhythmus," *English Historical Review*, XXXII (1917), 400-405.

Etienne de Bourbon. *Anecdotes historiques, légendes et apologues tirés du recueil inédit d'Etienne de Bourbon*, ed. A. Lecoy de la Marche (Soc. de l'histoire de la France, vol. 185). Paris, 1877.

Etienne de Fougères. *Livre des manières*, ed. J. Kremer (Ausgaben u. Abhandlungen aus dem Gebiete der romanischen Philologie, XXXIX). Marburg, 1887.

Feifalik, J. "Studien zur Geschichte der altbömischen Literatur, V," *Wiener Sitzungsberichte*, XXXVI (1860), 119-191.

Fierville, C. "Notices et extraits des manuscrits de la Bibliothèque de Saint-Omer," *Notices et extraits des manuscrits*, XXXI, i (1884), 1-156.

Flacius Illyricus, M., ed. *Varia doctorum piorumque virorum de corrupto ecclesiae statu poemata*. Basil, 1556.

Freidank. *Bescheidenheit*. Selections in *Deutsche National-Literatur*, IX 251-353. Stuttgart and Berlin, n.d.

Furnivall, F., ed. *Early English Poems and Lives of Saints*. Berlin, 1862.

Gerhoh of Reichersberg. *Libellus de eo quod princeps huius mundi iam iudicatus sit*. In MGH, *Lib. de lite*, III, 240-272

Gervais du Bus. *Le roman de Fauvel*, ed. A. Långfors (SATF). Paris, 1914-19.

Gillebertus. *Carmina*, ed. L. Tross. Hamm, 1845.

Giraldus Cambrensis. *Opera*, 8 vols., ed. J. Brewer and J. Dimock (Rolls Ser.). London, 1861-91.

Gower, J. *Works*, 4 vols., ed G. Macaulay. Oxford, 1899-1902.

Greene, R., ed. *Early English Carols*. Oxford, 1935.

Gregory I, St. *In primum regum expositiones*. In PL, LXXIX, 17-468.

—— *Moralium libri, sive expositio in librum B. Job*. In PL, LXXV, 509-1162, LXXVI, 9-782.

—— *XL homiliarum in evangelia libri duo*. In PL, LXXVI, 1075-1314.

Guido of Arezzo. *Epistola Widonis ad Archiepiscopum Mediolanensem*. In MGH, *Lib. de lite*, I, 5-7.

Guillaume le Clerc de Normandie. *Le besant de Dieu*, ed. E. Martin. Halle, 1869.

Guillaume de Lorris and Jean Chopinel de Meun. *Le roman de la rose*, 5 vols., ed. E. Langlois (SATF). Paris, 1914-1924.

Guiot de Provins. *Œuvres*, ed. J. Orr. Manchester, 1915.

Hagen, H., ed. *Carmina medii aevi maximam partem inedita*. Bern, 1877.

Hauréau, B. *Les mélanges poétiques d'Hildebert de Lavardin.* Paris, 1882.

—— "Notice sur un manuscrit de la Reine Christine à la Bibliothèque du Vatican," *Notices et extraits des manuscrits,* XXIX, ii (1880), 231-262.

—— "Notice sur les mélanges poétiques d'Hildebert de Lavardin," *Notices et extraits des manuscrits,* XXVIII (1878), 289 ff.

—— "Notice sur le numéro 1544 des Nouvelles Acquisitions (Fonds Latin) à la Bibliothèque Nationale," *Notices et extraits des manuscrits,* XXXII, ii (1886), 253-311.

—— *Notices et extraits des quelques manuscrits latins de la Bibliothèque Nationale,* 6 vols. Paris, 1890-93.

Heinrich von Melk. *Von des tôdes gehugde.* In *Deutsche National-Literatur,* IX, 69-99. Stuttgart and Berlin, n.d.

—— *Priesterleben.* In *Deutsche National-Literatur,* IX, 99-120.

Hélinant. *Vers de la mort,* ed. F. Wulff and E. Walberg (SATF). Paris, 1905.

—— *Helinandi Frigidi Montis monachi . . . Opera Omnia.* In PL, CCXII, 477-1084.

Henry of Huntingdon. "Satira communis," *Historiae liber undecimus.* In Wright, *Satirical Poets,* II, 164-166.

Herolt, J. *Promptuarium exemplorum.* Speier, 1483.

Hervieux, L. *Les fabulistes latins,* 5 vols. Paris, 1884-99.

Hildebert of Lavardin. *Carmina miscellanea.* In PL, CLXXI, 1381-1458.

—— *De Nummo.* In F. Otto, *Commentarii critici in codices Bibliothecae Academicae Gissensis.*

Hilka, A. and O. Schumann, eds. *Carmina burana,* 2 vols. Heidelberg, 1930-41; in progress.

Historical Collections of a Citizen of London, ed. J. Gairdner (Camden Soc., n.s., 17). London, 1876.

Hoccleve, T. *Minor Poems,* ed. F. Furnival (EETS, e.s., 61). London, 1892.

Holder, A. "Mittheilungen aus Handschriften," *Neues Archiv,* I (1876), 415.

Horace. *Opera,* ed. E. Wickham and H. Garrod (Scriptorum classicorum bibliotheca Oxoniensis). Oxford, 1947.

Hugh of Saint Victor. *Quaestiones et decisiones in epistolas d. Pauli.* In PL, CLXXV, 431-634.

Hugo von Trimberg. *Der Renner*, ed. G. Ehrismann (Bibliothek des Litterarischen Vereins in Stuttgart, 247, 248, 252, 256), 4 vols. Tübingen, 1908-11.

Humbert of Silva Candida. *Adversus simoniacos libri tres.* In PL, CXLIII, 1005-1212.

Innocent III, Pope. *De contemptu mundi.* In PL, CCXVII, 701-746.

Isidore of Seville, St. *Libri sententiarum.* In PL, LXXXIII, 537-738.

Ivo, Bishop of Chartres. *Epistolae.* In PL, CLXII, 11-299.

Jacob's Well, Part I, ed. A. Brandeis (EETS, o.s., 115). London, 1900.

Jacques de Vitry. *Exempla*, ed. G. Frenken (Quellen u. Untersuchungen zur lateinischen Philologie des Mittelalters, V, i). Munich, 1914.

Jeanroy, A. and A. Långfors, eds. *Chansons satiriques et bachiques du* XIIIe *siècle* (CFMA 23). Paris, 1921.

Jerome, St. *Commentaria in Isaiam prophetam.* In PL, XXIV, 18-703.

John de Hanville. *Architrenius.* In Wright, *Satirical Poets*, I, 240-392.

John of Salisbury. *Policraticus*, 2 vols., ed. C. Webb. Oxford, 1909.

Johnston, R. and D. Owen, eds. *Fabliaux.* Oxford, 1957.

Jubinal, A., ed. *Jongleurs et trouvères.* Paris, 1835.

—— *Nouveau recueil de contes, dits, fabliaux et autres pièces*, 2 vols. Paris, 1839.

Juvenal. *Saturae*, ed. S. Owen, 2d ed. (Scriptorum classicorum bibliotheca Oxoniensis). Oxford, 1908.

Keller, H. *Fastnachtspiele aus dem fünfzehnten Jahrhundert* (Bibliothek des Litterarischen Vereins in Stuttgart, 28-30). 3 vols. Stuttgart, 1853.

Kernstock, O. "Mittelalterliche Liedercompositionen," *Anzeiger für Kunde der deutschen Vorzeit*, XXIV (1877), 68-73.

Långfors, A. "Notice du manuscrit français 12483 de Bibliothèque Nationale," *Notices et extraits des manuscrits*, XXXIX, ii (1916), 579.

Langland, W. *The Vision of William Concerning Piers the Plowman*, 2 vols., ed. W. Skeat. Oxford, 1886.

Legrand d'Aussy, P., ed. *Fabliaux et contes*, 5 vols., 3d ed. Paris, 1829.

Lehmann, P., ed. *Parodistische Texte.* Munich, 1923.

Lewis, H., T. Roberts and I. Williams. *Cywyddau Iolo Goch ac Eraill.* Wales University Press, 1937.

Leyser, P. *Historia poetarum et poematum medii aevi.* Halle, 1721.

Liber exemplorum ad usum praedicantium, ed. A. Little (British Society of Franciscan Studies, I). Aberdeen, 1908.

El Libro de los enxemplos, ed. P. de Gayengos. In *Biblioteca de autores Españoles*, LI, 443-542. Madrid, 1952.

Ludus Coventriae, ed. K. Block (EETS, e.s., 120). London, 1922.

Lydgate, J. *Minor Poems*, ed. H. MacCracken (EETS, e.s., 107, o.s., 192), 2 vols. London, 1911-1934.

Map, Walter. *De nugis curialium*, ed. M. James (Anecdota Oxoniensis, XIV). Oxford, 1914.

Marbod of Rennes. *Carmina varia*. In PL, CLXXI, 1647-1686.

Matheolus. *Les lamentations de Matheolus et le livre de leesce*, ed. A.-G. Van Hamel (Bibl. de l'Ecole des Hautes Etudes, Fasc. 95-96). Paris, 1892.

Meyer, P. "Mélanges de poésie Anglo-Normande," *Romania*, IV (1875), 370-397.

—— "Notice du MS Rawlinson Poetry 241," *Romania*, XXIX (1900), 1-84.

Meyer, W. "Die Arundel Sammlung mittellateinischer Lieder," *K. Gesellschaft der Wissenschaften zu Göttingen. Philos.-hist. Klasse. Abhandlungen*, n. F. XI (1908-09).

Dan Michel. *Ayenbite of Inwit*, ed. R. Morris (EETS, o. s., 23). London, 1866.

Montaiglon. A. de and G. Raynaud, eds. *Recueil général et complet des fabliaux des* XIIIe *et* XIVe *siècles*, 6 vols. Paris, 1872-1890.

Morawski. J., ed. *Proverbes français antérieurs au* XVe *siècle* (CFMA, 47). Paris, 1925.

Mozley, J. "The Unprinted Poems of Nigel Wireker," *Speculum*, VII (1932), 398-423.

Mum and the Sothsegger, ed. M. Day and R. Steele (EETS, o.s., 199). London, 1936.

Neckam, Alexander. *De naturis rerum et de laudibus divinae sapientiae*, ed. T. Wright (Rolls Ser.). London, 1863.

Nigel de Longchamps. *Speculum stultorum*, ed. J. Mozley and R. Raymo (Univ. of California English Studies, 18). Berkeley and Los Angeles, 1960.

—— *Tractatus contra curiales et officiales clericos*. In Wright, *Satirical Poets*, I, 146-230.

Otto, F. *Commentarii critici in codices bibliothecae academicae Gissensis graecos et latinos*. Giessen, 1842.

Ovid. *Opera omnia*, 4 vols., ed R. Merkel, R. Ehwald, F. Levy (Bibliotheca scriptorum graecorum et romanorum Teubneriana). Leipzig, 1915-1924.

Peter of Blois. *Epistolae*. In PL, CCVII, 1-560.

Peter Cantor. *Verbum abbreviatum*. In PL, CCV, 21-528.

Peter Damiani, St. *Apologeticum de contemptu saeculi*. In PL, CXLV, 251-292.

—— *Carmina et preces*. In PL, CXLV, 917-986.

—— *Contra clericos aulicos, ut ad dignitates provehantur*. In PL, CXLV, 463-472.

—— *Contra phylargyriam et munerum cupiditatem*. In PL, CXLV, 529-642.

—— *Epistolae*. In PL, CXLIV, 205-498.

—— *Liber qui dicitur gratissimus*. In PL, CXLV, 99-160.

Peter Lombard. *Collectanea in epistolas D. Pauli*. In PL, CXCII, 9-520.

Petrus Pictor (?). *Versus de denario*. In J. de Saint-Genois, "Notice sur le *Liber floridus Lamberti Canonici*," PL, CLXIII, 1014-1015.

A Poem on the Times of Edward II, ed. C. Hardwick (Percy Soc., 28). London, 1850.

Quevedo y Villegas, F. de. *Obras*, 3 vols. In *Biblioteca de autores Españoles*, vols. 23, 48, 69. Madrid, 1926-30.

Rabanus Maurus. *Homiliae de festis praecipuis, item de virtutibus*. In PL, CX, 9-134.

Raynouard, M., ed. *Choix des poésies originales des troubadours*, 5 vols. Paris, 1819.

Li Renclus de Moiliens. *Romans de carité*, ed. A.-G. Van Hamel. Paris, 1885.

Richard, Son of Nigel. *Dialogus de scaccario*, ed. C. Johnson. London, 1951.

Ritz, Regierungsrath. "Mittheilungen aus dem Archiv der ehemaligen Abtei Malmedy," *Archiv. d. Gesellschaft für ältere deutsche Geschichtskunde*, IV (1822), 412-434.

Robert of Brunne. *Handlyng Synne*, 2 vols., ed. F. Furnivall (EETS, o.s., 119, 123). London, 1901-03.

Rodulf Glaber. *Historiarum sui temporis libri quinque*. In PL, CXLII, 611-698.

Le roman des romans, ed. I. Lecompte (Elliott Monographs in the Romance Languages and Literatures, 14). Princeton and Paris, 1923.

Li romans de Bauduin de Sebourc, 2 vols., ed. L.-N. Boca. Valenciennes, 1841.

Ruiz, Juan, Arcipreste de Hita. *Libro de buen amor*, ed. J. Cejador y Franca, 2 vols. (Classicos Castellaños, 6th ed.). Madrid, 1951.

Rutebuf. *Œuvres complètes*, 3 vols., ed. A. Jubinal, Nouv. éd. Paris, 1874-75.

Smaragdus, Abbot of St. Michael's. *Via regia*. In PL, CII, 931-970.

Suchenwirt. *Gedichte*. Selections in *Deutsche National-Literatur*, XII, i, 313-314. Berlin and Stuttgart, n.d.

Sylvester II, Pope. *De informatione episcoporum*. In PL, CXXIX, 169-178.

Theodulf, Bishop of Orléans. *Carmina*. In PL, CV, 283-300.

Tiberianus. *Carmina*. In A. Baehrens, *Poetae latini minores*, III, 263-268.

The Towneley Plays, ed. G. England and A. Pollard (EETS, e.s., 71). London, 1907.

Tractatus Garsiae Tholetani canonici, ed. E. Sackur. In MGH, *Lib. de lite*, II, 425-435.

Twenty-Six Political and Other Poems, Part I, ed. J. Kail (EETS, o.s., 124). London, 1904.

Vintler, Hans. *Blume der Tugend*. Selections in *Deutsche National-Literatur*, XII, i, 195-206. Berlin and Stuttgart, n.d.

von der Hagen, F.H. *Minnesinger. Deutsche Liederdichter des zwölften, dreizehnten und vierzehnten Jahrhunderts. . .*, 5 vols. in 4. Leipzig, 1838-61.

Walter of Châtillon. *Alexandreis sive gesta Alexandri Magni*. In PL, CCIX, 459-574

—— *Moralisch-satirische Gedichte Walters von Chatillon*, ed. K. Strecker. Heidelberg, 1929.

Walther von der Vogelweide. *Die Gedichte Walthers von der Vogelweide*, ed. K. von Kraus. Berlin, 1877.

Wattenbach, W. "Aus dem Briefbuche des Meister Simon von Homburg," *Anzeiger für Kunde der deutschen Vorzeit*, XX(1873), 70-78.

—— "Bericht über eine Reise durch Stiermark im August 1876," *Neues Archiv*, II (1877), 385-425.

—— "Kirklich-politische Gedichte des zwölften Jahrhunderts," *Anzeiger für Kunde der deutschen Vorzeit*, XX (1873), 99-103.

—— "Lateinische Reime des Mittelalters," parts III, V, VI, X, XI, XII, *Anzeiger für Kunde der deutschen Vorzeit*, XVII (1870), 87-90, 191-195, 320-323; XVIII (1871), 130-131, 202-203, 231-233.

—— "Mittheilungen aus zwei Handschriften der K. Hof-und Staats-bibliothek," *Bayerische Akademie. Philos.-philol.-hist. Klasse. Sitzungsberichte*, III (1873), 685-747.

—— *Monumenta Lubensia.* Breslau, 1861.

—— "Der Streit der Bauern mit dem Klerus," *Anzeiger für Kunde der deutschen Vorzeit*, XXIV (1877), 369-372.

Werner, J. *Beiträge zur Kunde der lateinischen Literatur des Mittelalters.* Aarau, 1905.

—— *Lateinische Sprichwörter und Sinnsprüche des Mittelalters.* Heidelberg, 1912.

Wilmart, A. "Poèmes de Gautier de Châtillon dans un manuscrit de Charleville," *Revue Bénédictine*, XLIX (1937), 121-169, 322-365.

Wimbledon, R. *A Famous Middle English Sermon*, ed. K. Sunden. Göteborg, 1925.

Wright, T., ed. *The Anglo-Latin Satirical Poets and Epigrammatists of the Twelfth Century*, 2 vols. (Rolls Ser.). London, 1872.

—— *Early English Poetry, Ballads, and Popular Literature of the Middle Ages* (Percy Soc., 23). London, 1848.

—— *Early Mysteries and Other Latin Poems.* London, 1844.

—— *The Latin Poems Commonly Attributed to Walter Mapes* (Camden Soc.). London, 1841.

—— *Political Poems and Songs*, 2 vols. (Rolls Ser.). London, 1859-61.

—— *The Political Songs of England* (Camden Soc.). London, 1839.

—— *A Selection of Latin Stories* (Percy Soc., 8). London, 1843.

Wright, T. and J. Halliwell, eds. *Reliquae antiquae*, 2 vols. London, 1845.

Wyclif, J. *English Works*, ed. F. Matthew (EETS, o.s., 74). London, 1880.

Wynnere and Wastoure, ed. I. Gollancz. Oxford, 1930.

York Plays, ed. L. Toulmin Smith. Oxford, 1885.

Yunck, J., ed. "The *Carmen de nummo* of Godfrey of Cambrai," *Duquesne University Studies Annuale Mediaevale*, II (1961), 72-103.

Zingerle, I. "Bericht über die Sterzinger Miscellaneen-Handschrift," *Wiener Sitzungsberichte*, LIV (1866), 293-340.

—— "Bericht über die Wiltener Meistersänger-Handschrift," *Wiener Sitzungsberichte*, XXXVII (1849), 331-407.

SCHOLARSHIP:

Arnould, E. *Le manuel des péchés: étude de littérature religieuse Anglo-Normande*. Paris, 1940.

Bourgain, L. *La chaire française au XIIe siècle*. Paris, 1879.

Boutemy, A. "Hildebert dépossedé une fois de plus," *Moyen âge*, LII (1946), 146-147.

—— "Le patrimoine poétique de l'abbaye de Saint-Trond," *Moyen âge*, LIV (1948), 393-395.

Bowden, M. *A Commentary on the General Prologue to the Canterbury Tales*. New York, 1948.

Brooke, Z. "Gregory VII and the First Contest between Empire and Papacy," in *Cambridge Mediaeval History*, V, 51-111.

Bryan, W. and G. Dempster., eds. *The Sources and Analogues of Chaucer's Canterbury Tales*. Chicago, 1941.

Carlyle, R. and A. Carlyle. *A History of Mediaeval Political Theory in the West*, 6 vols. Edinburgh, v.d.

Chambers, R. *Man's Unconquerable Mind*. London, 1939.

Coghill, N. *Visions from Piers Plowman*. London, 1949.

Cohen, H. *A History of the English Bar and Attornatus*. London, 1929.

Cornelius, R. "*Piers Plowman* and the *Roman de Fauvel*," PMLA, XLVII (1932), 363-367.

Coulton, G. *Five Centuries of Religion*, 4 vols. Oxford, 1923-49.

—— *Medieval Panorama*. Cambridge, 1936.

Curtius, E. *Europäische Literatur und lateinisches Mittelalter*. Bern, 1948.

Dawson, C. *Medieval Religion*. London, 1934.

Faral, E. *Recherches sur les sources latines des contes et romans courtois du moyen âge*. Paris, 1913.

Feavearyear, A. *The Pound Sterling: à History of English Money*. Oxford, 1931.

Fliche, A. *Etudes sur la polémique religieuse à l'epoque de Grégoire VII: Les prégrégoriens*. Paris, 1916.

—— *La querelle des investitures*. Paris, 1946.

—— *La réforme grégorienne*, 3 vols. (Spicilegium Lovaniense; études et documents, 6, 9, 16). Louvain, 1924-1937.

Francke, K. *Zur Geschichte der lateinischen Schulpoesie des* XII *und* XIII *Jahrhunderts.* Munich, 1879.

Ghellinck, J. de. *L'essor de la littérature latine au* XIIᵉ *siècle,* 2ᵉ éd. Brussels, 1955.

Gottlob, A. *Die Servitientaxe im 13. Jahrhundert: eine Studie zur Geschichte des päpstlichen Gebührenwesens.* Stuttgart, 1903.

Haskins, C. *The Renaissance of the Twelfth Century.* Cambridge, Mass., 1927.

—— *Studies in Medieval Culture.* Oxford, 1929.

Hazelmeyer, L. "The Apparitor and Chaucer's Summoner," *Speculum,* XII (1937), 43-57.

Hazeltine, H. "Roman and Canon Law in the Middle Ages," in *Cambridge Mediaeval History,* V, 697-764.

Heiserman, A. *Skelton and Satire.* Chicago, 1961.

Hélin, M. *A History of Medieval Latin Literature,* tr. J. Snow. New York, 1949.

Jacob, E. "Innocent III," in *Cambridge Mediaeval History,* VI, 1-43.

Jaffé, S. *Die Vaganten und ihre Lieder.* Berlin, 1908.

Jarcho, B. "Die Vorläufer des Golias," *Speculum,* III (1928), 523-579.

Jordan, K. "Zur päpstlichen Finanzgeschichte im 11. und 12. Jahrhundert," *Quellen und Forschungen,* XXV (1933-34), 61-104.

Jusserand, J. *Chaucer's Pardoner and the Pope's Pardoners* (Chaucer Soc. Essays on Chaucer). London, 1884.

Kane, O. *Middle English Literature.* London, 1951.

Labande, E. *Etude sur Bauduin de Sebourc.* Paris, 1940.

Laistner, M. *Thought and Letters in Western Europe*: *A.D. 500 to 900,* 2d ed. London, 1957.

Langlois, C. "La littérature goliardique," *Revue bleue,* LI (1893), 174-180.

Lehmann, P. *Erforschung des Mittelalters,* 5 vols. Stuttgart, 1941-62.

—— *Die Parodie im Mittelalter.* Munich, 1922.

Lenient, C. *La satire en France au moyen âge.* Paris, 1883.

Lunt, W. *Financial Relations of the Papacy with England to 1327.* Cambridge, Mass., 1939.

—— "The Financial System of the Medieval Papacy in the Light of

Recent Literature," *Quarterly Journal of Economics*, XXIII (1909), 251-295.

—— *Papal Revenues in the Middle Ages*, 2 vols. New York, 1934.

Manitius, M. *Geschichte der lateinischen Literatur des Mittelalters*, 3 vols. (Handbuch der Altertumswissenschaft, IX, 2). Munich, 1911-1931.

Manly, J. *Some New Light on Chaucer*. New York, 1926.

Mitchell, A. *Lady Meed and the Art of 'Piers Plowman'* (Third Chambers Memorial Lecture). London, 1956.

Morin, G. "Le Pseudo Bède sur les psaumes et l'opus super psalterium de Maitre Manegold de Lautenbach," *Revue Bénédictine*, XXVIII (1911), 331-340.

Müntz, E. "L'argent et le luxe a la cour pontificale d'Avignon," *Revue des questions historiques*, LXVI (1899), 5-44, 378-406.

Owst, G. *Literature and Pulpit in Mediaeval England*. Cambridge, 1933.

Peter, J. *Complaint and Satire in Early English Literature*. Oxford, 1956.

Poole, A. *Obligations of Society in the* XII *and* XIII *Centuries* (Ford Lectures, 1944). Oxford, 1946.

Post, G., K. Giocarnis, and R. Kay. "The Medieval Heritage of a Humanistic Ideal: 'Scientia Donum Dei Est, Unde Vendi Non Potest,'" *Traditio*, XI (1955), 195-234.

Raby, F. *A History of Secular Latin Poetry in the Middle Ages*, 2d ed., 2 vols. Oxford, 1957.

Rand, E. *Ovid and His Influence*. New York, 1928.

Robertson, D. and B. Huppé. *Piers Plowman and Scriptural Tradition*. Princeton, 1951.

Rocquain, R. *La cour de Rome et l'esprit de réforme avant Luther*, 3 vols. Paris, 1893-97.

Saltet, E. *Les réordinations*. Paris, 1907.

Sandys, J. *A History of Classical Scholarship*, 3 vols., 3d ed. Cambridge 1921.

Schletter, H. "Die poetischen Werke Hans Rosenplüts," *Serapeum*, II (1841), 353-358.

Spicq, P. *Esquisse d'une histoire de l'exégèse latine au moyen âge*. Paris, 1944.

Stammler, W. *Frau Welt: ein mittelalterliche Allegorie*. Freiburg, 1959.

Tanner, J., C. Previté-Orton, Z. Brooke, eds. *The Cambridge Mediaeval History*, 8 vols. Cambridge, v.d.

Tellenbach, G. *Church, State and Christian Society at the Time of the Investiture Contest*, tr. R. Bennett. Oxford, 1940.

Ullmann, W. *The Mediaeval Idea of Law as Represented by Lucas de Penna*. London, 1946.

Utley, F. *The Crooked Rib* (Ohio State Univ. Contributions in Language and Literature, No. 10). Columbus, 1944.

Whitney, J. "The Reform of the Church," in *Cambridge Mediaeval History*, V, 1-50.

Williams, A. *The Characterization of Pilate in the Towneley Plays*. East Lansing, 1950.

—— "Chaucer and the Friars," *Speculum*, XXVIII (1953), 499-513.

Wilmart, A. "Le recueil des poèmes et des prières de S. Pierre Damien," *Revue Bénédictine*, XLI (1929), 342 ff.

Winfield, P. *The Chief Sources of English Legal History*. Cambridge, Mass., 1925.

Yunck, J. "Dan Denarius: the Almighty Penny and the Fifteenth Century Poets," *American Journal of Economics and Sociology*, XX (1961), 207-222.

—— "Economic Conservatism, Papal Finance, and the Medieval Satires on Rome," *Mediaeval Studies*, XXIII (1961), 334-351.

—— "Medieval French Money Satire," *Modern Language Quarterly*, XXI (1960), 73-82.

—— "The Venal Tongue: Lawyers and the Medieval Satirists," *American Bar Association Journal*, XLVI (1960), 267-270.

INDEX